0812

£3

COLLINS
Complete Book of
HOUSEPLANTS

COLLINS
Complete Book of
HOUSEPLANTS

HALINA HEITZ
Consultant Editor: William Davidson

BCA
LONDON · NEW YORK · SYDNEY · TORONTO

First published in 1991 by
HarperCollins Publishers
London

First published in Germany in 1990 by
Gräfe und Unzer GmbH
München

This edition published 1992 by BCA by
arrangement with HarperCollins Publishers

CN 2735

Copyright © 1990 Gräfe und Unzer GmbH

All rights reserved.

**A CIP catalogue record for this book is
available from the British Library**

Photography by Friedrich Strauss, Max
Wetterwald, Hermann Eisenbeiss and others
Drawings by Ushie Dorner

Printed and bound
in Cordoba,
Spain by
Graficromo,
S.A.

**Note for Australian/
New Zealand
Readers**

Due to the climatic
differences between
Australia/New
Zealand and Europe,
readers in the
southern hemisphere
are advised to bear in
mind the different
weather conditions
prevailing there.
Hotter, drier seasons
will enable many
plants to adapt more
readily to outdoor
conditions and they
can be placed outside
in courtyards or on
balconies for longer
periods. The flowering
season may also be
extended and plant
growth will be more
vigorous in temperate
areas. (See 'Habitats
and climatic zones' on
page 12.)
Note: The Spider mite
referred to in the text
is commonly known
as the Two-spotted
mite in Australia and
New Zealand.

CONTENTS

*The bellflower
(*Campanula
isophylla*) is one of the
few houseplants that
can tolerate hard water.*

The striking pattern of a fan palm: this is a Washingtonia.

Lycaste skinneri, an epiphytic mountain orchid from Central America

The fruit of the kumquat (Fortunella margarita) is edible. New plants can be grown from the seeds.

Plants on previous spread
All the plants in this Mediterranean window are sun-loving. Back row, from left to right: Calamondin orange (× Citrofortunella mitis 'Variegata'), bougainvillea (Bougainvillea), rosette-forming succulent (Aeonium arboreum 'Atropurpureum'), kangaroo thorn (Acacia armata), bougainvillea hybrid and passionflower (Passiflora caerulea). Front row: China rose (Rosa chinensis), desert rose (Adenium obesum), lavender (Lavendula angustifolia), another china rose, crimson bottlebrush (Callistemon citrinus), wax-flower (Chamelaucium), oleander (Nerium oleander), Livingstone daisy (Dorotheanthus bellidiformis), her and-chickens (Echeveria) and stonecrop (Sedum species).

7

Preface

Houseplants were as costly and rare as gold or salt when they were brought to Europe from distant lands some 300 years ago. Early settlers to Australia and New Zealand brought their favourite houseplants with them. We still prize them highly today because they beautify our homes. But many plant-lovers have forgotten that our houseplants are almost exclusively from tropical or subtropical regions and therefore have special needs if they are to live happily in our homes. Anyone who understands these needs holds the key to success as a houseplant gardener.

Note: Virtually all the plants discussed in this book are grown commercially.

How can you have better success with houseplants? In the first part of this book I have cut through all the familiar complexities to come up with one simple solution: adopt the appropriate culture. This simply means learning about the living conditions of each tropical or subtropical plant and then imitating them. For instance, did you know that some plants have a rest period but that others do not? That a plant's shape and leaves indicate its light or water requirements? Someone who understands the origins and needs of his or her plants knows what is good for them and does not make any serious mistakes in caring for them.

Two other topics vital to the caring plant owner are also included in this first part: how to deal quickly with pests and diseases, and, for the owner who wants to increase or replace his or her plant stock, the rewarding practice of propagation. All this – supported by the easy-to-follow **Techniques** pages with clear step-by-step drawings and the **Glossary** (printed on green pages for rapid reference) – and a section on the role plants can play in the home offer, I hope, a thorough introduction to the subject.

But the real heart of this book are the **Plant Portraits** which make up the second, larger part of the guide. More than 300 houseplants for home, office and conservatory – popular, well-known ones, as well as interesting novelties and enchanting rarities – are introduced and described, using full-colour photographs and precise instructions that guarantee success even to the novice.

There is also much to be learned from the superb colour photographs – many commissioned exclusively for this book. They show, for example, how splendid properly cared for houseplants can look, and at the same time they offer a wealth of ideas and decorative possibilities – from hanging plants to combinations of plants in containers and lush groupings in windows.

So, read, learn and enjoy! I wish you much pleasure and success with houseplants.

HALINA HEITZ

Acknowledgements
Halina Heitz is one of Germany's greatest houseplant experts. She was for 15 years the editor of the houseplant department of the leading German garden magazine, *Mein schöner Garten.* Through her collaboration with gardeners and botanists, as well as hundreds of thousands of contacts with readers, she has gained an almost unparalleled experience in the care of ornamental plants.

Important Some of the plants described in this book are poisonous. To keep your pleasure in houseplants unspoiled please read the Warning on page 236.

Opposite
The enchanting umbels of this white hydrangea consist of sterile single flowers. Hydrangeas like slightly acid soil and must be kept moist.

*Modern amaryllis have
few peers among the
flowering plants.*

10

ALL ABOUT HOUSE PLANTS

Magnificent flowers do not happen all by themselves. It takes a little knowledge to be able to turn a love of plants into practical success in growing them. Understanding native conditions is perhaps the greatest secret of successful plant culture, but the following pages tell you everything you need to know about growing houseplants. In warm, frost-free areas, some plants mentioned here will make good balcony or patio plants for summer interest.

Venerable rubber trees with aerial roots reaching to the jungle carpet (see photograph, page 141), man-high hedges of flaming red poinsettias, coconut palms on golden tropical shores (see photograph, page 205), green swamps full of umbrella plants, gigantic tropical forests decked with magnificently coloured orchids and bromeliads (see photographs, pages 13 and 213), woods of eucalyptus and Norfolk Island pine, dense

Getting to know your plants

Botany and plant history are more exciting than many gardeners believe. Anyone who knows where a plant comes from, what its structure is, how it lives, and why it looks the way it does, understands its needs better.

thickets of bamboo, cacti standing like monuments in the sparkling desert light (photograph, page 223) – these are the native habitats of our houseplants.

They are, in effect, foreign visitors. Yet we expect them to feel at home in containers while getting used to our poor winter light and to air made dry by heating systems. So never be unsympathetic when your houseplants occasionally let their leaves hang limp. Try to make them feel at home, to gain insight into their needs. This is very easily done by learning all you can about them and observing them carefully.

Habitats and climate zones

Houseplants are not winter hardy and so must be protected all year long from low temperatures. They originate in tropical and subtropical regions and grow most happily in habitats which emulate those conditions. An overview of the most important climatic zones follows, but do not forget that these zones can frequently overlap and that geographical conditions can create islands of different types of climate within the basic zones.

Tropical habitats

The zone on either side of the equator is designated tropical. The tropics of Cancer and of Capricorn at latitudes 23.5° north and south, respectively, delineate its extent. The tropics circle the 'belly of the earth' like a wide belt and comprise about 40 per cent of its surface.

The climatic conditions of this zone are quite various and range from the sultry, humid climate around the equator, to the climate of the savannahs and grasslands, which are characterized by alternately rainy and dry spells, to the hot, dry high-lying prairies and cool, damp mountain forests within these regions. Tropical plants can, therefore, occur in very different native conditions, as far as rain, temperature and humidity are concerned. However, they all have two essential requirements for life.

● Tropical plants do not undergo any seasonal change of temperature and light.

● Tropical plants receive a uniform duration of light all year long because in the tropics the length of the day and night is always the same.

Plants from the tropical rain forest live in a natural greenhouse. The rain forest extends on both sides of the equator and is characterized by steamy, leaden heat with marked nightly cooling, humidity between 90 and 99 per cent and copious rainfall without any real dry season. The luxuriant flora consists of a canopy of evergreen trees, lianas and epiphytes and below it gigantic shrubs and plants, often large-leaved forms, which live above one another in three storeys, or layers. Rain-forest plants in the house tolerate sun and dry indoor heating very poorly. They do not require a resting period but our dark seasons seem to compel them to check their growth in autumn and winter.

Plants from tropical regions with rainy and dry spells include those from savannahs and steppes. Others belonging to this group are those from areas influenced by the monsoon and trade winds. These plants are accustomed to considerable alternation of humidity and dryness, something to remember especially if you place them beside a window.

Staghorn fern is epiphytic and in its natural habitat establishes itself in the forks of tropical trees.

Plants from the tropical mountain forests have a natural habitat distinguished by rainfall, mists, strong sunlight and coolness, and which can even include frost in the higher regions. Therefore, tropical mountain plants in the house need a lot of light, moisture and coolness, depending on the season.

Plants from desert regions are of necessity experts at survival. Fierce heat in the daytime, with temperatures up to 50°C (120°F) in the shade, a mercilessly glaring light, often a stiff breeze, and an evaporation rate that is far greater than the yearly rainfall, as well as night temperatures that go down almost to freezing point are indeed inhospitable conditions for plant life. Often there is no rainfall for months or even years at a time, and when there is, it comes in such cloudbursts that the ground cannot take up the water. Desert plants

have therefore learned to manage with condensed water, mists or dew. Anyone who grows them should not overwater them in summer and must keep them almost dry in winter. That they like bright light is obvious.

Subtropical habitats

The subtropical zones lie between the tropics and the temperate zones. The average temperature in the coldest months ranges from 10 to 18°C (50 to 64°F), with rainfall and hours of daylight varying according to season. The subtropical zones have warm summers and mild winters; rainfall comes either in winter or in summer. The winter rainy regions lie in the Mediterranean area, South Africa, California and parts of south and western Australia, the summer rainy regions in the southern United States, northern coastal areas of

Australia, New Zealand and in parts of China.

Subtropical plants are frequently equipped with water reservoirs and protection against evaporation. They love cooler temperatures at night and have a rest period. Representatives of the summer rainy regions need warmth and water in summer and in winter must be kept cool and relatively dry; those from winter rainy areas like more watering in winter – as well as sufficient light and warmth.

Ecological tip To anyone who would like to learn more about the various kinds of climatic conditions and their characteristic flora I recommend a visit to a good botanical garden.

TECHNIQUES

Naming of parts from root to flower

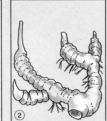

Underground plant parts

1 Roots, consisting of main and side roots
2 Rhizome (partially buried) with roots
3 Tuber with roots
4 Bulb with roots

The life goal of plants

The purpose of a plant's life is to reproduce itself in order to continue the species. The processes of growing, flowering and fruiting are all designed to serve that end. It is the single task towards which every cell, every part, of the whole organism is directed.

In nature, the above- and below-ground plant parts have worked harmoniously together towards this goal for millions of years. If that co-operation is disrupted, the plant attempts to reach its life goal through constant regeneration. Over the centuries gardeners have learned how to exploit this process for their own ends. Cutting a plant's flowers, for example, induces it to produce more flowers. But for the plant the flower is only a necessary transitional stage – the indication of its sexual maturity, whose purpose is reproduction.

Life underground

The underground parts of the plant – roots, bulbs, tubers or rhizomes (see drawings, Underground plant parts) – have no contact with light and are mostly brown or white. How they are shaped and whether they root near the surface or deeply, strongly or weakly, is a matter of species and location.
Roots provide anchorage in the ground and make possible the uptake and distribution of water and nutrients to other parts of the organism.
Root tubers or metamorphosed stems like rhizomes, stem bulbs/tubers or bulbs serve as underground storage places for water in some plants.

Above ground plant parts

The main stem, side stems, leaves, flowers and fruits: all are adapted to the plant's main purpose of reproducing itself.

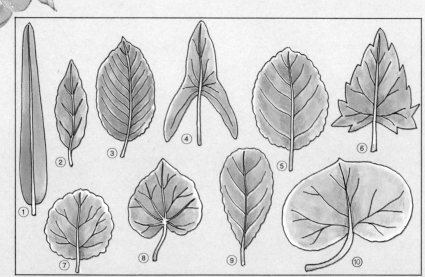

Selection of houseplant leaf shapes

1 linear (Chlorophytum) *2 long* (Brunfelsia) *3 ovate* (Beloperone)
4 arrow-shaped (Caladium) *5 roundish* (Saintpaulia) *6 triangular* (Ficus deltoidea) *7 shield-shaped* (Jatropha) *8 heart-shaped* (Sparmannia)
9 wedge-shaped (Euphorbia milii) *10 kidney-shaped* (Ceropegia woodii)

Important for culture: If a part of the root is damaged, for example by overwatering or injury during transplanting, the above-ground plant parts will suffer injury as well and may even die.

Life above ground

All the above-ground plant parts, such as stems, leaves, flowers and fruit, need light to survive. Those with deposits of the plant pigment chlorophyll are green and can transform or assimilate carbon dioxide and water into sugar in the presence of light.

Stems (also called shoots), like all other plant parts, display the wealth of nature's variety. They can be branched or unbranched, thin as a thread or so thick that a man cannot clasp his hands around them, herbaceous and juicy or woody and hard; they can creep, climb or twine. Their function is to bear the leaves and flowers, to provide them with nutrients, and to position the leaves for the best access to the light.

Leaves vary widely in size, shape and colour (see drawing, Leaf shapes) and are often very attractive. Whether they are small and needle-fine (see *Asparagus*, page 146), large and flat (see *Alocasia*, page 143), parchment-thin (see *Adiantum*, page 196) or as thick as your arm, they are always the central nervous system and the lungs of the plant. For it is mainly here that photosynthesis and transpiration take place.

Flowers frequently demonstrate nature's incredible refinement. They are structured exclusively to fertilize and be fertilized. To this end they are provided with male pollen grains and female egg cells (see drawing, Structure of a flower). Colour, shape (see drawing, Selection of flower forms) and scent have proven roles in the task of seduction. Together or separately they attract insects, which then pollinate the flowers. When it flowers, the plant becomes sexually mature and prepares internally for fertilization. All energies are directed towards later fruiting and seeding, which is why a flowering stem will often reduce its growth.

Fruit and seeds are the result of successful fertilization. The often colourful fruits serve as bait for the insects that will distribute the seeds. Development of seeds costs the plant a great deal of strength. Therefore, if you do not plan to propagate your houseplants, remove the flowers when they finish blooming.

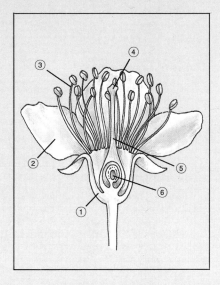

Structure of a flower

1 *Calyx of sepals*
2 *Corolla of petals*
3 *Male stamen, consisting of anther (top) and filament*
4 *Stigma*
5 *Style*
6 *Ovary with ovule*
The stigma, style and ovary are the female parts of a flower and together make up the pistil.

Selection of flower forms

1 *Bell-shaped* (campanulate) *flower, for example flowering maple* (Abutilon)
2 *Funnel-form flower, for example Cape primrose* (Streptocarpus)
3 *Butterfly-form* (papilionaceous) *flower, for example broom* (Cytisus)
4 *Tubular flower, for example lipstick vine* (Aeschynanthus)

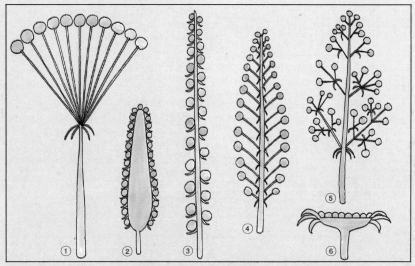

Selection of flower arrangements (or inflorescences)

1 *Umbel* (Pentas, Clivia, Ixora *and* Pelargonium grandiflorum) 2 *Spadix* (Anthurium *and* Spathipyllum) 3 *Spike* (Acalypha, Crossandra, Pachystachys *and* Vriesea) 4 *Raceme* (Cymbidium and Smithiantha) 5 *Panicle* (Phalaenopsis *and* Medinilla) 6 *Composite* (Chrysanthemum, Gynura *and* Senecio).

What appearance tells you

The reason for plants' extraordinary variety is the different habitats to which they have had to adapt, each according to its species.

As organisms bound to one spot, plants have been compelled over millions of years to perfect their life rhythms, length of life, habit and appearance until the survival of their species was ensured. For their innumerable problems they invented amazing solutions which offer us important hints for their care and maintenance.

Habit and life expectancy

Every plant, depending on its species, has its own genetic programme that determines how old and how large it will become and what shape it will take. However, trees and shrubs that grow to great heights in their own habitat will generally achieve only a fraction of their potential size in the confined area of a pot, in appearance will remain more or less juvenile plants and will rarely bear fruit.

The major habits

● upright, for example *Cordyline* or *Dracaena*
● climbing or twining, for example grape ivy (*Cissus*)
● creeping or ground-covering, for example mind-your-own-business (*Soleirolia*)
● trailing, for example lipstick vine (*Aeschynanthus*) or *Columnea*.

Furthermore plants can live to various ages. They grow as annuals, biennials or perennials, remain herbaceous or become woody like subshrubs, shrubs or trees.
Annual plants, such as *Browallia grandiflora*, or biennials, such as *Exacum affine*, go through a complete cycle of germination, growth, flowering, formation of fruit and ripening of seeds in one or two years respectively. After that they have fulfilled nature's reproductive requirement and they die. Naturally annual or biennial plants do not live any longer as houseplants, so the plant-lover must replace them after one or two years or propagate them.
Perennial plants (for example *Anthurium-Scherzeranum* hybrids, *Campanula*, *Chrysanthemum* hybrids or *Cyperus*) or bulbs (for example *Hippeastrum*) form roots, tubers or bulbs that bring forth new growth during every growing season. With optimum care these plants can last for years, even as houseplants.
Subshrubs (for example *Asparagus setaceus* or *Beloperone*) possess herbaceous parts that die back and woody parts that put out new growth every year. These are also relatively long-lived in pot culture.
Shrubs and trees (for example *Araucaria*, *Ardisia*, *Cupressus*, *Gardenia*, *Grevillea*, *Ficus*, *Medinilla* or *Sparmannia*) are particularly long-lived evergreen or deciduous woody plants that can, with good culture, achieve quite remarkable age, even in exile.

Plant survival strategies

Protection from strong light
Plants provide themselves with felt-like coverings of downy hairs, farina (a powdery, dust-like covering, composed of very short hairs) or a silvery- to blue-greenish waxy coating (for example *Crassula*, *Echeveria*).
What this tells us These plants can tolerate full sun.

Protection from water evaporation
Plants develop a waxy coating, many small or tough leaves reduced to thorns or needles, leathery leaves or thick hairy growth (for example cactus and euphorbia, *Hoya*, *Ixora*, *Leptospermum*, *Myrtus*).
What this tells us These plants can tolerate dry air.

Protection from dry periods
Some plants arm themselves with underground storage organs (*Achimenes*, *Cyclamen*, *Gloriosa*, *Sinningia*, *Zantedeschia*), succulent leaves (*Crassula*, *Hoya*, *Kalanchoe*) or stems (*Beaucarnea*, *Jatropha*, *Pachira*).
What this tells us These plants must be watered carefully.

Quest for light
Many rain-forest plants locate themselves in forks of trees. Still others provide themselves with gigantic leaves to catch as much light as they can or develop tendrils so that they can climb up to the top of forest trees.
What this tells us Tree dwellers (such as epiphytic orchids, bromeliads and ferns) do not belong in soil. Plants with huge leaves such as *Alocasia*, *Fatsia*, *Ficus elastica*, *Ficus lyrata*, *Philodendron* and *Tetrastigma* need relatively little light.

Quest for atmospheric humidity
Some plants develop absorption scales (for instance bromeliads), aerial roots (as in orchids) or hairs (as in African violets).
What this tells us These plants need damp air.

Opposite
Rhododendron simsii
hybrids, more commonly sold as florist's azaleas

1 'Euratom'	6 'Rex'
2 'Rosa Perle'	7 'Flamenco'
3 'Rosalie'	8 'De Waele's
4 'Memoria	Favourite'
Karl	9 'Stella Maus'
Glasen'	10 'Leopold
5 'Schnee'	Astrid'

Plant names

Plants not only have one or several popular names in each country, but as befits citizens of the world they also possess a valid international passport: their botanical or scientific name. This contains Latin or Greek elements and consists of the capitalized genus name, which always appears first, and the lower-cased species name, which always comes second, for example, *Clivia miniata* for the kaffir lily. Hybrid varieties also have a third name, the varietal name, for example *Camellia japonica* 'Barbara Clark'.

Carl von Linnaeus, who is known as the father of botany, introduced this binomial or two-named nomenclature in 1753 in his work *Species Plantarum*. His system banished the monstrously wordy descriptions of plants commonplace before that time. Descriptions such as *Cyclamen orbiculato folio inferne purpurascente*, which translated means 'sphere with circular leaves purple on the underside', could, for example, be replaced by *Cyclamen purpurascens*, the wild alpine violet.

But the new-style names did not lose all their descriptive and colourful elements. They are derived from the names of the discoverer, patrons or first describer, indicate the region of origin, characteristic qualities or the appearance of the plant, or are latinizations of the language of the native country. The species descriptions are particularly individual and informative.

Opposite
This delightfully airy grouping has been assembled from all over the world. From tropical South America come cane-type begonias and leopard lily, from tropical Africa dracaena and umbrella plant (in background from left to right). Mind your own business (front left) is native to the Mediterranean region, whereas rabbit's foot fern (centre and front right) comes from China.

Descriptive species names

hispida=stiff-haired, as in *Acalypha hispida* (see page 90)
infundibuliformis=funnel-shaped, as in *Crossandra infundibuliformis* (see page 104)
lyrata=lyre-shaped, as in *Ficus lyrata* (see page 165)
macrophylla=large-leaved, as in *Hydrangea macrophylla* (see page 116)
magnifica=magnificent, as in *Medinilla magnifica* (see page 123)
miniata=reddish-orange, as in *Clivia miniata* (see page 103)
nutans=nodding, as in *Billbergia nutans* (see page 96)
polyanthum=many-flowered, as in *Jasminum polyanthum* (see page 119)

The history of houseplants

It may be hard to believe – but the culture of houseplants began in Scandinavia, where for centuries people brought plants into the house when the desolation of the long winter began. Of course, in the beginning they were certainly not exotic plants. These probably first reached Europe when the great voyages of exploration began in the fifteenth century. In any event, interest in cactus started with the discovery of America, and presumably Christopher Columbus and his boat *Santa Maria* brought home a number of plant rarities from the New World.

● In 1570 an English apothecary advertised as a botanical rarity a *Melocactus*, which probably came from the legacy of the *Santa Maria*.
● In 1620 the belladonna lily was introduced from the Cape Colony.
● In 1644 arum lilies were already growing in the Royal Garden in Paris.
● In 1690 the pineapple was being successfully bred in the hothouses of royal palaces and the sea grape (*Coccoloba*) was brought to Europe.
● In 1698 *Aloe arborescens* was already growing in European winterhouses.
● In 1733 the first tropical orchid bloomed in Europe. It was *Bletia verrecunda* from the Bahamas.
● In 1770 the Swiss botanist Frederik Allamand collected seeds in South America, which were later named *Allemanda* for him, and sent them to Linnaeus.
● In 1774 and thereafter numbers of fragrant-leaved pelargoniums were introduced from Cape Colony.
● In 1779 Captain Cook and Sir Joseph Banks brought back the Norfolk Island pine from New Zealand.
● In 1819 an amaryllis species was brought to Europe from Brazil.

The majority of houseplants reached Europe during the nineteenth century. This was because of the development of internal heating and the greenhouse, which made it possible for the exotic visitors to be kept without injury.

Certainly the tale of the ways the plants reached us reads like an adventure story. Gardeners, botanists, missionaries and explorers risked their lives for them, but so did fortune-hunters and mercenaries utterly uninterested in plants. To get the highly prized rarities to Europe they had to cope with tropical illness, insects, poisonous snakes, predators, hostile natives and the unpredictable climatic conditions. In addition there was ruthless competition, corruption, espionage and possibly, because of the astronomical prices some plants commanded, even murder to be reckoned with.

And for the plants the journey to Europe was equally terrible. They languished for months in unventilated wooden boxes, and frequently they were eaten by vermin or insects, or simply rotted. Eventually, however, the English physician and naturalist Nathaniel Ward, through an accidental discovery, invented a glass container which could be closed and in which the soil retained constant dampness. This 'wardian case' became the ideal means of transporting tropical plant discoveries and was later the prototype of English ferneries as well as modern window greenhouses and terrariums.

It is often very tempting to make an impulsive purchase of a beautiful plant for the sheer joy of it. But ideally several considerations should precede any plant purchase so that the right plant gets to the right spot and the future 'cohabitation' will be a mutual pleasure for plant and human.

The first consideration What conditions (light and temperature) do I have to offer my chosen plant

Choosing, buying and positioning plants

Houseplants make an important contribution to your living space. They can hint of far-away places into your home, create colourful focal points or restful green areas, enrich your home with exotic fragrances or simply underscore the beauty of your furniture. The key to success is simple: the location must be right.

and does it to some degree match the conditions and circumstances in its natural habitat?

The second consideration What plants fit the size of my home and the style of my furnishings?

The importance of light

Light is one of a plant's most basic requirements. In its natural environment it receives light from all sides, in the house often only from one. And do not forget that many houseplants come from tropical regions with days and nights of the same length so that our autumn/winter season means a noticeable light deficiency for them.

Plants always thrive best when they receive the amount of light they are used to in their native locations. They have adapted to these conditions over thousands and thousands of years – their leaves, particularly, are structured for this purpose. The light requirements of many plants can be determined from their leaves (see pages 26–7). Before you buy a plant that you do not know, study its leaves and, to be safe, find out as much as you can about its light requirements.

Often plants are sold with very brief instructions for light requirements, such as sunny, bright, semishade or shady. The following table explains what these vague terms mean.

● Sunny=a place in a sunny window with maximum light intensity. Expressed as a light intensity of 20,000 lux and over.
● Bright=a place in a window with a short period of sun in the morning or in the evening, as is provided by an eastern or western location. Expressed as a light intensity of 10,000 to 20,000 lux.
● Semishade=a place in a large shaded window or near a window without direct sun. The light intensity ranges from 5000 to 10,000 lux.
● Shady=a place in a small shaded window or a location in a room with a light intensity of 2500 to 5000 lux.

On cloudy winter days the light intensity can be as little as 400 to 500 lux; on the other hand, on sunny summer days it can be as high as 90,000 lux. The minimum light that a plant needs for life ranges from 700 to 1000 lux but many plants only begin to thrive at 10,000 lux.

Determining light values

The light supply in a room is largely determined by the direction in which its windows face and its sources of artificial light. But other variables are involved too. Light values prove only really consistent where light can enter freely and unhindered. So an unimpeded shady window on the fourth floor of an apartment house will receive far more light than a sunny window on the ground floor with a balcony extending over it or a large tree in front of it.

If you do not want to put a plant directly in front of a window, you must bear in mind that not only closely woven draperies but even almost transparent curtains and venetian blinds filter out considerable light. Besides, the light intensity diminishes according to the distance from the source of light.
● At a distance of 1m (39in) the plant receives 80 to 50 per cent of the light
● At a distance of 1.5m (59in) the plant receives 50 to 25 per cent of the light
● At a distance of 2m (79in) the plant receives 25 to 10 per cent of the light

Right
Pachystachys lutea
*needs a very bright but
never sunny location.
Standard forms such as
this are very rare. The real
flowers are the white
tubular shapes that peep
out of the sun-yellow
bracts.*

Professional tip Before you decide to buy a large, expensive houseplant check its future location with a luxmeter. This light-measuring instrument, which is comparable to the light meter used in photography, is an invaluable once-only purchase for the houseplant gardener. You should only buy plants that need sunny or bright locations if you can offer them a place in a window that faces the sun – or if you have a plant light. If you want to place them in a darker position for a short period, for instance as a table decoration, you need not supply any additional light.

The importance of room temperature

Remember to check the warmth of the location of your future houseplant. In summer a pool of intense heat can sometimes form very quickly behind windows in certain positions. In winter there are more things to consider. Radical changes of temperature at night are harmful to the more tender plants. Heating units under windows and low-level heating especially offer the rising warmth prized by plants since both help to warm the soil. What is bad, however, is the drying of the air and the soil that accompanies such heating. Thin-leaved plants in particular can be harmed by hot air passing through their leaves. The solution is to widen shelves above heat sources to redirect the ascending air. Many plants need increased humidity during this period (see page 43).

In colder climates a number of plants like to be overwintered in a cool, bright situation. Before you buy such plants, consider whether you can set up the appropriate winter quarters for them such as a glasshouse.

Types of location

In every household and in every room, individual light and temperature conditions determine which plants will thrive well there. Here are some classic types of location.

The warm all-year-round, sunny place offers mean daytime temperatures of 20°C (68°F) and more, and at night does not fall below 15°C (59°F). As a rule these conditions are found in a window location in a constantly used living area and in the comfortably heated conservatory. On the window sill the plants receive sunlight for several hours a day: and in the heated conservatory they benefit from it nearly all day long. For the hot window with its strong midday sun the only plants suitable are those that live in the hot sun in their native habitat, for example flaming nettle (*Coleus*) or ponytail (*Beaucarnea*). Semi-shaded windows, on the other hand, are ideal locations for all light-hungry plants that cannot stand the full glare of the midday sun.

The humid, bright place offers much light without direct sun, humidity over 60 per cent and temperatures that never go below 18°C (64°F). This environment can be achieved in a warm humid climate from tropical to temperate zones and in a climate-controlled plant window, terrarium, growing cabinet and greenhouse. Tropical rain-forest dwellers like the prayer plant, ferns, many gesneriads and members of the arum family, as well as epiphytic orchids, bromeliads and tillandsias, flourish admirably here.

Cool, sunny to bright places offer several hours of good light with temperatures between 10 and 15°C (50 and 59°F) and warmer in summer than in winter. Such conditions are found, for example, in a window in a cool bedroom, in a bathroom that is warm only periodically, in a hallway or in a conservatory that is not part of the living area. Plants of the subtropics flourish here, as do those of the Mediterranean region and from the tropical high mountain regions, such as flowering maple (*Abutilon*), Norfolk Island pine (*Araucaria*), orange trees (*Citrus*), *Coelogyne*, Monterey cypress (*Cupressus*), sago palm (*Cycas*), dendrobium (*Dendrobium*), silky oak (*Grevillea*), myrtle (*Myrtus*) and azaleas (*Rhododendron* hybrids).

The warm, shady place provides temperatures of 15 to 21°C (59 to 70°F) and receives no sun. It can be directly in a window that is shaded or in the middle of a very bright room. All manner of forest dwellers thrive here since they are used to shadows or filtered light; these include ferns, tropical palms and members of the arum family.

The cool, shady place offers average temperatures of 10 to 15°C (50 to 59°F). This can be any area that is slightly heated in winter and shady in summer. The plants to thrive in such conditions come from tropical and subtropical mountain forests, such as cast-iron plant (*Aspidistra*), bird's-nest fern (*Asplenium*), ivy (*Hedera*), Cretan bracken (*Pteris cretica*), reed rhapis (*Rhapis*) and mind-your-own business (*Soleirolia*).

Decorating with houseplants

Remember when you are selecting and buying houseplants that they have decorative qualities with which you can define or emphasize the atmosphere and furnishing of your home. Take a little time to study the plants at your local garden centre and you will find in every plant some essential feature or characteristic form or colour that will harmonize particularly well with a certain lifestyle (see table, page 25).

Houseplants need space

No plant stays the size it was when you bought it. How large it will become depends on several factors: its genetic growth programme, the container in which you cultivate it and the care that you bestow on it (see Growth factors, page 36). Species that in their native habitat grow into tall trees or shrubs, such as the spineless yucca (*Yucca*), *Ficus* species, African hemp or dumb cane (*Sparmannia africana*) or the sentry palm (*Howea*), can, with good care, reach the ceiling indoors or grow very broad, like the screw pine (*Pandanus*). So, when choosing a houseplant to complement your living space, keep two things in mind. A plant needs a place where it can flourish undisturbed and where its own individual style of growth will be the most effective visually. The space requirement of a large solitary plant is comparable to that for a piece of furniture.

Choose a container that complements the plants.

Flowering bulbs can make a bold statement.

Ideas for interiors

● Large plants work best alone or as key plants in groups of smaller plants. In small areas use one at the very most.

● Large-leaved plants mitigate busy wallpaper patterns and form an unfussy background for small-leaved varieties.

● The graphic contours of palm fronds, ferns or *Yucca* crowns are particularly well set off by backlighting.

● Smaller plants look nicer in groups. For example, a basket or dish with a dozen African violets (see photograph, page 128), spring primulas, mini cyclamen or cape primrose hybrids in various violet and pink shades.

● Repeat the colours of curtains, wallpaper, sofa cushions or pictures with flower colours, or set up points of contrast, for instance red flamingo flowers (*Anthurium*) with black furniture.

● Make your hallway inviting with beautiful plants. Install plant lights if necessary (see Measured light, page 45).

● Turn your walls green with climbing plants. But make sure before you begin that they will get enough light. A traditional espalier trellis is the prettiest way to help plants climb. You can also anchor trellis in a large box and use it as a room divider, covered with plants.

● Hang greenery in the roof space of high old conservatories. For example, a grid of bamboo sticks bound together and supported by loops attached to the roof beams can provide stations for quantities of hanging baskets of every imaginable size.

Furniture for plants

When your windowsills are full and the nicest places on chests of drawers or console tables are already occupied, do not despair. You can resort to 'plant furniture'. Today the market offers a variety of flower benches, side tables, planters and flower stands or *etagères* (see photograph, page 146). Plants on glass shelves that allow the light to shine through produce a very attractive effect. Jardinières or wooden flower-holders are very good for displaying single plants, especially gracefully trailing ones, such as spider plant (see photograph, page 151), sword fern (see photograph, page 200) or the other classic hanging plants.

Attractive cachepots and containers

Decorative jars and pots designed to hold potted plants set off houseplants to the best effect. They come in enchanting colours and wonderful forms and are available in a wide variety of materials from pottery, porcelain, wood, wicker and rattan to plastic, metal and glass.

Make sure when you choose cachepots that they are larger than the plant pot (there should be a finger's thickness of free space between plant pot and cachepot) and that plant and container harmonize in colour and shape. White cachepots, terracotta pots and naturally coloured baskets always look good. Here are a few suggestions for attractive alternatives.

● For coloured-leaved plants such as Joseph's coat (*Codiaeum*), flaming nettle (*Coleus*) or rex begonia (*Begonia*), choose a monochrome pot in the dominant leaf colour, for instance red or purple, to make a dramatic statement.

● Very sturdy Mediterranean plants like the money plant (*Crassula*) or miniature orange (*Citrus*) look best in plain pots of terracotta, stoneware or glazed pottery.

Plants enliven any work area and can improve the climate of a room.

● Old-fashioned plants like cyclamen, fragrant-leaved geranium (*Pelargonium*), miniature roses (*Rosa*) or African violets (*Saintpaulia*) look pretty in porcelain cachepots with flower patterns or lacquered baskets in the appropriate colour.

● Green-white or green-silvery variegated plants like *Aglaonema* or *Fittonia* go well in olive or sea-green containers.

● Popular favourites for interior effects, such as palms, spineless yucca (*Yucca*), *Ficus* species and African hemp or dump cane (*Sparmannia*), could, in the right context, be planted in square or round metal drums.

● Cactus, as long as they are not blooming, look especially jolly in brilliantly coloured small pots.

Advice on buying

It does not matter where you buy your plants as long as you check carefully how well they have been looked after.

● Reject any plant that is standing in a dark corner or a draughty passageway. Pavement locations and garage forecourts can spell death for the more tender plants.

● Green plants should be growing well, with several shoots and juicy, spotless leaves. Avoid plants with yellow-brown spots on the leaves or leggy shoots (long shoots with wide intervals between leaves).

● Flowering plants should have lots of buds that are just about to open. Do not choose one in full bloom or one with 'left-behind' buds that look dried out. Both chrysanthemums and azaleas should have some flowers fully open, otherwise the buds may be too tight to ever open indoors.

● Only take plants that are insect-free. Inspect the ends of shoots

carefully (for aphids) and the undersides of leaves (for spider mites and scale). On the flowers, small, elongated thrips are the easiest to recognize. (See Diseases and pests, pages 54–5).

● Also avoid plants whose soil is completely dried out or covered with moss. In both cases the roots may be damaged.

Availability

As a rule you can obtain foliage plants all year around, but flowering plants are only available at their natural blooming time or when brought on by nurseries. Some flowering plants, such as African violets (*Saintpaulia*), winter-flowering begonias (*Begonia*), flamingo flowers (*Anthurium*) or flaming Katie (*Kalanchoe*), bloom for months at a time or are obtainable in bloom almost all year round.

Diversity of plants

Thanks to the demands of fashion, the selection of houseplants now available is extremely varied. Breeders and growers no longer attempt merely to manipulate flowering seasons or to achieve new flower colours and forms or variegations of leaves through hybridization. They 'invent' plants that do not exactly conform to species norm but are decorative or they keep them small, either by reduction of the pot size (for example by culture in almost thimble-sized pots), by treatment with inhibiting chemicals or through breeding. The following list gives some idea of the diversity that is now available.

Flowering-plant minis from chrysanthemum, spathiphyllum (see photograph, page 133), flamingo flower, flaming Katie (see photograph, page 120), roses (see photograph, page 128) and African violets (see photograph, page 128)

Foliage-plant minis of dracaena, ferns, Joseph's coat, palms and pepper

Standard forms of chrysanthemum (see photograph, page 101), broom, *Pachystachys lutea* (photograph, page 21), hibiscus, poinsettia and non-hardy azaleas

Hanging baskets of plants that have a creeping, climbing or trailing growth habit (see photographs, pages 30–1)

Bonsai of various *Ficus* species (photograph, page 48), bottle tree, myrtle, lady palm, *Azalea indica* and Norfolk Island pine

Plants trained on hoops of bougainvillea, dipladenia (see photograph, page 106), jasmine (see photograph, page 119), glory lily (see photograph, page 112), stephanotis (see photograph, page 133), glory-bower, passionflower (see photograph, page 124) and wax vine

Twisted or braided stems in *Ficus* species (see drawing, page 44)

Planted dishes or other arrangements (see photographs, pages 23 and 29), in which often more attention has been paid to the visual effect than to the correct conditions for the particular plants

Bottle gardens planted with mini plants that need high humidity

Professional tip In Europe, tillandsias are often sold fastened to stones. Apart from the fact that they are frequently endangered species plundered from their native habitats, this is not the correct culture for these plants. A real tillandsia-lover only buys plants that are domestically reproduced from seed or vegetative propagation and are bound to branches (see photograph, page 46). Your national bromeliad society will be able to recommend suppliers.

Plants are good for you

Plants are not only wonderfully decorative, they also contribute to our well-being. Their beauty is a spiritual pleasure and taking care of them can reduce stress and anxiety by offering a little contact with the soil and closeness to nature. A research programme into plants in the workplace showed that houseplants had a positive effect on the health and mood of the test subjects. But plants can do still more.

Improving the air Plants humidify dry centrally heated air and filter out dust, which settles on the leaves and can be washed off or wiped away. They also produce oxygen, even if in relatively small amounts.

Filtering pollutants A study completed by NASA proved that the spider plant, philodendron, ivy and mother-in-law's tongue could reduce the formaldehyde concentration in the air. Chrysanthemums and gerbera displayed the best effects against benzene and trichlorethylene.

Houseplants for every interior

Antique and reproduction furniture The following are especially good: cyclamens, azaleas, winter-flowering begonias or various bush begonias, ivy, ferns, gloxinias, camellias, palms and African violets.

Art Deco and Art Nouveau furniture Use plants whose contours are sharply defined or that have an ornamental, elegant effect, for example alocasia, amaryllis, flamingo flower, spathiphyllum, cheese plant, gardenia, calla, stephanotis, string-of-hearts and passionflowers.

Exotic furniture Rattan harmonizes well with all tropical and subtropical plants, but especially with members of the arum family, bromeliads, *Ficus* species, flowering gesneriads, marantas, medinillas, orchids, palms and passionflowers.

Oriental furniture Lacquered pieces go well with austerely formal or oriental plants like azaleas, bamboos, calamus and lady palms, as well as all bonsai.

Contemporary designer furniture Steel, glass and marble need plants with a graphic or sculptured effect, for instance asparagus, dracaenas, euphorbias, ferns, monsteras, large *Ficus* species, cacti, palms, schefflera, aspidistras, emerald trees, yucca, Norfolk Island pine and grape ivy.

Country furniture Traditional and Swedish furniture needs cheerful, colourful flowering plants like cyclamens, winter-flowering begonias, flaming Katie, busy Lizzie, campanulas, Easter and Christmas cacti, geraniums, primulas, winter-flowering begonias, poinsettias, billbergia or sturdy green plants, such as staghorn fern, schefflera and Japanese fatsia.

Pine furniture harmonizes particularly well with agave, aloe, bougainvillea, mind-your-own business, echeverias, elephant's foot, euphorbias, sedums, jade plants, hibiscus, cacti, myrtle, button fern, yucca and with miniature orange and lemon trees.

Leaves that reveal light requirements

Leaves constitute the real charm of most plants. Often, to the knowledgeable observer, they also reveal the plant's light needs. (The numbers in brackets refer to the key to the illustration below.)

Leaves that are fleshy or reduced to thorns Full sun and light. Examples: hen and chickens, stonecrop (1), flaming Katie, cacti, euphorbias, mother-in-law's tongue

Leathery leaves A lot of light, but no sun. Examples: rubber plant, ixora, coffee tree, camellia, stephanotis, wax vine (2)

Small, often needle-fine leaves Full sun. Examples: asparagus, crown-of-thorns, myrtle (3)

Large, usually soft leaves No sun, bright to semi-shade. Examples: calathea, gloxinia, gynura, indoor linden (4)

White or yellow-green variegated leaves Never sunny but always brighter than the green-leaved varieties. Examples: ivy (5), devil's ivy, spider plant, piggyback plant, goosefoot plant, screw pine, spindle tree, wandering Jew. Exceptions: leopard lily and aglaonema, which do better in semi-shade

Coloured leaves Bright to semi-shade but never sunny. Examples: rex and other rhizomatous begonias, calathea, ctenanthe, dracaena, polka-dot plant, Joseph's coat, prayer plant (6), neoregelia, nidularium, pepper, earth star. Exceptions: flaming nettle and bloodleaf, which like full sun

Pinnate leaves No sun, bright to semi-shade. Examples: ferns (7), aralias, palms

Grey-green leaves A lot of light. Examples: silky oak, rosary vine (8), grey tillandsias

Soft leaves arranged in rosettes Semi-shade. Examples: cape primrose, primulas, African violets (9)

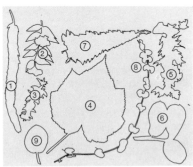

Plants for different locations

Plants for hot, sunny places

Adenium, desert rose
(see page 91)
Aeonium, aeoniums
(see page 142)
Aloe, aloes
(see page 144)
Beaucarnea, bottle ponytail
(see page 147)
Bougainvillea, bougainvillea
(see page 139)
Brachychiton, bottle tree
(see page 149)
Crassula species, crassulas
(see page 155)
Echeveria species, echeverias
(see page 107)
Euphorbia species (succulents),
euphorbias
(see pages 108 and 163)
Haemanthus, shaving-brush plant
(see page 113)
Haworthia, star cactus
(see page 168)
Hibiscus, China rose
(see page 113)
Jatropha, bottle plant
(see page 119)
Kalanchoe, flaming Katie
(see page 120)
Pachira, shaving-brush tree
(see page 174)
Passiflora, passionflower
(see page 124)
Pelargonium, fragrant geraniums
(see page 176)
Phoenix canariensis, Canary Island
date
(see page 210)
Plectranthus, Swedish ivy
(see page 180)
Senecio, string of pearls or Danish ivy
(see page 193)
Yucca, yuccas
(see page 190)

Fragrant plants

Citrus, dwarf orange
(see page 102)
Exacum, German violet or indoor
violet
(see page 110)
Gardenia, gardenia
(see page 111)
Hoya bella, Hoya carnosa, wax plant
(see page 115)
Jasminum, jasmine
(see page 119)
Pelargonium, fragrant geraniums
(see page 176)
Stephanotis, Madagascar jasmine
(see page 133)

Plants for shady places

Adiantum species, maidenhair ferns
(see page 196)
Aglaomena, Chinese evergreen
(see page 143)
Aspidistra, aspidistras
(see page 147)
Begonia, rhizomatous begonias
(see page 148)
Chlorophytum, spider plant (green
variety)
(see page 151)
Cissus rhombifolia, Venezuela
treebine or grape ivy
(see page 152)
Cyrtomium, holly fern
(see page 198)
Davallia, Rabbitsfoot fern
(see page 198)
Dracaena marginata, dragon tree
(see pages 160 and 161)
× Fatshedera, tree ivy
(see page 163)
Howea, sentry palm
(see page 209)
Microlepia, microlepia
(see page 199)
Peperomia species, radiator plant
(see page 177)
Philodendron scandens, heart-leaf
(see page 178)
Platycerium, staghorn fern
(see page 202)
Pteris, brake
(see page 203)
Rhoicissus rhomboidea, grape ivy
(see page 183)
Tolmiea, piggyback plant
(see page 189)
Yucca elephantipes, spineless yucca
(see page 190)

Plants for indoor water gardens or very sunny patios

Swamp Plants
Cyperus alternifolius, Cyperus
haspan, Cyperus papyrus, umbrella
and papyrus plants
(see page 158)
Scirpus, Bullrushes
(see page 185)
Humidity-loving houseplants
Acorus gramineus, grassy-leaved
sweet flag
(see page 142)
Ophiopogon jaburan, jaburan lily
(see page 193)
Spathiphyllum, white sails
(see page 133)

Plants for children

The most exciting plants are those
that 'do something'. The following
are all proven favourites.
The peanut (*Arachis hypogaea*)
blooms for only a few hours and
wilts after self-pollination. Then the
flower stalk lengthens, reaching
towards the ground, and burrows
into the earth, where the ripening of
the seed takes place (hence its
alternative name, 'ground nut'.) If
you want to show your children this
strange behaviour, sow peanuts in
late winter (unsalted ones, of
course). Remove the brown shell or
husk from the seed and put a group
of three in a pot. Place the pot in a
warm, light place and keep damp.
Cotton (*Gossypium herbaceum*), like
the peanut, can be sown in the
spring. Keep it in good light at
moderate temperatures 10 to 16°C
(50 to 60°F). It blooms about six
months after sowing, with a mallow-
like creamy-yellow flower that is
self-fertilizing. After nine weeks a
green capsule forms; later this
bursts and white 'cotton wads' are
released.
Mimosa (*Mimosa pudica*), otherwise
known as the sensitive plant, has
leaves which collapse alarmingly,
even unnaturally, when touched.
Like the cotton plant, it requires
good light and moderate
temperatures to thrive.
Venus fly-trap (*Dionaea muscipula*)
also reacts when touched. When an
insect alights on the 'hinged' leaves,
touching the sensitive hairs on
either side of them, the two sections
snap shut to imprison it. (See page
192 for culture instructions.)

Opposite
*A glass container filled
with water-retaining clay
granules is ideal for
bulrushes, sedges and the
calla lily, which all love
constant humidity. If you
want the calla to bloom
again, however, you must
be sure to remove it in late
spring. It needs a rest
period so keep it dry in
another container for two
months and then repot it
with the others.*

Hanging pots

No more room on the windowsill? Hanging pots are the best way to use overhead space.

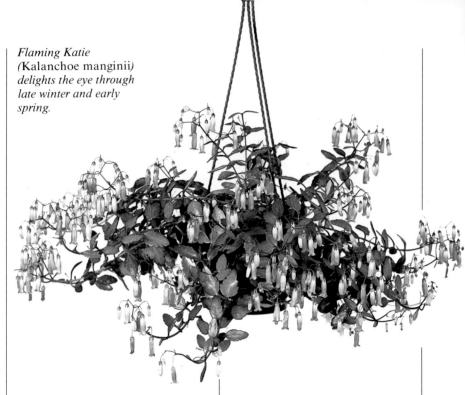

*Flaming Katie (*Kalanchoe manginii*) delights the eye through late winter and early spring.*

Streptocarpus saxorum loves a sunny place and its fleshy little leaves indicate that it requires very little water. Keep it cool in winter.

Cascades of flowers and foliage

Hanging baskets offer trailing, climbing and creeping plants the chance to develop a balanced all-round shape. The effect can be spectacular as leaves cascade like a waterfall, flowers foam over and offspring or shoots dangle free. Of course, hanging plants are not exactly easy to maintain.

How much to water becomes a question of instinct. It is not so easy to employ the standard tests of feeling with the fingertips or judging the weight of the container. Since the plants are often very leafy, they lose a lot of water through evaporation and furthermore they dry much faster in their lofty location than down below. When temperatures are warm it is advisable to make sure the potting medium stays moist. The best equipment for this purpose is a plastic watering can with a curving spout about 60cm (24in) in length.

Important Only give as much water as the plants are able to absorb: remember most hanging pots have no drainage holes. So, to avoid standing water (which will rot the roots), put a 2cm (¾in) layer of clay-pot pieces in a solid-bottomed pot before setting the flowerpot in it. For containers with a drainage hole, it is best to take them down once a week, put them in a sink and spray them thoroughly but gently with lukewarm water. (To protect furniture and floors, only rehang the plants when they have stopped dripping.)

The threadlike runners of the mother of thousands make it a charming hanging plant.

Recommended plants

Especially robust *Asparagus, Billbergia, Ceropegia, Chlorophytum, Cissus, Hoya, Saxifraga stolonifera,* succulent *Senecio* species, *Setcreasea, Tradescantia, Zebrina*

Plants for areas that are only moderately warm *Ampelopsis, Ficus pumila, Hedera, Jasminum, Pelargonium odoratissimum, Peperomia, Schlumbergera* hybrids, *Scirpus, Tolmiea*

Plants that need warmth and high humidity *Aeschynanthus, Columnea, Hypocyrta, Dipladenia, Episcia, Epipremnum, Ficus sagittata, Monstera, Nepenthes, Philodendron, Syngonium,* as well as rhizomatous and winter-flowering begonias and, of course, many ferns. Since it is difficult to mist plants *in situ* because of the furniture, the use of a humidifer is recommended for these. Alternatively, take down the hanging plant and mist in the bath or shower.

Professional tip With skilful use of plant lights it is even possible to place hanging plants in the middle of a room.

*The root ball of parrot's beak (*Lotus berthelotii*) should never be allowed to dry out.*

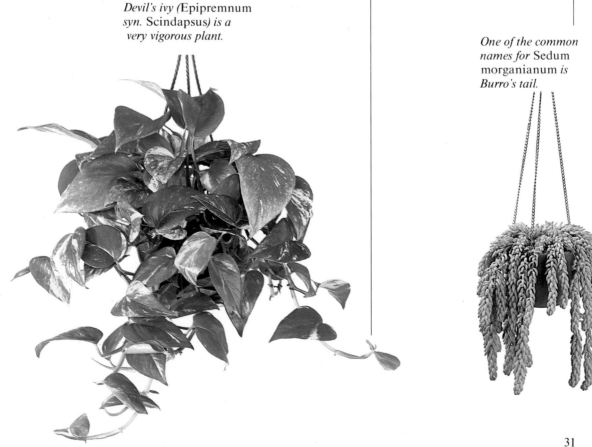

*Devil's ivy (*Epipremnum syn. Scindapsus*) is a very vigorous plant.*

One of the common names for Sedum morganianum *is Burro's tail.*

Cultivating houseplants successfully

Proper watering, feeding, potting on and training are important and must be learned. But cultivation also includes observation, instinct and understanding of what each individual plant needs.

There's a wise old gardener's saying which goes, 'Your garden wants to see you every day.' This applies to plants that live indoors too. Like pets, plants need human care and suffer when they do not get it. But care does not consist only of watering and feeding. Rubber plants and cyclamens thrive demonstrably better in a relaxed, positive atmosphere. So be sympathetic toward them – or, better still, only deal with plants that you really like. Cultivating a plant you are fond of is not work but a constant pleasure, for which you will gladly sacrifice a little time.

First care after purchase

Imagine how a houseplant feels just after you buy it. How much stress it has already suffered before it comes under your protection. At first it was pampered in a horticultural nursery with every possible refinement. Then it was taken from this not native, to be sure, but nevertheless caring environment to be stacked in palettes in a truck and sent cross-country, perhaps for hundreds of miles. Next it spent a little time at the garden centre, was sold, transported again and finally came to rest on your windowsill. Each time it has to get used to a new environment. Each time light, temperature, location and water quality change.

Examine the surface of the potting medium, and if it is dry, water once thoroughly and after half an hour pour away the water that has drained through. Orchids should be only misted at first.

Acclimatize every newly acquired plant for several days in a 'neutral' place. That is, one that is semi-shaded and where the temperature is around 18°C (64°F). If it is wintertime, do not put the new plant in an artificially heated room, even if it likes warmth. In a florist's shop plants are often kept at cooler temperatures than those prescribed. Great temperature changes are shocks to which many plants will react with flower, bud or leaf drop.

Do not transplant, even if the plant is completely potbound and the pot seems to be too small. Wait about two weeks until the plant has got used to your living conditions. Do not pot on plants bought in autumn and winter until the end of late winter. The nutrients in the new soil are then available to the plant at the right time: the beginning of the growth period. When you are repotting, do not use too large a pot. Potting mediums in pots that are too large frequently retain too much water.

Dish gardens often contain combinations of species and varieties which frequently do not have the same care requirements. Place these gift arrangements in bright, warm (around 20°C/68°F), but not sunny places. Separate the plants before their roots become intertwined and pot them singly or in roomier containers. This is best done in the spring.

Equipment for plant care
- Hand rake and trowel
- Watering can with long, thin spout
- Watering can with a rose
- Spray bottles for spraying water, insecticides and foliar fertilizer
- All-purpose household shears
- Garden shears
- Sharp knife
- Wood and bamboo stakes
- Florist's wire, twine and string
- Charcoal powder or fungicide for disinfecting cut places
- Fertilizer
- Water softeners
- Various soils, soil components and additives
- Plant lights (for very dark locations)
- Holiday or time-controlled watering systems

These delightfully patterned prayer plants will not tolerate dry, centrally heated air.

Establishing a plant schedule

Plants are extraordinarily adaptable and most will not suffer if you occasionally do not follow the care plan exactly. But naturally they thrive best when care is right. So you should learn the basics about every new plant on its arrival in your home.

● Study the care instructions in the appropriate plant portrait (see pages 84–229).

● Compare them with your conditions and care habits.

● When establishing individual timetables for culture, take into consideration basics like growth factors (see page 36) and vegetative rhythms (see right).

● Try to improve less favourable locations by installing plant lights (see page 45), increasing the humidity (see page 43), shading or insulating windowsills (see page 45).

Vegetative rhythm and its implications

The growing season

For all plants the growing season is triggered by an increase in available light. For houseplants it begins when the days grow longer.

Distinguishing signs Appearance of fresh green new shoots.

What to do Starting in spring, slowly increase the amount of water and begin fertilizing.

The rest period

For many plants, for example those from tropical and subtropical latitudes with unfluctuating climate, there is no rest period. As houseplants in the temperate zone they are forced into a rest period, which is conditioned by the decreasing amount of sunshine and shorter days in the autumn and winter months.

Plants on pages 34–5
Green on green: a stunning collection of leaf shapes and textures. Back row, from left to right Calathea veitchiana, *sword fern (*Nephrolepis exaltata*), stromanthe (*Stromanthe 'Stripe Star'*) and scented-leaved geranium (*Pelargonium graveolens*). Front row Sword fern (*Nephrolepis exaltata 'Linda'*), bulrush (*Scirpus cernuus*), inch plant (*Callisia repens*), guzmania (*Guzmania*), desert privet (*Peperomia obtusifolia*), bead plant (*Nertera granadensis*), umbrella plant (*Cyperus*), brittle maidenhair ferns (*Adiantum tenerum*) and another umbrella plant.*

However, a rest period can also be part of the genetic programme of some species. This is true in the case of plants that die back and regenerate themselves from tubers and bulbs (like amaryllis, cyclamen and many gesneraids) or in the case of deciduous plants. Also, plants that in their native habitat must live through periods of drought manage to survive by treating them as rest periods. It is important to bear in mind that these rest periods do not always coincide with our autumn and winter. In the case of the calla lily, for instance, the rest period does not begin until the end of late spring.

Distinguishing signs Growth decreases until it is at a standstill; leaves yellow and drop.

What do do Many houseplants need to maintain the rest period if they are to begin to grow again and set flowers. This means that the houseplant gardener must provide a dry, cool period. Since the processes which keep the plant alive diminish when less light is available, the other growth promoters, such as water and warmth, must be reduced at the same time, although very low temperatures must be avoided. Moreover, feeding must stop because a plant in a resting condition or with light deficiency cannot process nutrients. For example, cacti that are compelled by warmth and nutrients to grow during the winter do not produce very hardy tissue and do not bloom the following year.

Professional tip Plants from the tropical rain forest do not need a rest period, and you can give them excellent, appropriate care under plant lights, which provide the constant optimal condition for growth. Of course, constant warmth and a consistently high humidity are essential too.

The five growth factors

The growth factors of light, warmth, water, air and nutrients are the engine that gets plant life started and keeps it going. They are mutually dependent on each other and mutually influence each other and they must be coordinated correctly for the species and for the time of year. The plant portraits (see pages 84–229) make very clear, under the headings of 'Location' and 'Watering, Feeding' what each plant's growth factors are.

1 Light

By means of light, through photosynthesis, the plant manufactures the carbohydrates that it needs for growth. Light affects the direction of growth and influences the shape of the plant, leaf colour and flower development. Diminish the light intensity and the life processes are reduced to mere survival levels. Light intensity is expressed in lumens and can be measured with a luxmeter (see drawing, page 45). The minimum light needed by plants varies between 700 and 1000 lux. Below this, growth and flower development stand still. Optimal growth becomes possible above 10,000 lumens.

The period during which a plant needs light varies with the individual and depends on its natural habitat. On the average, a plant needs 12 to 16 hours of light daily.

Tips for care The brighter a plant's location, the more vigorously it will grow and therefore the more warmth, water and fertilizer it tolerates. In a darker position, the other growth factors should be reduced accordingly.

2 Warmth

Warmth promotes growth, nutrient uptake and vigorous root growth. Plants from the tropical rain forest need constant warmth; other tropical and subtropical plants will not be harmed by slightly lower winter temperatures; and tropical mountain-dwellers and Mediterranean species must be cool when the dark season begins. But bottom warmth is important for all plants. Many plants fail because their roots are much too cold, so a

heated pad is of considerable benefit to more delicate plants placed on a windowsill. If you have lots of plants grouped together, in a conservatory for example, it will pay to install electric warming cables in the peat or gravel on which the plant pots are resting.

Tips for care The warmer and brighter a plant's location, the more water it needs. Water less when it is cool. Coolness plus dampness spell poison for houseplants.

3 Water

Water, a main constituent of the plant, serves as the transporter of nutrients (also of fertilizer) and maintains pressure in the cells. If it is lacking, the plant becomes limp. If there is too much of it, the same symptom appears because the water actually squeezes out the oxygen that the roots need to absorb from the soil.

Opposite
Camellia japonica *is an ideal tub plant for the conservatory.*
1 'Ima Kumagai'
2 'St Ewe'
3 'Imbricata Rubra'
4 'Jury's Yellow'
5 'C.M. Wilson'
6 'Bob Hope'
7 'Fred Sander'
8 'Ezo Nishiki'
9 'Betty Sheffield Supreme'

Water is constantly evaporating, more in sunny places, in high temperatures and in dry air than in shady places with lower temperatures and humid air, and from large, soft and thickly foliaged plants more than from small- and hard-leaved ones.

Tips for care Water all plants more during the growing season, especially those in a bright location, in heat and when air is dry. Water less during the rest period as well as in a shady spot, in cool areas and where humidity is high.

4 Air and humidity

Air is needed by plants to breathe. But if they are to be healthy the air must be reasonably fresh. Stagnant air (as when the plants are crowded together) promotes fungal problems and straggly growth. Draughts and air that is contaminated with exhaust or poisons (such as cigarette smoke) can produce leaf, flower or bud drop.

Humidity is important for all houseplants that are not furnished with their own protection against evaporation (see page 16), or that can take up water from atmospheric moisture alone (epiphytes), or that come from the constantly moist rain forest and are not at all adapted to dry centrally heated air.

The humidity requirement of some tropical plants lies between 60 and 80 per cent. Most houseplants need between 50 and 80 per cent humidity. A healthy indoor climate for people, animals and plants should have 50 to 60 per cent humidity. In winter the humidity in a centrally heated room is around 40 to 50 per cent, presenting dry air that most plants cannot tolerate. You can measure with a hygrometer whether there is enough moisture in your home.

Tips for care The higher the humidity, the more warmth a plant can tolerate.

5 Potting medium and fertilizer

Potting medium provides plants with their nutrients. Furthermore it serves to contain and anchor the roots and should be so constituted that they are always surrounded by slight dampness while enabling air to get to them. This means that a good potting medium should be able to retain moisture and still be air-permeable.

Potting medium can be made up by the gardener from various components or bought ready-mixed. In my experience, plants grow best in commercial potting mixtures and in the ready-made special mediums for particular plant groups (see page 40). Use only high-quality commercial potting products for your houseplants. Inexpensive ones may not have satisfactory water-retention capacity and permeability for air circulation; their nutrient or humus content or pH-value may be insufficient; and their condition may not be hygienic. It is also important that the soil should be reasonably fresh so check the condition of the bags in which it is sold: you may be able to spot those which have been lying around the shop for ages.

Other plant materials or soil additives Gravel, sand, polystyrene pieces, pumice, lava and vermiculite are frequently mixed into commercial potting mediums to make them lighter and therefore more permeable to air. It is possible to buy these materials separately at most good garden-supply shops, and some plants do require added help of this sort. Portuguese bark and old branches are used for supporting epiphytes.

Environmental tip At present there is much concern regarding the use of peat in potting mixtures because of the large quantities that are being extracted from moorland regions so it is advisable to use this material sparingly. Alternative materials are currently being experimented with, but much work still needs to be done before recommendations can be made.

Tips for care Never allow mediums containing peat to dry out. Peat does, of course, have a good water-storage capacity, but once it has become completely dry, it takes up water very poorly. Plunging a very dry pot into water is the most effective first-aid measure.

Fertilizer is necessary because any potting medium offers only limited nutrients, and plants, if they are to continue to grow and thrive, need additional supplies.

The principal nutrients are nitrogen (the chemical symbol for it is N), phosphorus (P), potassium (K) and magnesium (Mg).

Nitrogen makes plants grow, providing for the growth of stems and leaves and for the development of chlorophyll. But too much nitrogen makes plant tissue soft and subject to disease.

Phosphorus is necessary for the development of roots and buds as well as for the ripening of fruits and seeds. Flowering plants need more of it than foliage plants.

Potassium makes plant tissue strong and resistant to disease and insect pests and is important for photosynthesis.

Magnesium is used principally in the formation of chlorophyll.

Trace elements are those nutrients that the plant must have for life but nevertheless takes up only in tiny or 'trace' amounts. For efficiency the plant requires iron, copper, manganese, molybdenum, zinc and boron.

A good complete fertilizer must contain the four chief nutrients and all the trace elements necessary for life. They can of course be supplied in various compositions, some to suit specific groups of plants (orchids and cacti, for example). Growth-promoting fertilizers have slightly more nitrogen, whereas flower-promoting fertilizers always contain more phosphorus and potassium than nitrogen. Fertilizers are available in various forms. Especially suitable are the liquid fertilizers, which can be watered in, or fertilizer sticks, which you simply poke into the soil.

The correct dosage depends on the roots' sensitivity to salts. For most plants 2 grams or 2 ml (0.7 oz) of fertilizer to 1 litre (1 qt) of water is enough. Follow the manufacturer's instructions, use the measuring spoon provided and make the solution too weak rather than too strong. Salt-sensitive plants, like orchids and ferns, should receive very low dosages.

A small aquarium makes a delightful container for ferns. The lava rock provides humidity.

Tips for care

● The rule of thumb is: feed houseplants every two weeks during the growing season. However, vigorously growing plants can be fed weekly; slow-growing ones should only be fertilized every four weeks or so.

● Never fertilize a dry root ball or in full sun.

● It is better to feed often and at low concentrations than to do it seldom and in high dosages.

● Only feed when the plant is growing.

● Fertilize less when the plant is receiving less light than it needs for growth. When light is deficient the nutrients are not utilized and with inorganic fertilizers the soil can become oversalted.

● Plants without rest periods also need fertilizer once a month in winter.

● Remember that for very large plants feeding can take the place of potting on.

Talking to plants

I know plenty of plant-lovers who attribute their success to the fact that they talk with their charges, and every so often I catch myself 'talking to myself' around plants in the garden or in the house.

It still is not clear what kind of sensory apparatus plants possess, but trials with lie detectors have shown that plants react 'anxiously' to attack (from fire or cutting implements, for example), and new discoveries are being made all the time. So far scientists know that ultrasound stimulates growth, an anaesthetized tree survives transplanting better and plants thrive more with chamber music than with hard rock. Why this should be so is not clear. But the fact that we cannot explain it, and cannot demonstrate the reasons for it by means of technology, does not render the phenomena any less true. We may smile now at those who talk to their plants, but perhaps in

the future scientists will be able to confirm that such people were really applying sound principles of plant care.

For all that, even today it is possible to hear the sound made by thirsty plants. In England a sensor has been developed that picks up the alarm sound of plants that need water. The tone, which lies in the region of ultrasound at 1 MHz is caused by movements in the tiny capillaries that transport materials around the whole plant.

We know so pitifully little about all living things that it seems to me very inappropriate for us to scorn the notion that communication between plants and people is impossible. So speak with your plants, and stroke them gently on their leaves. The evidence that it does not do any good has not yet been produced.

TECHNIQUES

Potting mediums and the secrets of potting on

Potting composts consisting mainly of peat, loam, sand and nutrients serve most plants well. Proof of this is the fact that underground the medium is quickly permeated by healthy roots and above ground many new shoots develop.

Expanded clay aggregate induces many houseplants to thrive. The lightweight, water-retentive granules (they come in various sizes) give the roots good support. Nutrients are provided by water and a special nutrient solution.

Epiphyte medium provides good rooting conditions for tree dwellers such as ferns, bromeliads and orchids. These plants look especially attractive if the medium is bound to an epiphyte support, a piece of bark or an old branch.

Types of potting medium

The potting medium is both culture medium and foundation. In other words, plants need to be able to draw nutrients and water from it as well as using it for support. A good potting medium should be well aerated, warm and permeable to water but also water-retentive, rich in nutrients and slightly acid (pH value 5 to 6.5). See also page 38. The most common types of potting mediums are listed below.

● Soil-less compost: based on peat, this medium is prepared ready for use with no added nutrients required. Seeding compost contains only a little fertilizer; potting compost is more heavily fertilised and is used for maintaining growth. Mixtures vary slightly depending on the manufacturer. Some are prepared for specific potting operations, for example planting in hanging baskets. Soil-less compost is now the preferred potting medium for general indoor use. Its characteristic lightness means both that it is easier to handle and that it remains better aerated than soil-based compost.

● Soil-based compost: not so freely used today, this is the formula of seven parts loam, three parts peat and two parts sand with nutrients added, the quantities dependent on the use to which the medium will be put (either for propagation or for potting on).

● Cactus soils: sandy, free-draining mediums.

● Azalea soils: leafy, spongy, ericaceous mediums containing peat and leaf mould.

● Orchid soils: consist of varying materials, including coarse shredded peat, polystyrene pieces, charcoal and mineral materials like vermiculate, lava and pumice.

● Epiphyte planting materials: see orchid soils.

● Clay granules: consist of marble-sized pieces that are water retentive, aerated and stable in structure.

Root ball in clay granules

Ideal for all who usually water too much or too little. The pea-sized clay granules can absorb up to a third of their own weight in water and release it to the roots as needed.

How to convert to hydroculture

1. *Thoroughly wash the potting medium out of root ball under running water.*
2. *Remove any obviously damaged roots.*
3. *Set plant on wet clay granules in special basket; add granules to fill.*
4. *Place basket in outer container and fill with lukewarm water.*

How to pot on

It is time to pot on when:
- the plant is too large for its pot.
- leaves are becoming discoloured from lack of food.
- the plant has too much root for its current pot when removed for inspection.
- when young plants are growing vigorously at the start of the season.

The ideal time for potting on for most plants is spring into early summer, when growth is most vigorous.

Preparation begins several hours beforehand. Water the plant thoroughly and select the new container, which should be about 2cm (¾in) larger than the old one. Soak terracotta pots for two hours before using.

Removing the old pot can be difficult. Try turning it over and rapping it sharply on the edge of a table. If the plant refuses to be dislodged, you may have to break the pot. Crumble away the topmost layer of soil. Loosen tight networks of roots very gently.

Trimming the roots is necessary when they are brown-black and rotten or with very old plants that you do not want to keep putting into larger pots. Powder the cut places with charcoal. The branches can be lightly trimmed back too so that balance above and below ground is maintained.

Cutting back is recommended for leafless plants (see page 44).

Drainage and its importance cannot be overemphasized for bad drainage rots roots. Plastic pots with several holes do not need special treatment, but when potting plants into terracotta pots with a single drainage hole in the bototm, it is important to ensure that drainage material is placed in the bottom of the pot before introducing the potting mixture. Lay a piece of broken flower pot over the drainage hole or cover it with a 3cm (1in) layer of clay granules, pebbles or polystyrene pieces; for large pots use 5 to 10cm (2 to 4in) of the chosen material.

Replanting Water the plant and place it in a bright position where the roots will be warm. Warm potting mixture promotes the development of roots. Do not put it in a sunny spot.

Initial care is very important too. Water sparingly – only enough to prevent the soil from drying out. As soon as new growth appears, begin care according to the plant's requirements. Fertilize six to eight weeks after transplanting.

Top dressing, or replacing the top layer of potting mixture is recommended for large plants that, for reasons of space, you do not want to keep potting on into larger pots and for plants that should not be potted on.

Converting to hydroculture demands extremely careful washing of the root system to remove all the potting medium (see drawings, How to convert to hydroculture).

Potting on foliage and flowering plants

1 *Placing your hand over potting mixture, turn pot upside down. Carefully remove root ball from pot. Very gently untangle root network. Do not disturb sections permeated with roots. Trim away injured roots.*
2 *Provide drainage by covering drainage hole with curved piece of broken flower pot or layer of clay granules.*
3 *Put some fresh potting mixture in pot. Place plant in middle of pot and at about same level as before. Fill up with potting mixture and press firmly. Leave a 2-cm (¾-in) space to allow for watering.*

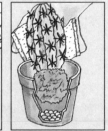

Potting on cactus

1 *Lift cactus out of pot. Wear stout gardening gloves and use pieces of polystyrene to protect your hands.*
2 *Remove hard crust of potting medium from top of root ball.*
3 *Arrange drainage granules or crocks at base of pot. Put some fresh potting mixture in pot and set cactus at same height as before.*
4 *Fill with potting medium and firm it around cactus.*

How to secure orchids to supports

1 *Wrap the roots in sphagnum moss.*
2 *Position the plant centrally on bark or branch anchorage.*
3 *Bind carefully to support with plastic-covered wire.*

TECHNIQUES

Watering, softening water and providing humidity

Watering from the top is recommended for most houseplants. The potting medium is dampened uniformly and any fertilizer in the water can be evenly distributed. Tip: a watering can with a long spout helps to keep the leaves from getting wet.

Watering from the bottom is good for plants with tubers, stems or leaves that are particularly susceptible to dampness (for example, African violets). Disadvantage: the possibility that the potting medium will become much too wet from standing too long in water.

Soaking is the best way to provide thorough watering for epiphytes and orchids, which have a particularly porous potting medium. It is also an ideal method for hanging plants, which are often in pots or baskets with inadequate saucers beneath them.

Nine golden rules of watering

How much water a plant needs depends on its individual requirements (see descriptions of individual species, pages 89–229), its vegetative rhythms and the potting medium, as well as on light, temperature and humidity. However, the following most important list contains the ten principles of watering.

1 Water when the potting medium feels dry to the touch or when the pot feels light in weight. (It is important to know how heavy the pot feels when the plant is properly watered.)

2 Water most plants from the top; in some exceptional instances, water from the bottom. It is best to soak dried-out plants, epiphytes and hanging plants. (See drawings)

3 Ideally water for almost all plants should be hand-temperature and soft. If your kettle rapidly gets 'furred up', you live in a hard-water area and should soften the water you give to your plants beforehand (see drawing, Softening water).

4 In general tap water should be left to stand overnight so that chlorine can evaporate and the lime precipitate.

5 The following plants must be watered more often: plants in dry, warm air; in bright, sunny places; abundantly leaved and large-leaved plants; plants in terracotta pots and plants with high water requirements, which are usually planted mainly in clay or peaty soils.

6 The following plants must be watered less often: plants in high humidity; in lower temperatures; in light-poor conditions; plants in plastic pots and plants with lower water requirements, which are frequently planted in sandy soils.

7 During the growth period water thoroughly but not too often.

Watering bromeliads

Pour the water directly into the cup of overlapping leaves. For any other plant, standing water of this sort would be lethal, but bromeliads supply themselves with water and nutrients from the cup, which must never be allowed to dry out.

Softening water

1 With peat: suspend a 1 litre (1qt) bag of dried peat in 10 litres (10qt) of water overnight.
2 With filtered watering can containing an ion exchanger: lime and other impurities are removed.
3 With the liquid or solid softening agent: let water stand for several hours.

'Thoroughly' means watering until water runs out of the drainage holes at the bottom of the pot. Small quantities of water dampen only the surface and never reach the fine roots in the interior of the pot.

8 The amount of water is usually decreased in autumn and winter.

9 Always remove the superfluous water in saucers and outer pots.

How to improve humidity

A humidity of 60 or 70 per cent is the ideal climate for most houseplants. In summer low humidity is less of a problem, but in winter in a warm room it can very quickly drop to under 40 per cent, which causes problems for plants.

Direct humidity can be provided with direct spraying (see drawing 4, Humidity). In this way you are imitating the falling of dew, which is indicated for tillandsias and other epiphytes, for example. It is important, when employing this technique, to use soft water and a fine spray, and do not spray flowers or in sunlight.

Indirect humidity is appreciated by most houseplants. Besides the methods illustrated (see drawings 1 to 3, Humidity), there are the following other possibilities.

● Install an electric humidifier, aquarium or indoor fountain.

● Place plants on saucers with peat, sand or pebbles that are kept constantly damp.

Professional tip If you want to increase the humidity by spraying, you should not direct spray onto leaves that are particularly sensitive to water (for example, begonias, streptocarpus, gloxinias, mimosas, *Miltonia*) but only in their vicinity (see drawing 3, Humidity). In such cases it is even better to use some other method of indirect humidity.

Watering while on holiday

If you are going to be away from home for only a few days, water the plants thoroughly, give them a cooler place or tuck them into clay granules, which can take up 33 per cent of their own weight in water (see drawing, Root ball in clay granules, page 40).

For longer absences a friendly neighbour prepared to stand in for you is probably the happiest solution, but there are various 'plant sitters', which all work on the principle of capillary action. As the potting medium dries out, the plant sucks water from a reservoir through an inserted terracotta spike (see drawing

3, Automatic watering), wicks (see drawings 1 and 2, Automatic watering), woollen cord or a block of wood or through capillary matting of various types (see drawing, Holiday watering).

Important Try your plant-sitter system out ahead of time to make sure it works and to estimate how long the water supply lasts.

Humidity for several plants
Lay grid rack in dish and add enough water to reach bottom of grid. The plants will avoid being waterlogged but be enveloped in evaporating water.

Humidity for individual plants
1 *Sink pot in larger pot filled with peat or clay granules.*
2 *Put plant on overturned saucer in larger, water-filled container.*
3 *Use indirect misting: not on plant itself but in air around it.*
4 *Tillandsias and epiphytes like to be sprayed directly.*

Automatic watering
1 *Introduce fibreglass wick through drainage hole with larding needle or when potting on . . .*
2 *. . . and arrange upper end on surface of potting medium, allowing lower end to hang down into water container. Cover with potting mix.*
3 *Use terracotta spike attached to special tube to draw water into dry soil.*

Holiday watering
Place sheet of capillary matting on draining board, making sure the end hangs into water-filled sink. The water-absorbent mat can take care of a collection of plants. But make sure it does not extend beyond the draining board or water will drip onto floor.

TECHNIQUES

Cutting, pinching back and pruning

1 Cutting: the place to cut is just above a bud.
2 Pinching back: nipping out the end of a shoot, especially in young plants, to create a bushier effect.
3 Pruning: for rejuvenating, shaping or making plants smaller, used especially on older specimens.

Cutting back, training and culture hints

Training on a hoop

For twining and climbing plants
1 Form wire into hoop and insert ends deep into potting mixture.
2 Carefully wind shoots round hoop and tie in position.

Establishing a moss stake

For aeroids such as philodendrons
1 Place moss stake in pot, firming potting mix around it.
2 Settle plant next to it and fasten shoots to it.

The right way to cut back

Plants are cut back for several reasons: to rejuvenate them, to make them grow bushier and to keep them small.

The optimum time for pruning is spring, before the plant begins to put out new growth, or just after flowering (often in the autumn).

The correct way to prune is to make a clean, sharp cut 2.5 to 5cm (1 to 2in) above a bud (see drawing 1, Cutting). Large cut areas are best disinfected with a little damp potting medium.

How much to take off? This depends on the kind of plant, its growth and your purpose in pruning.

● In pinching back (see drawing 2, Pinching back) the ends of the shoots are nipped off with the fingers.

● In pruning (see drawing 3, Pruning), if you want to shape the plant, it is simply a matter of trimming out untidy growth. More drastic pruning is recommended only when the plant is growing too vigorously, is bare underneath or has formed straggly shoots with large intervals between the leaves.

Methods of training plants

For training on a frame (see drawing, Hoop) or espaliering choose plants with long, soft stems.

Moss stakes (see drawing, Moss stake) can be purchased from most garden centres and are ideal for *Philadendron* and *Monstera*.

Make your own standard (see drawing, Training a standard). It can take five years to achieve a finished standard. To allow for losses, it is a good idea, if you have space, to begin with several plants at once.

Tree with intertwined stems

The still-pliable stems of three young weeping figs can be braided to make a charming standard.

Training a standard

1 Keep removing side shoots of sturdy young plant.
2 Introduce a support and secure with string at intervals. When desired height is reached, trim the top.
3 Remove growing tips at first to produce bushy crown.

Ten hints for successful culture

Each of these suggestions takes a little time, but it is time well spent when the result is a healthier, happier plant.

1 *Helping bromeliads to flower* (see drawing, Culture tricks). Ripening apples and citrus fruits give off ethylene gas, which is a plant hormone that bromeliads need to develop flowers. Shut your bromeliads (they must be mature plants) in a transparent plastic bag with an apple for one to two weeks. Some four months later the flower development will occur.

2 *Regularly removing old flower heads* (see drawing 2, Culture tricks). The development of seeds actually costs the plant a great deal of energy and makes a second flowering less likely. However, some plants (such as the *Hoya*) produce their second flowers on the flowerstalks of the first.

3 *Making a mark on the pot* (see drawing 3, Culture tricks) is a help in orienting the pot so that it is replaced facing the light the same way, after it has been removed for spraying, dusting or window washing. This is important for sensitive plants like the Kaffir lily, azalea and gardenia, which otherwise react very easily with flower drop.

4 *Insulating windowsills with polystyrene boards* (see drawing 4, Culture tricks) is the simplest way to protect from cold. Still better are electric warming pads, which are available in garden supply stores.

5 *Dusting, washing or a warm June rain* (see drawing 1, Plant cosmetics) allow the leaves to 'breathe' and help increase photosynthesis efficiency.

6 *Removing brown leaf tips* (see drawing 2, Plant cosmetics). Leave a small brown margin or freshly cut area will dry out again.

7 *Rinsing the potting medium* (see drawing 1, Rinsing and soaking) under a slow stream of lukewarm water washes out the superfluous fertilizer salts. Helpful with plants that cannot be potted often or that you do not want to pot on because of their location.

8 *Soaking in a bucket* (see drawing 2, Rinsing and soaking) is often the last resort for a limp plant with a completely dried-out root ball.

9 *Using a plant light* (see drawing 1, Measured light) allows you to put both foliage and flowering plants in the darkest corners.

10 *Checking the light values* with a light meter (see drawing 2, Measured light) is a sensible precaution when installing plant lights or considering poorly lit locations.

Culture tricks

1 *The scent of apples induces bromeliads to flower.*
2 *Remove spent flowers: seed development takes too much energy. But lilies and amaryllis must be left to seed.*
3 *A mark on pot can indicate window side of plant.*
4 *Polystyrene or a warming mat insulates against cold.*

Plant cosmetics

1 *Wipe off smooth leaves with lukewarm water. Dust hairy leaves with soft brush.*
2 *When trimming brown leaf tips, leave a margin.*

Rinsing and soaking

1 *Remove superfluous fertilizer salts by running lukewarm water through potting medium.*
2 *If root ball has dried out, immerse pot in a container of lukewarm water, deep enough to cover pot, and leave until bubbles no longer rise to surface.*

Measured light

1 *Plant lights can make it possible to grow plants in dark interiors.*
2 *Brightness can be checked with a luxmeter (available from garden and photographic suppliers).*

A bizarre, twisted branch fixed in a sturdy pottery container with plaster or cement is an ideal place to display grey tillandsias. They are best attached with soft, pliable, plastic-covered wire. Since they take up water through the absorptive scales on their leaves, they should not be watered but misted all over with soft, room-temperature water.

Mistakes in culture that make plants sick

- Too little light in too warm a location
- Too much sun for shade-lovers
- Too much shade for sun-lovers
- Strong spring sunshine
- Fluctuating temperatures
- Heat pool behind the windowpane
- Cold air between windowpane and curtain
- Cold roots
- Cold, hard water
- Too much water in too cool a location

- Waterlogged potting medium
- Oxygen starvation in a poorly ventilated room
- Poisoned air (caused by gas from leaky gas pipes or fires, or vapours from wood preservatives)
- Draughty position
- Too small or too large a container
- Musty, mouldy and compacted potting mediums
- Not maintaining winter rest
- Open windows in late spring when aphids appear

Clay versus soil

Clay pellets have long been used in hydroculture as well as for a combined soil–gravel culture. With the latter, the plant is simply transplanted from its soil-filled pot into the potting medium, which it soon fills happily with roots (see drawing, page 40).

Clay granules, hydroculture equipment and the chemicals necessary for this type of culture are obtainable from specialist suppliers.

Advantages of clay pellets

- They have a plant-friendly pH value somewhere between 6.0 to 6.5.
- They do not deteriorate or compact (and therefore are aerated and stable in structure), providing a good supply of oxygen and water which is beneficial to the roots.
- The equipment includes a water gauge which indicates when the plants must be watered again so there is little danger of over- or under-watering.
- The water supply lasts for three to four weeks, as a rule, so you can be away for short trips without worrying.
- Special long-acting nutrient solutions last for four to six months.
- It is not necessary to pot on so often provided the original container is a reasonable size.

Switching from soil culture to hydroculture

This process is not without problems and works best when the plants are young, growing well and healthy. Furthermore, all soil must be completely removed from the roots (see drawing, page 40) so they do not begin to rot. Use only special hydropots for potting on. Best time: early spring to early autumn.

A number of foliage and flowering plants are suitable for this type of culture (see Plant portraits, pages 89–229, carrying the symbol ⌗).

Switching from soil culture to clay granules

This is much simpler because the plant roots are not disturbed. You can also transplant older plants to this medium. In fact, all houseplants that thrive in soil can also be cultivated this way. The new pot must be considerably larger and without a drainage hole (see drawing, page 40); the ideal proportions are one third earth ball and two thirds clay granules. The best time for potting on is early spring to early autumn.

Professional tip Since the salt content of clay granules varies widely, they must be rinsed thoroughly before being used.

The ancient art of bonsai

Translated, *bonsai* means 'a tree in a dish'. These miniatures are not, as their size might suggest, an 'immature' or juvenile form but tiny adults with the growth characteristic of the mature form. A bonsai can be five years old and look as if the storms of decades had passed over it. However, a bonsai does look curious when it blooms and fruits. Its branches and leaves may be small, but the flowers and fruits develop at their original size.

Every bonsai tells a story when you study it closely. The little sageretia grove on page 49, for example, could be titled 'The Whisper of the Leaves – the Quiet of the Forest'. To me it suggests a coppice of trees on a high plateau of rock. I can imagine the trees' struggles for light, with the outermost ones victorious, bearing abundantly leaved branches almost to the ground, while those inside are bare at the bottom. Below them shade-loving moss spreads a thick carpet over the entire crown of the rock, muffling the whisper of the sageretia leaves – the stillness of the forest. The fact that this little group, made small as though by magic, makes the essential form of the tree more apparent is extraordinary, and is perhaps the most fascinating aspect of the art of bonsai.

In Japan, where bonsai first originated, the miniature tree has been an object of meditation for almost two thousand years. There they use outdoor plants exclusively, such as pine or maple. When bonsai was first brought to Europe, there was bitter disappointment when these outdoor plants perished after being brought inside in order to admire their beauty. As a result bonsai gardeners began to experiment with the idea of creating indoors rather than outdoor subjects. What could be more appropriate than to choose tropical, subtropical or Mediterranean trees and shrubs that had already demonstrated their usefulness indoors as house or tub plants? After years of experimental work, experts have now discovered some very successful candidates.

Bonsai for interiors

Culture requirements

Basically they have the same requirements for light, water, temperature and nutrients as do the non-miniaturized pot plants of the same name (see Plant portraits, pages 89–229). The following principles generally hold true.

Mediterranean shrubs are imprinted by their habitat in the Mediterranean, South Africa, Chile and California. They love the freshness of summer outdoors but must be brought inside before the first frost and overwintered in a bright, cool place (average temperature about 10°C/50°F).

Subtropical shrubs come from regions with hot, humid summers and mild, rainy winters. They also summer happily outdoors and should be moved indoors in early autumn and overwintered in a place that is bright and somewhat warmer (around 15°C/59°F).

*An evergreen or Chinese elm (*Ulmus parvifolia*) whose trunk has been trained to slant.*

Tropical shrubs are used to warm, damp air the whole year round. Some can get along with astonishingly little light. Cultivate them in the house all year long, keeping them warm and as light as possible, but never sunny. Provide humidity (see page 43).

Shrubs from the dry plains are used to dry periods and do not mind if you

*In the pomegranate (*Punica granatum*) the flowers appear on one-year-old wood.*

Serissa foetida overhangs its container as a wild tree would a cliff.

forget to water them once in a while. They do best in a sunny place that is not too warm in winter.

Palms are really not suited for use as bonsais. Only the runner-producing lady palm (see Plant portraits, page 210) permits development of a tiny forest form.

Suitable plants

Mediterranean shrubs Monterey cypress (*Cupressus macrocarpa*); myrtle (*Myrtus communis*)

Subtropical shrubs camellia (*Camellia japonica*); kangaroo vine (*Cissus antarctica*); tender azalea (*Rhododendron simsii* hybrids); Chinese elm (*Elmus parvifolia*); sageretia (*Sageretia thea*); serissa (*Serissa foetida*)

Tropical shrubs weeping fig (*Ficus benjamina*); box-leafed fig (*Ficus buxifolia*); *Ficus neriifolia*; creeping fig (*Ficus pumila*); glossy-leaf fig and subspecies (*Ficus retusa*); schefflera (*Brassaia actinophylla*); Ming aralia (*Polyscias fruticosa*)

Shrubs from the dry plains desert rose (*Adenium obesum*); money plant (*Crassula arborescens*); spurge

Ficus retusa: this gnarled specimen is 60cm (23in) high.

(*Euphorbia balsamifera*); narrow-leaved bottle tree (*Brachychiton rupestris*)

Palms lady palms (*Rhapis excelsa, Rhapis humilis*)

Caring for bonsai

In the cultivation of all bonsai, it is most important that they are planted in very little soil in a very shallow dish. This means that the soil dries out faster than it would in a normal pot and nutrients are used up faster. Certain special care is therefore necessary.

● Mist the soil well before watering. Otherwise the water cannot penetrate and will run down the hill of earth unused and erode the potting medium.

A grove of sageretia, about 30 years old and 56cm (17½in) high

● Ideally fertilize very weakly and often, using a special bonsai fertilizer (available from specialist suppliers). This will avoid root-burn and salt deposits in the potting medium.
● Do not fertilize just before and during flowering, after repotting, after root pruning or if the bonsai looks sick.

Expert advice
If you have bought an indoor bonsai and would like to know more about these special houseplants, you should join your nearest bonsai club. Another bonsai gardener in the area can offer invaluable support to the beginner.

Fruit-bearing brush cherry (Syzygium paniculatum)

49

The he main reasons for disease and parasites – as I know from the countless letters from readers that I have answered in the course of 15 years – are mistakes in culture and poor location (see table, page 47). These weaken the plant and make it vulnerable. So, pay close attention to the culture instructions in the plant portraits (pages 89–229) and choose the best possible location.

First aid for your plants

No plant is proof against ailments and parasites. But you can do something to protect against them. Avoid mistakes in culture, feed your plants carefully and, if something does go wrong, root out the reason and eliminate the cause.

Preventive measures

The best prevention is to give the plant the care it requires. Besides this, there are a number of further measures to prevent disease or to help you recognize it early.

Hygiene Regularly remove leaves or flowers that have dried out, rotted or look sick to avoid sources of blight. Cut stems off cleanly at the base. Always disinfect the cut places with charcoal. Keep pots and soil clean. Loosen the surface of the soil with a fork now and again so that algae or moss cannot take hold. Regularly wash lime and salt deposits off the outsides of clay pots.

Strengthening plant tissue Water your plants with a brew made from horsetails, which contain silicic acid (see Recipe, page 52).

Regular check-up Make time to observe your plants and watch for any changes. Stem tips and buds are easily attacked by aphids. Be sure to check both sides of all leaves. This way you will often detect insects and disease in the early stages, which makes controlling them considerably easier. If you are at all in doubt, use a magnifying glass.

Breathing space Avoid putting plants too close together. Air must be able to circulate between them.

Isolate if necessary Sick plants must be separated from the healthy ones so that they cannot infect them or transfer parasites.

Control procedures

Do not automatically reach for the poison. In many instances you can get the same results with 'harmless' methods.

Mechanical controls should always be the first step.

● Remove the infested or ailing parts of the plant.

● Collect or wipe off insect pests. Also rinse in the shower.

● Submerge the above-ground plant parts in lukewarm water with a little washing-up liquid added. First enclose the pot in a plastic bag and fasten it to keep the pot and soil from getting wet.

Alternative control methods involve the use of traditional plant remedies, but they do not always prove successful.

● You can spray aphids with an extract of stinging nettles (see Recipe, page 52).

● Horsetail broth (see Recipe, page 52) combats mildew. Use once a week.

● Garlic is a powerful fungicide. Press a peeled clove into the soil.

● A wide-necked jar buried up to its neck and filled with beer entices slugs to the death by drowning.

● Agents from the pyrethrum flower combat many chewing and sucking insects, especially aphids. But they must not come into contact with open wounds or skin irritations. If they get into the bloodstream, they are highly poisonous.

Biotechnical controls make use of the natural reactions of parasites to physical or chemical stimuli.

● Yellow cards smeared with glue attract whiteflies and various flying pests with their colour.

● Using a 'plant sauna' (see drawing, above) you can destroy spider mites with extremely high humidity. To use this method, water the plant well, enclose it in a transparent plastic bag (for large plants use a dustbin bag), tie it at soil level and leave for several days. Important: not all plants will tolerate this procedure. Watch out for mould.

Most bathrooms offer warmth and good light and are an ideal setting for a fern collection.

Chemical means should be used only when other measures have not worked. Always read the product instructions carefully and follow the manufacturer's advice concerning dilution when handling insecticides of any kind. There are no agents to treat viral illnesses.

● Insecticides kill insects and can be sprayed, watered in or scattered over the potting medium or pushed into the ground in stick form.

● Agaricides kill mites.

● Fungicides are agents that destroy fungi.

● Substances containing oil (for example, white oil) or soap solutions (see Recipe, page 52) clog insects' breathing mechanisms or destroy their protective waxy covering. Oily sprays for making leaves shine work the same way and are now available in environment-friendly forms.

Essential precautions

● Before using any insecticide, make sure it has been passed safe for garden use.

● Follow the instructions for use and the dosage requirements exactly. Observe the recommended treatment intervals so as to destroy the second generation of pests.

● Protect the environment by using only environmentally friendly sprays.

● Spray plants out of doors.

● Wear gloves and do not inhale the insecticide fumes.

● Keep the insecticides in their original packages, out of reach of children and animals and under lock and key.

● Do not keep old, partially used cans around (the effectiveness of the preparation diminishes very quickly). Do not throw them away with the household rubbish; they should be taken to a toxic-waste collection centre.

Alternative sprays to make at home

Extract of stinging nettles for aphids
Let 500g (17½oz) fresh, young stinging nettles (before blooming) soak in 5 litres (5qt) water for 12 to 14 hours. Spray fresh and undiluted. (Also available from specialist shops as a herbal extract.)

Horsetail broth for mildew
Soften 500g (17½oz) fresh or 150g (5¾oz) dried field horsetails in 5 litres (5qt) of water for about 24 hours, and then boil for half an hour. Allow to cool, strain and thin 1:5 for spraying. (Also available from specialist stores as a herbal extract.)

Spirit-soap solution for scale and mealy bugs
Dissolve 1 tablespoon of soft soap or a generous squirt of washing-up liquid in some warm water. Add 1 scant litre (1 qt) of water and 1 tablespoon of methylated spirits. Paint the solution onto the affected areas. Alternatively, spray the whole plant with it, not forgetting the undersides of the leaves. Rinse tender-leaved plants after 15 minutes in clear, lukewarm water to lessen the risk of 'burning'.
Caution Do not smoke while handling spirits.

Treatment for growth problems

Failure to grow Eliminate errors in location or culture as well as root injury resulting from same (see below) or control root mealy bug with insecticide.

Sunscorch Remove spotted leaves. Place plant in a bright but not sunny location. Do not water the leaves of plants that are in the sun – the effect will be the same as if you held a magnifying glass to the leaves.

Iron deficiency (chlorosis) Dissolve iron sequestrin (from the garden centre) in water according to the directions, and spray the leaves or water the plant with it. Soften the water used for watering (see page 42). Pot on the plants in spring.

Corky growth Remove affected leaves. Keep the plants in a brighter location and uniformly damp.

Root injury Unpot the plant, remove ailing roots with a clean, sharp knife, dust with charcoal and pot on in fresh potting mixture.

Accordion growth in orchids Cut off injured roots, dust with charcoal and resettle in new potting medium.

Blossom rot Eliminate culture errors, such as wrong location, fertilizer too rich in nitrogen, disregarding the rest period or wrong overwintering.

Treatment for pests

Scale and mealy bugs Keep plants cooler and brighter. Scale can be cleaned off with a firm sponge or painted with spirit-soap solution (see Recipe, above). Use pyrethrum spray or insecticide; for hard-leaved plants use white oil or leaf-polishing spray.

Plant lice Use stinging-nettle extract (see Recipe, above), soap solution, pyrethrum spray or other insecticide.

Root mealy bug Remove potting medium and clean roots. Pot on and after about two weeks drench with insecticide. Repeat several times.

Thrips Rinse off with lukewarm water. Use yellow sticky cards or insecticide. Alternatively, use a host plant (such as potted gerbera) in the vicinity to attract them.

Spider mites (for instance, red spider) Increase humidity (see page 43), plant sauna (see page 50) or multiple rinsings with lukewarm water. Treat with spider-mite spray, changing product if necessary because the mites quickly develop resistance.

Whiteflies Lower the temperature because this tropical insect does not like coolness. Use yellow sticky cards or insecticide.

Mites Lower temperature and humidity. Remove and destroy infected plant parts.

Leaf eelworms Remove damaged leaves and destroy them. Damp foliage encourages them so do not get water on the leaves.

Root eelworms Destroy the plant.

Scariad fly (fungus gnats) Drench potting medium with insecticide.

Springtails (collembola) Drench the potting medium with malathion solution; it is strong smelling so treat outdoors. Less water in winter.

Vine weevil Remove potting medium from the roots and kill larvae before potting into fresh mixture.

Slugs Put down slug pellets. In large greenhouses set out beer traps.

Treatment for fungal infections

Powdery and downy mildew Remove afflicted leaves and destroy them. Use horsetail broth (see Recipe, above) or specific fungicide.

Grey mould (botrytis) Remove infected plant parts and dust remainder of plant with a fungicide. Place in airier, brighter location with lower humidity.

Leaf-spot fungus Remove infected plant parts. Use specific fungicide.

Rust fungus Remove fallen leaves. Use specific fungicide.

Sooty mould Remove completely blackened leaves and wash the less blackened ones with warm water. Get rid of cause (aphids, scale or whitefly).

Rot in roots, tubers, stalk or stem base There is no cure.

Mould Scratch off the superficial milky white layer on the surface of the potting medium. Raise the temperature and water well, but allow to dry out slightly between waterings. Pot on in the spring.

Opposite
These orchid beauties will all thrive on a windowsill. Here among the green of the ferns grow hybrids of Dendrobium nobile *and* Phalaenopsis, *the multigeneric hybrid* Vuylstekeara cambria 'Plush' *and* Odontoglossum *hybrids.*

TECHNIQUES

Healthy leaf
A healthy leaf has a firm structure as well as unblemished margins and tip.

Faulty culture
Brown leaf margins
Causes: too little water or too much, overfertilization, exhausted soil or dry air. Remedy: correct culture.

Brown leaf tips
Cause: air too dry or root ball too dry. Remedy: provide higher humidity (see page 43) and more water.

Diseases and pests: what the leaves tell

Yellow leaves
Cause: overwatering, too little nitrogen or too dark, too warm or too cool a location. Remedy: water less, fertilize and improve location.

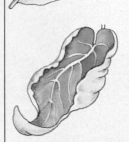

Curled leaves (see also Leaf curl)
Causes: air too dry, root ball too dry, root injury or caterpillars. Remedy: correct mistakes in culture and pot on as needed.

Pale leaves (chlorosis)
Leaf veins are still green. Causes: water too hard or iron deficiency. Remedy: use iron sequestrin in solution when watering.

Light spots on leaves
Causes: temperature shocks, water too cold or too warm and spraying in sunlight. Remedy: improve location and correct culture mistakes.

Silvery spots
In some plants also may be red or brown spots. Causes: sunscorch. Remedy: improve location and do not water in sunlight.

Corky growth
Causes: flagrant temperature changes, too much water in too little light or too wide a fluctuation of dampness in potting medium. Remedy: correct mistakes in culture.

Pests
Spider mites
Symptoms: pale brown discoloration on surface of leaves; pitting on undersides. Cause: air too warm and dry. Remedy: see page 52. If webs have formed, destroy plant.

Scale
Symptoms: brown scale, which conceals the insect, and leaf drop. Cause: air too dry. Remedy: see page 52.

Aphids
Symptoms: sticky and deformed leaves. Causes: draught, open windows in spring or air too dry. Remedy: see page 52.

Thrips
Symptoms: finely punctured, silvery leaves. Cause: dry air. Remedy: see page 52.

Mealy bugs
Symptoms: cottony formations and stunted growth. Cause: air too dry. Remedy: see page 52.

Whitefly
Symptoms: on undersides of leaves small white flies with wings overlapping like roof tiles. Cause: spread from contaminated plants. Remedy: see page 52.

Mites
Symptoms: rolled, crumpled leaves and no growth. Causes: contagion, promoted by warmth above 23°C (73°F) and humidity over 85 per cent. Remedy: see page 52.

Leaf eelworms
Symptoms: glassy spots, later becoming brown, leaf veins become more prominent and leaf drop. Remedy: None.

Slugs
Symptoms: leaves eaten and slimy trails. Cause: brought in from outside. Remedy: slug pellets.

Fungal diseases
Powdery mildew

Symptoms: white to dirty-brown powdery deposits on tops and undersides of leaves. Cause: airborne fungal spores. Remedy: see page 52.

Downy mildew
Symptoms: white to dirty-brown powdery deposits on undersides of leaves. Cause: airborne fungal spores. Remedy: see page 52.

Grey mould (botrytis)
Symptoms: brown-grey deposit on leaves, stems or flowers. Causes: overcrowding, too cool and damp or humidity too high. Remedy: see page 52.

Leaf-spot fungus
Symptoms: scattered yellow to brown leaf spots, some with encircled spore deposits. Cause: infection. Remedy: see page 52.

Rust
Symptoms: rust-coloured little heaps of powder on undersides of leaves and light spots on tops of leaves. Cause: brought in from outside. Remedy: see page 52.

Sooty mould
Symptoms: blackish, dirty deposit on the leaves. Causes: aphids, scale or whitefly. Remedy: see page 52.

Bacteria and viruses
Damp rot

Appears on cyclamen, dieffenbachia and calla. Symptoms: rot at base of stem and later throughout plant. Remedy: none.

Oil-spot disease
Appears on begonias and ivy. Symptoms: discoloured spots on tops of leaves and stems. Remedy: none.

Mosaic virus
Especially afflicts flamingo flowers, orchids, hydrangeas, gloxinias and amaryllis. Symptoms: light- and dark-green spots. Remedy: none.

Leaf curl
Afflicts fuchsias and geraniums particularly. Symptoms: stunted, unnaturally crimped leaves. Remedy: none.

anyone who does his or her own propagating is constantly astonished at how eager plants are to reproduce. They propagate themselves in two ways.
Vegetatively from plant parts The young plants which develop are exact copies of the mother plant. This is asexual propagation.
Generatively from seeds The young plants inherit the characteristics of the father and mother plant and a completely new individual plant is

Propagation made easy

Propagation is not only fun. It also helps you duplicate your favourite plants and create delightful memories of times and places past. Planting the seeds of exotic fruits is especially interesting for children and adults alike.

produced. This is called sexual propagation.

Vegetative propagation

With many plant species, this is the best way to get plants that are ready to bloom in a relatively short time. Propagation is done by rooting a cutting in water or soil (see page 59) or by division of the plant.
Rooting Almost all plants can develop roots from the cambium, the growth tissue under the outer skin. The process is induced by a wound, a cut or a tear. This stimulates the wound-healing development of callus, which is essential for root development. Some plants like African violets, begonias, cape primroses or sansevierias can even regenerate themselves from leaves or pieces of leaf.

The most difficult form of vegetative propagation is meristem culture, in which an entirely new plant is produced from a microscopically small group of cells. Since laboratory equipment is necessary for this technique, it remains the province of the experts.
The ideal time Propagate in spring or early summer if possible. This means the young plants will be growing during the months when there is plenty of light, which will help them to develop better. In some plants, top cuttings become

available in the spring as a result of cutting back, and you can use them to increase your plant stock. Other plants can be divided when they are potted on. By early summer the mother plants are strong enough to stand having cuttings taken. Cuttings of woody plants can also be taken in summer. Naturally you should always wait until after the spring-flowering plants have bloomed to divide them or take cuttings. Tubers are divided at the end of the rest period.

Propagation from seed

This method is fast only when propagating from annual plants (that is, those that develop completely and flower in one year). For them, from seed to flowering as a rule takes 8 to 12 weeks. With other plants (such as palms) it often takes months for the seeds to germinate and then months or years until the plants are ready to flower.

Propagation by seed offers those who like to experiment a full palette of species that are not obtainable as plants. Plant dealers and mail-order specialsits offer seeds of countless flowering and foliage plants, palms and cacti. But do not forget that other source: the seeds of exotic fruits (see pages 63–5), which remain after the fruit is eaten.
Sowing When seeds germinate, they take up water and swell. In the process the seed coat splits and the growth enzymes are activated. At first the root begins to grow, then the stem, with its simply structured seed leaves, and finally the true leaves emerge. The seed leaves wither, the stem extends itself, developing more and more leaves, and the plant grows towards maturity.
The ideal time Sowing is best done in the spring. If you want to use plant lights, you can sow all year long and cultivate the young plants that grow in autumn and winter under artificial light.

Before you propagate

Some plants contain poisons that are released when they are cut and will irritate the skin or mucous membranes (there are warning notes in the specific plant portraits), and you can receive injury from

Propagation is often child's play. Herbaceous top and stem cuttings root easily in water.

cactus spines. Therefore, wear gloves when working. Do not rub your eyes as you work, and make sure that plant juice does not get into open wounds. Hold the cut surfaces of plants that 'bleed' (spurges, for instance) under water, which stops the milky flow.

Equipment for propagating

- Seeding compost (or peat pots)
- Propagating tray with a cover, heated propagator, propagating bed with a heater (alternatives: mini greenhouse or heating mat for plants that need warmer potting-medium temperatures)
- Transplanting pots of pressed peat or plastic
- Pricking-out sticks
- Plant labels
- Waterproof pencil for labelling
- Sharp knife
- Root hormone powder
- Charcoal powder or pieces

Correct medium for propagating

Almost all plants germinate and root well in a potting medium that is poor in nutrients and not only permeable to water and air but also able to retain both of them.
Basic requirements The medium must be free of harmful microorganisms. Suitable are a mixture of two parts unfertilized peat and one part of quartz sand, one of the commercial seeding composts or peat pots, which contain a small amount of nutrients. (If available, it is advisable to use an alternative to peat.)
For cacti a mix of fine grit, coarse sand and a good potting mixture is used. To kill weeds and fungal spores, the material should be first sterilized in the oven for two hours at 170°C (350°F) and allowed to stand for two days. A ready-made mix will be more convenient for most people.

For succulents or other cuttings that need a particularly efficient air-permeable medium you can use quartz sand or fine polystyrene granules for rooting. Do not use builder's sand.
For hydrocultivated young plants fine-ground expanded clay granules can be used. Alternatively, they can be propagated in the normal way, potted up and then have all the potting medium washed from their roots before being transferred to the hydroculture method of growing.

Plants easily rooted in water include *Aglaonema*, *Begonia*, Joseph's coat (*Codiaeum*), flaming nettle (*Coleus*), devil's ivy (*Epipremnum*), creeping fig (*Ficus pumila*), wax vine (Hoya), African violets (*Saintpaulia*), spiderwort (*Tradescantia*) and inch plant (*Zebrina*).

TECHNIQUES

Successful propagation from offsets and cuttings

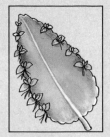

Mother plants, such as air plant (*Kalenchoe pinnata*), devil's backbone (*Kalenchoe daigremontiana*) and mother spleenwort (*Asplenium bulbiferum*), produce already-rooted plantlets that need only be potted up.

Bulbils develop on some flowering bulbs, for instance on amaryllis. They are removed when they reach a diameter of about 6cm (2½in) and potted up. It can take one to three years until first flowering.

Offshoots or stolons develop in bromeliads right next to the mother rosette. When they are a reasonable size, they are separated and potted up. The more roots a particular offset has, the more easily it will grow. The interval before flowering varies.

Propagating from offsets
Offsets are mature young plants which form on the stem, leaves or roots of a plant, some possessing a root or roots before making their first contact with a potting medium. The following list includes the major types of offset.
● Mother plants like *Kalenchoe pinnata* (air plant), *Kalenchoe daigremontiana* (devil's backbone), *Asplenium bulbiferum*, (mother spleenwort), *Tolmiea menziesii* (piggyback plant, see photograph, page 189) and *Begonis hispida* var. *cucullifera*, whose offsets arise on their leaves and are called plantlets (see drawing, left)
● Plants with bulbils like the blood lily or the amaryllis (see drawing, left)
● Offsets of the bromeliads (see drawing, left)
● Stolons of the spider plant (see drawing, Runners), strawberry begonia, kaffir lily, ferns, various cacti and succulents.
● Keikis, which are the offsets of orchids, for example of *Phalaenopsis* or *Dendrobium*.

Young plants are separated when they have reached a reasonable size and simply potted in a good potting medium or placed in water. Bulbils should be half as large as the mother bulb. With bromeliads the offset should already have formed its own cup. Keikis are cut off with a piece of stem and pegged down into the potting medium.

Runners root easily
Spider plants form young plants on long shoots, which can be cut off and potted up.

Types of cuttings
1 Top cuttings are taken from flowerless growth tips of annuals. They should have at least two firm leaves and, if from woody plants, be semi-wooded. Always cut just under a leaf node and remove any lower leaves.
2 Stem cuttings are taken from middle and lower part of stem. Cut and treat like top cuttings.
3 Leaf cuttings are táken from a single leaf plus its stem.
4 Leaf-section cuttings are especially good for propagating begonias and sansevierias (see drawing, page 60).

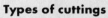

Propagating from cuttings

Cuttings are parts of the mother plant taken for the purpose of propagation. *Top cuttings* (see drawing 1, Kinds of cuttings) are cut from annual shoots, flowerless if possible. These include leaf crowns (see drawing 1, Crown and stem cuttings), for example of dracaena, and the umbrella of the umbrella plant (see drawing, page 60).

With leaf crowns it is advisable to remove several rosettes from a very dense crown some time before propagation so that the remaining rosettes are a good size.

Stem cuttings (see drawing 2, Types of cuttings) are cuttings with leaves from not-yet-hardened stems without the growth tip.

Top and stem cuttings may be herbaceous, woody or half-woody, depending on the particular plant species. Herbaceous cuttings are the most delicate but root most easily. Woody cuttings do not damp off so easily but are very slow to develop roots.

Cuts are made just below a leaf node. The cutting should be about 5 to 10cm (2 to 4in) long and have at least 2 firm leaves. Remove any lower leaves because contact with the medium is likely to cause rotting.

Leaf cuttings (see drawing 3, Types of cuttings) consist of a leaf with a little piece of stem. Plants that can be successfully reproduced this way are African violets, various kinds of sedums, peperomias and begonias. If you are rooting leaf cuttings in water, you should put a little piece of charcoal in with it to disinfect the water properly.

Leaf-section cuttings (see drawing 4, Types of cuttings) are pieces of leaves, which will develop roots along the central vein. With begonias, the leaves are cut straight across and the leaf pieces stuck in the soil in the direction of growth. With *Streptocarpus* you can also cut along the central vein and press the severed edges into the potting medium.

Stalk cuttings are taken from fleshy, not-too-woody shoots. Every piece should have at least one eye (or node). You can plant them horizontally or upright (see drawings 2 to 4, Crown and stem cuttings). Suitable for this method are dieffenbachia, philodendron, dracaena or *Yucca*. When planting upright, the direction of growth must be the same as it was on the mother plant because the eye must point towards the light.

The plastic-bag trick

To promote rooting, insert cutting into a pot of propagating mix and seal, as shown, in a polythene bag. Humidity will increase there, just as in a greenhouse, and this keeps the still rootless cutting from evaporating too much water from its leaves. You can also cover large, shallow trays of cuttings with transparent plastic wrap. Warming the soil is another aid to successful propagation.

Rooting leaf cuttings in water

1 Fill a jar with water, add piece of charcoal and cover with plastic film. Poke holes in the film and stick leaf stems through.
2 Pot up rooted young plants.

Rooting leaf cuttings in propagating mixture

1 Cut off leaf with stem.
2 Dip cut end in rooting hormone powder.
3 Stick cutting in moist propagating mix and firm mixture round it.
4 Tie in plastic bag. Place warming mat underneath. As soon as new growth appears, remove plastic bag.

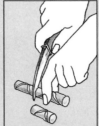

Crown and stem cuttings

1 Cut off crown of dracaena or yucca and root in potting mix, as above.
2 Cut stem in pieces and dust cuts with charcoal powder.
3 Pot stem pieces vertically . . .
4 . . . or press into potting medium horizontally, eyes upwards. Cover closely with plastic film. As soon as new growth appears, remove film.

TECHNIQUES

Root division requires both care and firmness. Pull the plant apart, using a sharp knife if necessary to cut a matted root ball. Untangle twisted roots. Shake out as much of the old potting medium as possible and pot on both halves of the plant in new earth.

Rooting umbrella plant is very simple. The 'umbrellas' can be placed in water head down or right side up. They will root in either case. All the sedges can be rooted in this way.

Propagating from seed, by division and layering

Layering can be done with long-stemmed plants (ivy, creeping fig, columnea, for example). Lay the young stem on the soil of a small pot, make a scratch on the underside of a leaf node and fasten it down with wire. When rooted, separate from the mother plant.

Simple propagation methods

Root division (see drawing, left). Strongly growing, bushy plants can also be controlled by dividing the plant into sections.

Division of tubers Tubers are first forced until growth becomes visible and then cut into pieces, each with an eye. Important: disinfect the relatively large pieces with charcoal powder.

Rhizome division Rhizomes are divided so that each piece has at least two eyes (leaf buds).

Rooting umbrellas (see drawing, left). Cut off the topmost leaf crown, leaving a 5cm (2in) stem below it, shorten the leaves by one third with scissors and place the umbrella in hand-temperature water or in damp sand. The new leaves appear in the middle of the umbrella.

Layering (see drawing, left). In this method the top cuttings are not separated from the mother plant until the shoot is well established.

Propagating from seed

Species and hybrids of many houseplants can be raised from seed. The fresher the seed is, the more likely it is to germinate. Many seed firms therefore seal them in a protective packet that must be opened before you sow. It is important to follow the instructions on the seed packet exactly. They will tell you whether the seeds should be covered with soil (dark germinators) or not (light germinators), whether they must be soaked in lukewarm water before sowing or be scratched, as well as the specific germination temperature, which will be around 18°C (64°F) at the minimum and at the maximum 25 to 28°C (77 to 82°F).

How to sow seed Large seeds are sown in peat pots; small fine seeds in trays. Cover the base of propagating trays

Propagating from seed

Even beginners succeed in growing from seed with the aid of compacted peat pots. They are soon thoroughly permeated with the roots of the seedling and keep the root ball together when being planted, pot and all, in a larger container.

Propagating from pieces of leaf

For begonias, streptocarpus and sansevierias (above)
1 *Cut healthy leaf from sturdy plant.*
2 *Cut horizontally into large pieces 5 to 8cm (2 to 3in) long. Allow the cut pieces to dry.*
3 *Stick shallowly in sandy soil in direction of growth.*

60

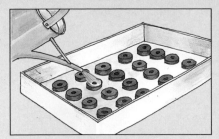

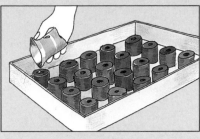

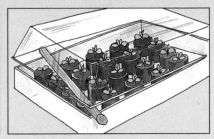

Sowing in peat pots
1 Lay compacted pots in tray of heated propagator and sprinkle with luke- warm water until swollen to full size.

2 Place a seed in each pot and cover with propagating mix if a dark germinator. Put covered propagator in bright, not sunny, warm place.

3 After germination, ventilate often so that condensed water can escape and young seedlings do not damp off.

with a finger-thick layer of clay granules or pebbles and then fill it with seeding compost up to within 3cm (1in) of the top. Smooth the soil and make furrows for the seeds. Spread the seeds along the furrows. For dark germinators sift potting mix over them, making the layer double the thickness of the seed, and press lightly. Sprinkle the soil with soft, lukewarm water until it is damp all the way through. Cover the tray, using polythene or a plate of glass if it has no cover.

Style tip Very fine seeds are easier to spread along the furrow if they are first mixed with fine sand and then sown. Or place the seeds in a folded piece of paper and then let them trickle slowly into the potting mixture.

Grafting cacti
Grafting is limited in use as a propagating method, but with the slow-growing cactus (see drawing, Cactus grafting) it quickly produces plants ready to bloom. Having the correct stock is important for success. *Echinopsis* species, *Eriocereus jusbertii*, *Hylocereus* hybrids and *Selenicereus* and *Trichocereus* species have proven especially suitable for this purpose. Ideal time: mid-spring to early autumn. The scion must be kept slightly damp, warm and in constant bright light but it must not stand in the sun.

Air layering
This is a useful technique for propagating plants that are hard to reproduce from cuttings or for rejuvenating very large, old branches that are bare at the bottom, and it involves rooting from the leafy area. It is suitable for rubber plants, dracaenas, philodendron, false aralia, cordyline, schefflera, fatsia and Joseph's coat. Ideal time: spring; for the rubber plants early/mid summer.

Pricking out
Wait until seedlings have two seed and two real leaves.
1 Loosen seedling from seeding medium with slender end of a dibber.
2 Shorten root tip.
3 Using thick end of dibber, bore a hole in prepared potting medium.
4 Plant seedling (medium up to lowest leaves) and firm medium lightly.

Cactus grafting
1 Cut horizontally under base of growth tip, bevelling edges of cut with sharp knife.
2 Cut off scion and bevel cut edge at a sharp angle.
3 Before joining base and scion together, cut another thin slice from each of cut areas.
4 Matching conducting channels, fasten graft with rubber bands.

Air layering a tall plant
1 Make upward cut in stem at leaf node and dust with rooting hormone. Prop open with piece of matchstick.
2 Fasten strip of plastic below cut. Fill with damp moss.
3 Fasten plastic above cut to prevent moss from drying out.
4 When well rooted, remove bag, cut off stem and pot.

Caring for seedlings

Until germination, you must make sure that the potting medium never dries out and stays warm at all times.

Germination times vary greatly. Some plants sprout after a few days, others (like palms) need months. Large seeds need an especially long time. Do not give up if they seem not to be doing anything.

Successful germination is indicated when you can see one or two 'seed' leaves that look different from the characteristic or true leaves. This is the time to lift the covering for several hours each day to enable the plants to get air and to help them to harden off slowly.

Pricking out is the term given to the next step, when the first two true leaves or leaf pairs have formed and the plant can be handled (see Pricking out, page 61).

For further development it is very important to give the young plants a lot of light. But be careful – avoid direct sun. With too little light the tiny plants grow leggy and develop unnaturally long intervals between leaves. You might try placing a sheet of white polystyrene behind the young plants; this will reflect the light.

Do not fertilize yet; the nutrients in the growing medium are enough to last for the first weeks. However, the fast-growing annuals may be fertilized for the first time after four weeks with a weak dosage.

Opposite
A beautiful palm needs a solitary position in any interior. Other plants will simply diminish the elegant effect it creates.

Plants from exotic fruits

It is a shame to throw away the seeds or plant parts of exotic fruits. Anyone who likes to experiment can get attractive plants from them, and they are likely to be just a little unusual. Another advantage is that seeds from fruits are superfresh, which for many tropical plants is essential for successful germination. Tropical fruits come from the same regions as many of our houseplants. However, for the most part they are not available in the trade as houseplants and so reports on experience with them and instructions for culture are incomplete.

The tropics produce plants such as papaya, star apple, mango, guava, mangosteen, pineapple, coconut and ginger. This means that you are dealing with subjects that need warmth. In winter they will not stand temperatures cooler than 15°C (59°F).

The tropical highlands give us Andes berries and cherimoya. These plants need a lot of light and warmth in summer and cooler temperatures in autumn and winter.

Subtropical or Mediterranean regions are the habitat of the avocado, Japanese persimmon, date, pomegranate, orange, lemon, lychee, fig and passion fruit. Plants from these regions like to be outside in the summer and during the winter will want a situation around 10°C (50°F).

Collecting seeds

Obviously you are dependent on when the fruit is available in the market. A brief summary of the main sales months follows.

All year: avocados (see pages 64–5), tree tomatoes, dates (see pages 64–5), guavas, star apple, coconut, mango, passion fruit (see pages 64–5) and most citrus fruit (see pages 64–5).

Available only at certain seasons: pineapple (September to December), cherimoya (September to February), pineapple-guava (March to July), pomegranates (June to December), Andes berries (January to June), lychee (January

to March and May to December), rambutan (January to February, June to October, and in December).

The best time for seeding and vegetative propagation of pineapple crowns or ginger rhizomes (page 65) is spring.

Seeds which will not germinate
● Seed from fruit bought in winter which encountered frost
● Damaged seed
● Seed from fruit that was half-ripe when harvested because they are also half-ripe. You recognize such fruit by colour comparison with ripe fruit and by their faded taste and still-green seeds.

Sowing

Some fruit seeds (avocado, for example) must be removed from the flesh before the fruit is eaten; others may not be discarded until eaten. After washing, dry the seeds with kitchen paper and then leave them to continue drying in the air for several hours. You can sow them, preferably in a heated propagator, the day you collect them or several days later.

Germination times

These vary widely. Plants that in their native habitats grow into trees as a rule germinate more slowly than herbaceous plants, such as the *Passiflora* (see page 64). Some seeds do not germinate at all because they are 'sterile'. Do not abandon the attempt if you have no success immediately. Just keep on trying.

Flowers and fruits

You can expect flowers or fruit from only a very few of the exotic plants you raise from seed yourself. Remember that most of them are trees in their habitats and always remain juvenile plants in pots. But some plants will surprise you by producing flowers, even in a pot or a tub. If they do form fruit, as a rule they will not taste like the original fruit, often being bitter, because they do not reach full maturity.

Raising and caring for popular exotics

Fortunella margarita (kumquat)

Sow seed in a heated propagator (20–22°C/68–72°F). Plants raised from seed will bloom after 8 to 10 years.
Location and care Put young plants in a bright spot at first, later in full

sun, preferably outdoors from the middle of late spring. Water well in summer and fertilize lightly every 14 days. From early autumn, keep drier, bring into house, place in a bright, cool location (10°C/50°F). Pot on young plants yearly in spring adding polystyrene pieces to the potting compost.

Passiflora edulis (passion fruit)

Wash and dry seeds. Sow, but do not cover: they are light germinators. Germination after two to four weeks.
Location and care See page 124.

Persea americana (avocado)

Remove stone from flesh and bury the broad end 2 to 3cm (¾ to 1in) deep in potting medium.
Location and care Keep in a bright place all year long; in summer warm, in winter cool (15°C/59°F). Keep damp throughout year.

Carica papaya (papaya)

Wash seed and sow, covering lightly with propagating medium. Invert a plastic bag over it. The seed will germinate after a few days.
Location and care Keep warm, bright and humid all year long. Water only moderately.

Passion fruit

Kumquat

Phoenix dactylifera (date palm)

Soak date pits from packaged dates in warm water for two or three days. Push about 2cm (¾in) deep into propagating medium. The seeds germinate after two to six months.
Location and care Keep light to sunny all year long; warm in summer, in winter around 10°C (50°F). Water moderately.

Papaya

Date

Lemon

Ginger
rhizome

Avocado

Zingiber officinale (ginger)

Lay the rhizome flat on the surface of the potting medium with the eye pointing upward and cover lightly. Put in a shady, warm place. The first shoots appear after two months. *Location and care* Keep bright, warm and constantly slightly damp from spring till autumn. In autumn let it die back. Overwinter the rhizome in its pot at room temperature and force it again in the spring.

More and more homeowners are building conservatories and turning them into 'green' living-rooms. In spaces such as this, plants can receive light from all sides obviously better than conventional, often mono-directional window light – and the area can provide a place for a collection of foliage and flowering rarities. Ventilation windows and adjustable blinds are vital to avoid stagnant air and keep out the midday sun, especially in summer.

66

This beautiful plant grouping includes two money plants (placed like sentries in the foreground), a roof-high fiddle-leaf fig (left), a light-hungry coconut palm (floor, right) and a philodendron (right). At the far end of the room, on the windowsill, are a fruiting dwarf orange, a passionflower and a quartet of unassuming aspidistras. The two tubs behind the table contain a pair of flowering oleanders.

**Horticultural
and botanical
terminology**

Words in **bold
type** crossrefer to
other entries in
the Glossary.

A

Absorption scales
Scales on the grey tillandsias which can absorb moisture. These plants can therefore be provided with water and nutrients through sprays and dipping.

Acaricide
A specific agent that is most effective against mites – red spider mite in particular. Most prepared **insecticides** for the control of mites will contain this agent, although it may or may not be mentioned on the container.

Adventitious roots
Roots that develop above ground, arising from stems to support a plant on a trunk or wall (in ivy, for example).

Aerial roots
Among houseplants, these are mostly seen in members of the Aracea family (the philodendrons, for example). Aerial roots anchor plants to trees as they climb and eventually reach 'ground level' to both nourish and stabilize the plant.

Air layering
A method of **vegetative propagation** which involves rooting from the stem of a plant (see drawing, page 61). Used for plants which are difficult to propagate from cuttings, or to reduce the height of plants such as the rubber plant and produce a new plant at the same time.

Air plant
Plant (also called **epiphyte**)that in its tropical habitat establishes itself in the crown or branch fork of trees and shrubs, the seeds being deposited there by birds or insects. Most form **aerial roots** to secure themselves and for the uptake of nutrients and humidity because they cannot get them from the earth. Air plants are not parasites.

Algae build-up
Caused by compacted soil and excess dampness. Algae builds up on the surface of the potting medium and should be removed when seen. Following removal, the medium should then be disturbed with a pointed stick to improve aeration.

Alkaline
In plant culture a soil or potting medium is alkaline when it has a **pH value** over 7. A soil is designated slightly alkaline or limey if it has a pH value of 7.1 to 8. Alkaline soils develop primarily from watering with hard water containing lime salts and are bad for almost all houseplants.

Alkaloids
Nitrogenous plant compound that adversely affects the human nervous system. The leopard lily and glory lily are both examples of alkaloidal plants, as are most members of the nightshade family. Alkaloids can often be lethal, even in very small doses.

Alternating leaves
Arrangement of leaves along a stem in which the leaves do not grow directly opposite each other in pairs but are spaced on alternate sides at intervals.

Annual
Plant that completes its life cycle from seed to flower and fruit within one growing season, for example cineraria.

Aphid
Small insect which feeds by sucking plant juices. See page 54.

Areolas
Woolly cushion on the end of cactus tubercle (or swelling) or on the edge of a rib, from which thorns sprout and which usually also produce the flowers and buds. Every cactus species has its own typical form of areola.

Assimilation

The process by which a plant converts substances foreign to itself into its own bodily substances. Differentiation is made between carbon dioxide assimilation (also called **photosynthesis**), by which sugar is produced and which in green plants needs light to take place, and nitrogen assimilation, by which protein is produced.

Axil

Angle between the upper surface of the leaf stalk or branch and the stem or trunk from which it is growing.

B

Bacteria

The oldest single-celled organisms on earth and present practically everywhere. They feed on organic substances, causing them to disintegrate and decompose. Some species play a part in the process of creating soil and other potting mediums rich in **nutrients**, particularly nitrogen. Others cause serious plant illnesses that are indicated by wilting or damp rot and for the most part cannot be treated.

Ball

Term for soil or potting medium thoroughly grown through with roots (root ball, earth ball) or for a compacted quantity of peat.

Ball dryness

Lack of moisture in the root ball of a pot plant, recognizable when the soil draws away from the edge of the flowerpot. Most plants tolerate ball dryness for only a very short period. See drawing, page 42, for treatment.

Biennial

Plant that takes two years to complete its life cycle, forming only leaves in the first year and in the second year flower and fruit, for example the German violet (*Exacum affine*).

Biotechnical insect control

Control of insects by reactions to natural chemical or physical stimuli, for example by yellow-painted, water-filled saucers or yellow sticky cards (for aphids and whiteflies).

Bleeding

The seeping out of the milky juice contained in the stalk and shoots of plants such as rubber plant or poinsettia when injured by cutting or breakage.

Bonsai

Term for the Japanese art of forming miniature trees on the model of the full-sized specimens by root and branch pruning and for the resulting miniature tree in its pot (from *bon*=pot, *sai*=tree).

Botanical name

Internationally used scientific descriptive name for a plant. The botanical name normally consists of two or three parts: 1 the genus name, for example *Ficus*; 2 the species name, for example *elastica*: 3 the variety name, if there is one, for example 'Decora'. The complete name is thus *Ficus elastica* 'Decora'.

Bracts

Modified leaves that are situated higher than the true foliage leaves and function to protect the flower and lure insects. Some bracts are splendidly coloured and substitute for the petals, as in the poinsettia and bougainvillea.

Breeding

The process, through crossing and selection, of developing new varieties that enjoy particular characteristics. Breeding goals include larger and more double flowers, new flower colours and resistance to disease and climatic influences.

Brood plantlet

Tiny plant which forms in leaf axil, at leaf edge or in place of flower on a mother plant and is adapted for propagation, for example on the devil's backbone (*Kalanchoe daigremontiana*).

Bud

Plant organ from which stems, leaves, flowers or entire plants develop. A distinction is made between terminal buds (at the end of a shoot), axillary buds (in the leaf axils), dormant buds (which can remain in the bud stage all year and only begin to grow under special circumstances, for instance if the stem or branch above it is removed), and adventitious buds, which are produced from meristem tissue. Flower and leaf buds develop into their respective organs; whole plants develop from **brood plantlets**.

Bulb

From the Latin *bulbus* (onion) and composed of fleshy modified leaf bases or scales, wrapped closely one on top of another like an onion and comprising a storage organ (mostly underground). Not to be confused with the **pseudobulbs** of orchids, which are thickened branch internodes.

Bulbil

Also called bulblet or brood bulb. Small bulb which develops at the base of mature bulbs on certain flowering bulbs (for example, amaryllis) or on stems above ground (as on lilies) and may be used for propagation.

Bush

Plant with several similarly sized woody shoots growing out of the ground.

C

Cactus fertilizer

Nitrogen-poor complete fertilizer that is formulated for the particular requirements of cacti and other succulents but not for epiphytic species. Commercially available.

Calcium (Ca)

White metal that is an essential building material during the entire life-span of a plant and one of the principal nutrients.

Callus
Wound-healing tissue that a plant forms after injury. Cuttings produce roots only after callus tissue has been formed.

Calyx
Rounded, bell-, funnel- or tube-shaped, outer protective leaf structure surrounding a flower, which consists of fused sepals.

Capillary action
The process by which water in thin tubes is persuaded to travel over shorter or longer distances. Gardeners utilize capillary action in arrangements for watering while on holiday (see drawings, page 43).

Carbon dioxide (CO_2)
Colourless and odourless gas that occurs in the air and in the soil. A very important compound for plant life because it is the basic building unit for the manufacture of carbohydrates through **photosynthesis**.

Chemical control methods
Control and prevention of insects using chemical agents, which with misuse or carelessness can endanger human beings. Chemical controls include agents to combat diseases and pests, such as **insecticides**, **fungicides** and **acaracides**.

Chemical fertilizer
Water-soluble inorganic fertilizer whose nutrients are compounded in salts and are thus more readily available to the plants. Danger: overdosage. In contrast, **organic fertilizers**, in which the nutrients must first be released and processed by micro-organisms to be suitable for plant absorption take longer to work.

Chlorophyll
Green pigment without which **photosynthesis** cannot take place. Its structure is similar to that of human blood. In chlorophyll magnesium plays the same part as iron in haemoglobin.

Chlorosis
Deficiency of **iron** or **magnesium** which disrupts production of **chlorophyll** and results in a yellowing or bleaching of the leaves (see page 54).

Clay granules
Expanded clay aggregate is the standard planting medium for hydroculture. The material is obtained from selected clays fired at 1200°C (2192°F) The granules are formed by liquifying the clay and then cooling it rapidly. During the process the water contained in the clay is vaporized, giving the resulting granules a porous structure and a hard skin. Being stable in structure, clay granules will not decay; nor will they compact or sour. Their porous nature permits excellent air and water exchange. Furthermore, roots find extraordinarily good anchorage in this potting medium. Clay granules also offer one solution to the problem of how to water plants while on holiday (see page 43).

Climber
Plant that climbs spontaneously on branches, tree trunks or walls, or can be trained, using organs developed for just this purpose, for example with adventitious roots, hooking tendrils or leaves, barb-like side shoots, spines, thorns or by winding back on themselves.

Common name
Popular name for a plant, (for example, busy Lizzie for *Impatiens*). Some plants have merely an anglicized version of the scientific name, but there are many plants that do not have English names.

Contact poison
Plant pesticide that affects insects when they come into contact with it. Respiratory, food and **systemic poisons** have other methods of controlling pests.

Cool house
A greenhouse whose temperature in winter is maintained between 2 and 12°C (36 and 54°F). Plants that need cool overwintering are sometimes called cool-house plants.

Corky scab
More correctly called oedema. It produces brown, scab-like growths on the leaves. Not a disease, the principal causes are low light levels and very wet soil.

Creeping plant
Plant with rooted **runners** or horizontally growing branches. Suitable for ground cover. Examples: strawberry begonia and creeping fig.

Crown
Point at which the root joins with the upper part of the plant (or stem). Extremely sensitive in some plants.

Culm
Stem of a grass plant, being either round and (usually) hollow (notably in corn and sugar cane) or triangular and filled with marrow. Giant grasses like the bamboos possess the strongest, thickest and longest culms.

Cultivar
See **Variety**.

Cup
Also called an urn or vase. Term for a bromeliad's rosette-like arrangement of leaves, which serves the plant in nature as the 'catch-basin' for water, dew and the rotting material that provides nutrients. Hence the bromeliads are sometimes called cup bromeliads.

Cutting back
Necessary measure for plant shaping, rejuvenation and producing new growth, bushy growth and good branching.

Cutting
Term for plant section that can be placed in soil or water to root. A cutting can be a top cutting, a piece of stem, a leaf or a piece of a leaf (see page 58).

Cyme
Form of inflorescence (see drawing, page 15).

D

Damping off
Disease of seedlings and cuttings that is caused – especially under crowded conditions – by fungus in the potting medium. Injury to root tissue and lower stem causes the young plants to wilt.

Dark germinator
Plant whose seeds will sprout only in absolute darkness. The sown seeds must therefore always been closely covered until germination so that no light can reach them.

Deficiency disease
Disease symptoms that appear with incorrect or neglected feeding of plants (see page 54).

Dicotyledonous
Term designating plants with two germinating leaves (*dicotyledoneae*) situated side by side. The main root often develops like a taproot; the leaves are multiform and furnished with a network of veins.

Dioecious
Plants which have male and female flowers growing on separate plants. Examples in the houseplant category include the chenille plant (*Acalypha hispida*) and palms.

Division
Method of **vegetative propagation** suitable for plants with many shoots. Examples include: spathiphyllum, aspidistra and aglaonema.

Dormant
See **Rest period**.

Double flower
A flower that has a greater number of petals than the characteristic number on the single flower.

Double-potting
Technique for increasing humidity in the immediate environment of a plant (see drawing, page 43).

Downy mildew
Fungal disease caused by airborne spores (see page 55).

Drainage
Measures for removal of excess water in the potting medium. This is important is plants are to avoid the dangers of standing water and should not be overlooked, particularly with larger pots or tubs. For this purpose broken crocks, clay granules, gravel or pieces of polystyrene should be placed in the bottom of the container.

Efflorescence
Deposits of lime and fertilizer salts on the outer walls of a clay pot. They occur when hard water has been used for watering or when fertilizing has been too frequent. Efflorescences can be removed with a vinegar-water solution and a stiff brush.

Enclosed plant window
Window of generous proportions that is closed off like a greenhouse and can be furnished with humidifiers, heating and aeration equipment. Ideal for tropical plants, which need warmth and high **humidity**.

Epidermis
Outermost tissue layer of the entire plant body. In many plants contains calcium or silicic acid for greater tissue strength.

Epiphytes
Plant that in its natural habitat does not grow on the ground but on tree branches, as for example many ferns, bromeliads and orchids. For this reason epiphytes are also called air plants.

Epiphyte support
An artificial 'perch' made of bark, or a slatted basket or wooden raft (see drawing, page 42), used in the home culture of **epiphytes**. Alternatively firm tree branches can be used, to which the plant is tied using plastic-covered wire after the root ball has been liberally covered with **sphagnum** moss.

Ericaceous
Belonging to the Ericaceae family, which includes heather, rhododendron, azalea and arbutus plants, all typically having bell-shaped flowers. Ericaceous compost or potting medium is a lime-free mixture suited to the culture of these lime-hating plants.

GLOSSARY

Ethylene
Gaseous plant hormone that is given off during the ripening phase of fruits (such as apples and citrus plants). Promotes flowering in bromeliads but orchids and hibiscus react to the fragrance of apple and citrus by dropping flowers and buds.

Evaporation
See **Transpiration.**

Evergreen
Plant that does not shed its leaves in autumn. Of course, such plants do renew their leaves. But in general this is not apparent because it happens gradually throughout the year.

Evolution
Science of development. Like all other living organisms, plants have progressed from simple structures to ever more specialized life forms in the course of their history. As organisms bound to their locations, they must continually adapt to their environment throughout millions of years if they are not to become extinct.

F

Family
In botanical terms, a group of genera (see **Genus**) with certain specific characteristics in common. The largest plant family may be that of the orchids. It represents almost 10 per cent of all flowering plants.

Family name
Indicates membership in a particular family. Thus for example, the lady's slipper belongs to the family of orchids (Orchidaceae), the African violet to the family of gesneriads (Gesneriaceae) and the rubber plant to the mulberry family (Moraceae).

Fasciation
Abnormal, growth form of stems of cacti and other succulents. The **vegetative cone** broadens to form a linear or band shape like a chicken's comb.

Fertile
Technical term for fruitful. The opposite of sterile. Flowers with sex organs (that is with stamens and pistil, see page 15) are fertile; flowers without these organs are sterile.

Fertilization
Merging of a male pollen grain with a female egg cell.

Fertilizer
Material produced to provide plants with **nutrients** necessary for sound growth and development. A complete fertilizer contains all the principal nutrients essential to plant life and the **trace elements** as well. A distinction is made between **chemical** and **organic fertilizers.**

Flower
Plant organ whose purpose is to effect sexual reproduction and thereby continue the species. The essential elements are the anthers, which produce pollen (or male cells) and the female ovaries, which bear the seeds. These are usually surrounded by coloured petals, which in turn are protected by sepals. Many variations on this basic arrangement are to be found (see drawings, page 15). Some plants (termed dioecious) have single-sexed flowers.

Foliar feed
Fertilizer that is applied to the leaves of a plant and absorbed by them.

Forcing
Advancing the flowering time by regulation of light and warmth. This is an especially common practice with flowering bulbs. For instance, crocuses, hyacinths or tulips can be forced as early as late autumn in a warm room so that they are blooming at Christmas.

Fungal diseases
Variety of conditions caused by airborne spores, infection, insect infestation or poor culture (see page 55).

Fungicide
Chemical agent for controlling fungal diseases.

Fungus

Plants whose bodies consist of threadlike filaments and contain no chlorophyll. They serve as 'garbage eaters' because they can digest cellulose and wood pulp. They are either decay dwellers, parasites (causes of disease in humans, animals and plants) or live in symbiosis with other plants, for instance orchids. Some produce substances (penicillin) or cause certain processes (such as fermentation) useful for human beings. Dampness and specific temperatures are essential to them but the **pH value** and concentrations of oxygen and carbon dioxide in their environment are also determining factors.

Generative propagation

Sexual reproduction of a plant through seeds. The seeds contain the plant embryo, which develops after the sex cells combine. The offspring need not resemble the mother plant. Compare with **vegetative propagation**.

Genus (pl. genera)

Term for a group of species that have certain characteristics in common. For example, the fig or *Ficus* genus comprises all the various types of fig tree.

Germinating temperature

Optimum ground and air temperature for plants to begin germination. It can vary widely depending on the species: some plants need warmth, others need coolness.

Germination

The sprouting of a seed or spore, the first stage in the development of a plant.

Greening

Reaction of coloured or variegated leaves to light deficiency. Plants can afford chlorophyll-free areas only in bright locations. In dark locations the leaves must become green all over in order to gain additional areas for the absorption of light to assist **assimiliation**.

Growth period

See **Vegetative period**.

Growth point

See **Vegetative cone**.

Growth problems

Diseases induced by mistakes in culture or poor location of plants (see page 54).

Growth regulators

Material either sprayed on the foliage or watered into the soil to inhibit growth and to encourage development of side shoots, thus achieving compact, bushy plants, generally available only to professional growers. As soon as the growth regulators are metabolized, the plant resumes its normal pattern of growth. Some of these agents can also initiate or precipitate flower development.

Habit

Botanical term for the general appearance of a plant, for example bushy, trailing, upright or climbing.

Hanging plants

Plant with trailing or creeping stems that look particularly attractive in a hanging container.

Hardening off

Careful programme designed to acclimatize a plant to changing temperature and light conditions.

Herbaceous

Any plant which does not in maturity have a woody stem. The description is strictly used of **annual**, **biennial** or **perennial** plants, but it has come to be used of perennial plants which die back in autumn and sprout again in springtime.

Honeydew

Sticky excretion of aphids and scale that is found not only on leaves but also on windowsills, floors and furniture. Honeydew attracts ants, and also sooty mould which can make the leaves very dirty. Wash off immediately.

Hormone

Substance produced by plants that can, even in small amounts, stimulate or inhibit growth and development. Also called phytohormone.

Horsetail broth

Home remedy for control of mildew (see recipe, page 52).

Humidity

Water vapour present in the air expressed as percentage: 0 per cent=absolutely dry, 100 per cent=saturated with water vapour, or mist. Houseplants need between 50 and 70 per cent humidity, depending on where they come from. Artificially heated air is invariably too dry. Various measures can be used to increase the humidity (see drawings, page 43).

Hybrid

A plant derived from the crossing of plants of different varieties, subspecies, species or (sometimes) genera. Such plants may show either a mixture of characteristics from both parents or favour only one parent.

Hydroculture

Plant culture without soil. The plants stand in a special medium that gives them support (for example, clay granules) and are supplied with a nutrient solution.

Hygrometer

Instrument for measuring humidity.

GLOSSARY

I

Inflorescence
The arrangement of the flowers on a plant (see drawing, page 15).

Insecticide
A plant-protective material used to control insects.

Insectivorous
Insect-eating plants, such as the Venus fly-trap, pitcher plant (see page 173), sundew or butterworts.

Internodes
Intervals along a stem between leaf nodes (Latin *inter*=between, *nodus*=node).

Ion exchanger
Slow-release fertilizer used by commercial growers in hydroculture. The fertilizer is made available to the plant as the acidity level of the water changes. One application will usually last for about six months. Soft water is essential when using such products.

Iron (Fe)
Important **trace element** that is necessary for plant growth and for making chlorophyll and protein. In alkaline soil or in the presence of hard water iron can be bonded to calcium and is then no longer available to the plants, resulting in symptoms of deficiency. The plants can actually starve because they lack the iron necessary for synthesizing **chlorophyll**.

Iron sequestrin
Chemical substance that enables iron in the soil or potting medium to dissolve better and thus be more readily available to the plants. Used to treat chlorotic conditions in ericaceous plants (see **Chlorosis**).

K

Keiki
Term for **offsets** from orchids.

L

Labellum
The middle, most conspicuous petal of an orchid flower. It is formed into a lip and serves as a 'landing pad' for pollinating insects.

Lava
Porous mineral pebbles of volcanic origin used in potting mixtures for cacti and in water culture.

Layering
A method of **vegetative propagation** by which one- or two-year-old plant shoots are laid on the potting medium, fastened firmly and covered with potting mixture. Root development is promoted by scratching or cutting into the underside of the shoot at the point where it is to be covered. See also **Air layering**.

Leaf
Important plant organ that assists in nutrition (see **Photosynthesis**), provides the plant with oxygen (see **Respiration**) and regulates the water supply (see **Transpiration**). It can take a great variety of different shapes and be flat and paper thin, fat and fleshy or needle- or tube-like.

Leaf eelworm
Type of insect pest (see page 55).

Leaf loss
Lower leaves can be lost because of poor care or too dark a location. However, leaf loss is normal for some species, such as in *Dracaena marginata*.

Leaf-spot fungus
Type of plant infection (see page 55).

Leaf vein
Branching vessel or tube which conveys water and nutrients to the leaf to aid the processes of **photosynthesis** and **transpiration**.

Legginess
Term for the development of long, weak, pale shoots with large intervals between the leaf nodes and no leaves. Cause: too little light and too high a temperature.

Liana
Strong roots of plants such as the philodendrons that assist in anchoring the plant to supports such as trees and eventually find their way to soil level, where they take in nourishment.

Light
Essential for plant life. Light is necessary for **photosynthesis** and it also regulates growth, flower development, **germination**, leaf colouring and leaf fall.

Light germinator
Plant whose seeds need light to germinate. The seeds of such plants should not be sown too thickly and should never be covered with potting medium.

Light mark
Marking on plant container that enables it to be replaced exactly as if was before it was moved for cleaning a window or for watering.

Lime-hating
Plants that either will not tolerate lime in water and potting medium or tolerate it badly. For instance, azaleas, camellias and miniature orange trees prefer a low lime-content.

Lithophyte
Plant that lives on rocks and stones (from Greek: *lithos*=stone, *phyton*=plant.

Long-day plant
Plant that needs long daily periods of light and short dark periods to set flowers (for example, poinsettia). Compare **Short-day plant**.

Luxmeter
Instrument for measuring light. Obtainable from garden and photographic suppliers.

M

Magnesium (Mg)
Important building material for plant cells and therefore a major **nutrient**. Necessary for the synthesis of **chlorophyll**.

Mealy bug
An insect pest frequently found on plants kept in air which is too dry (see page 54).

Metabolism
Conversion and processing of **nutrients** and elimination of waste by-products.

Microclimate
Climate in immediate vicinity of one or several plants. Can be affected by other plants, walls, heating units or humidifiers.

Micronutrient
See **Trace element**.

Mildew
Various fungal diseases found on plants (see page 55).

Milky sap
Milky, sometimes poisonous, fluid that some plants secrete if they are injured, for example spurge plants like poinsettia and other euphorbia species.

Miniature plant (Mini)
Plant kept small by means of breeding, reduction of potting medium and sometimes by use of growth-inhibiting hormones. They are useful when creating dish gardens, bottle gardens or for window greenhouses.

Minimum–maximum thermometer
Instrument that establishes the highest and lowest temperature so that the temperature differences between day and night can be determined. Important for orchid culture, in which a lower night temperature is essential for flower development.

Mite
Insect pest found on plants, thriving in hot humid conditions (see page 55).

Mixed fertilizers
Fertilizers that contain various organic and inorganic nutrients. See **Organic fertilizer**, **Inorganic fertilizer**.

Monocotyledonous
Plant that has only one seed leaf on germination, for example palms and grasses. The group of monocotyledonous plants is called the Monocotyledonea.

Monoecious
Plant which bears both male and female flowers on the same plant. In dioecious plants, on the other hand, male and female flowers are borne on separate plants.

Monopodial
Plant which characteristically grows on a single axis. Monopodial growth is recognizable by an unbranching, vertical main stem, from which side branches are produced (for example, Norfolk Island pine). Compare **Sympodial**.

Moss stake
A moisture-retentive support for plants with aerial roots, for example *Philodendron* and *Syngonium* species (see drawing, page 44).

Mother plant
Plant that has developed **offsets**, from which propagating material can be taken.

Multigeneric hybrid
Plant which results from crossing three or more genera. Especially common with orchids. To avoid gigantic botanical names when four or more genera are involved, a completely new name is invented for the hybrid. Example: *Potinara*, developed from *Brassavola*, *Laelia*, *Cattleya* and *Sophronitis*.

Mutation
Change in a plant's genes that appears spontaneously or can be artificially induced by irradiation (ultraviolet, roentgen or radioactive rays) or chemicals (for instance the poison colchicine from the autumn crocus), employed during hybridization.

N

Necrosis
Dead tissue, caused by various factors including incorrect use of fertilizers, too much sun, too much or too little water and too low a humidity, as well as disease or parasites.

New growth
Appearance of new shoots. A signal that the vegetative phase is beginning again, for example after the winter when light is poor. A plant that shows good new growth is healthy and vigorous.

Night-time temperature
Lower temperature during the dark period. Important requirement for orchids to set flowers.

Nitrogen (N)
One of the three most important plant **nutrients** and contained in every complete fertilizer. Nitrogen is used mainly for the synthesis of protein compounds and is responsible for leaf and shoot development.

Node
Point of origin of leaves or branches on a plant stem. Some plants (for example those of the carnation family) have prominent, thickened nodes.

NPK
Fertilizer formula indicating the three primary nutrients that a plant needs: N=nitrogen, P=phosphorus, K=potassium. How much is contained in each fertilizer and in what proportions is expressed in numbers (for example, 14+7+14 or 14/7/14, which means: 14 per cent nitrogen, 7 per cent phosphorus, 14 per cent potassium).

Nutrients
Specific elements that plants need for growth and good health. The principal nutrients consist of nitrogen (N), phosphorus (P) and potassium (K), and in addition calcium (Ca), magnesium (Mg) and sulphur (S). The **trace elements** are mainly heavy metals. Plants obtain nutrients from the fertilisers that we give them.

O

Offset
Young plantlet that is produced from the stem, forms roots and can then be separated from the mother plant and planted (see drawing, page 58). Examples: agave, bromeliads, spider plant and screw pine.

Opposite leaves
Leaves that are situated opposite each other at a leaf node.

Organic fertilizer
Fertilizers based on plant or animal products, such as manure, dried blood, hoof and horn meal, stinging nettle broth or guano. You can produce it yourself but it is also supplied commercially for use on garden and house plants. Organic fertilizers must first be broken down by soil bacteria into a form that plants can utilize. Because this takes time, they are slow to take effect. They are less useful for pot plants than in outdoor situations because the soil organisms in the confined area of a pot are greatly diminished.

Oxygen
The gas taken up by the plant in **respiration** and used to break down organic materials. Through this process energy is released for growth and development. The oxygen content of air is 21 per cent.

P

Panicle
Multiple-branched, pyramidal inflorescence (see drawing, page 15).

Peat
Sphagnum peat, which is milled and dug from the moors before being bagged for transit. Used in the preparation of potting soil. Alternatives are being sought to replace peat but they are still very much at the experimental stage.

Peat pot
Small pot of compressed peat. Best suited for seeding and growing of young plants. Later the plants can be potted on, pot and all, into a larger container.

Perennial
A woody or herbaceous plant that lives for at least three years, dying back each winter and putting out new growth in the spring.

Petals
Usually coloured, a modified leaf which forms part of a flower (see drawing, page 15). Designed to protect the reproductive organs and to attract pollinating insects.

pH value
(From Latin: *potentia hydrogenii*). A scale of measurement indicating the hydrogen concentration in the soil or potting medium and expressed in numbers that range up and down from 7, which equals neutral. Anything below 7 indicates an acid medium, anything above it an alkaline reaction. Almost all houseplants thrive best with a pH value of 5.5 to 6.5. The pH can easily be measured with indicator sticks (available in garden centres).

Phosphorus (P)
One of the three most important **nutrients** for plants. Phosphorus plays a large role in the energy economy of the plant, affecting the development of roots, flowers and fruits and promoting the processes of maturation.

Photoperiodism
Plant dependency on light. Plant maturation processes like setting flowers and the developing of storage organs (tubers and bulbs) are controlled by the length of daily light and dark periods. Commercial growers manipulate this dependency to control the development of flowers, for example with chrysanthemums and poinsettias. See also **Short-day plant** and **Long-day plant**.

Photosynthesis
The process whereby green plants make use of the energy of sunlight to convert simple chemicals into complex carbohydrates (or sugars) (from Greek: *photos*=light, *synthesis*=putting together). Photosynthesis depends upon the green colouring material of **chlorophyll**, found in the leaves, and often also the young stems, of plants. Without plants and their ability to use light as a source of energy, life on our planet would be impossible. See also **Assimilation**.

Phototropism
Movement of plant organs according to the influence of light. As a rule, stems turn towards the light whereas roots do not react to it.

Pinching out
Breaking off the soft ends of shoots with the thumb and forefinger (see drawing, page 44). Leads to better branching and thus to bushier growth.

Pinnate
Term for a leaf that consists of several pairs of leaflets growing opposite each other on a stem.

Pistil
Female organ of the flower, consisting of ovary, style and stigma (see drawing, page 15).

Pollen
The pollen grain is the male sex cell. The word 'pollen' may also refer to all the pollen grains contained in the anther or terminal part of the stamen.

Pollination
Transport of the (male) pollen to the (female) stigma by wind, water, insects, birds or the human hand, as with a brush.

Pores
Another term for the openings (or stomata) that are usually situated on the underside of the leaf. They provide for the gas exchange in **photosynthesis** and **respiration** and give off water vapour.

Potassium (K)
One of the three most important plant nutrients. Potassium produces resistance to drought, frost and certain plant diseases and insect pests and is important for **photosynthesis**. It is contained in every complete fertilizer. High-potassium fertilizers can be given after flowering to all plants that need to enter winter with woody stems because potassium also helps to build strong tissue.

Potting medium/mixture
See **Soil-based compost** and **Soil-less compost**.

Potting mixture
Potting mediums prepared either for seeding or potting on and formulated to meet specific plant requirements.

Potting on
Term used for transplanting into larger containers with new, unused potting medium.

Pricking out
Separating out seedlings into individual pots so that the young plants have more space to develop (see drawing, page 61).

Propagation
See **Generative propagation** and **Vegetative propagation**.

Prop roots
Develop from the stems of plants such as the pandanus and members of the *Ficus* family, helping to anchor them in stormy conditions.

Pruning
Controlled cutting back of plants, especially those with woody stems, to limit size, to train to a chosen shape or to encourage flower and bud formation.

Pseudobulb
The thickened, distinctively covered stem of an orchid that serves as a storage place for water and nutrients and helps the plant to survive dry spells. Every year a new plump, smooth pseudobulb grows, developing two or more leaves. The old one shrivels and loses its foliage but provides the younger one with nourishment.

Pumice
Volcanic, industrially fabricated 'pebbles' that provide good drainage and aeration, do not rot and retain few nutrients. Pumice is used as a potting medium for orchids, cacti and for propagation when mixed with other materials.

Pyrethrum
Natural insecticide from chrysanthemum species that is not harmful to bees and is quickly broken down. It is considered nontoxic to humans and other mammals because it is poorly absorbed by the stomach. According to the latest findings, it may be injurious if it gets into open wounds because it can reach the nervous system through the blood. Be careful with all wounds and skin ailments, especially allergies. Wear gloves when spraying and spray only when there is no wind. Still more questionionable are insecticides with pyrethroid, which is a synthetic pyrethrum.

R

Raceme
Form of inflorescence (see drawing, page 15).

Raphide
Needle-shaped crystal of calcium oxalate that occurs in many plant cells. Raphides are found in most plants of the arum family, especialy in dieffenbachia, the spider plant and cordyline. Located in special cells that open swiftly at the lightest touch to expel them, they can easily get into the mucous membranes of mouth and throat, producing burns and irritation.

Resistance
Inherited or developed ability to withstand disease, insects (in plants) or chemical substances (in insects). Plays an important role in plant breeding, one of whose goals is to produce varieties that can resist pests and disease.

Respiration
Plant cells, like human cells, require oxygen to function. The oxygen taken in is used to release energy for **photosynthesis**, and carbon dioxide and water vapour are given off.

Rest period
Period in which a plant does not grow, putting out no new leaves or shoots. With many houseplants the rest period occurs in the autumn and winter months, when the amount of light is also diminished. During this period plants need less water, no fertilizer and a cooler location. Also referred to as the dormant period.

Rhizome
Underground, horizontal stem axis that forms shoots on top and roots underneath. Rhizomes are also called root stalks or rootstocks and differ from roots in that they develop buds and scales. They occur in various Gesneriacea species, for example, and in the arum lily.

Root
Function in most plants is to anchor the plant in the ground, to take up water and nutrients and send them to other parts of the plant or to store nutrients. Examples of specialized root forms include **aerial roots**, **prop roots** and **adventitious roots**.

Root ball
Term for the soil of a pot plant completely laced with roots.

Root hair
The finest side roots, designed to take up water and nutrients from the soil or potting medium. Root hairs are also called sucking or short roots.

Rooting hormones
Hormone preparation in powder, liquid or paste form that promotes the rooting of **cuttings**.

Root rot
Disease caused by soil fungus, for which there is no cure.

Rosette
A circular cluster of leaves growing (usually) from the base of a very short stem. Rosette plants include bromeliads, echeverias, bird's nest fern and African violets.

Runners
Side shoot, above or under ground, that can grow from the base of the stem, the flower rosette or the root crown. Runners are also called stolons and appear on the strawberry begonia, for example, and the sword fern.

S

Salt burn
Arises from over-feeding or through the concentration of fertilizer salts in 'old' potting medium. Can be expressed in growth reduction, **chlorosis** or dying tissue.

Salt sensitivity
A common characteristic in plants and one which necessitates care in the administration of fertilizers containing high concentrations of fertilizer salts. In the plant portraits vulnerable species and varieties are clearly indicated. They should receive half to a quarter of the prescribed quantity of fertilizer, at most, or an organic fertilizer.

Scale
An insect pest which frequently occurs on indoor plants and may be seen on both leaves and stems (see page 54).

Scariad fly
Otherwise known as fungus gnats. See page 52.

Seed
Fertilized egg cell of a flowering plant, which can germinate and bring forth a new plant. It is provided with a food reserve and a protective coat.

Seed leaf
The first leaf or leaves of a plant, which appear after the seed germinates. Of simple, basic shape, they frequently do not resemble the complex, 'true' leaves characteristic of the plant. As soon as they reach light, **chlorophyll** is formed in them, which enables the plant to begin nourishing itself through the process of **photosynthesis**. There are plants that produce only one seed leaf (see **Monocotyledonous**) and those that produce two (see **Dicotyledonous**).

Seedling
New plant that has germinated from fertilized egg cell. The seedling consists of seed root, seed stem, seed bud and seed leaves. It is bipolar: the root system develops from the seed root, the stem and leaf system from the seed bud.

Self-climbing
Plant provided with a natural means of climbing, for example with tendrils or with **adventitious** roots.

Self-pollination
Method of pollination in which a **stigma** is dusted with the pollen of the same flower. Thus the hereditary factors of the single plant are passed on in a process called inbreeding.

Sensitive plants
Many plants react to external stimuli, such as changes of light or temperature or even to touch. A very striking reaction is shown by the so-called sensitive plant (*Mimosa pudica*). Its leaflet stems have hinges that snap together at the slightest touch, one after another down the leaf stalk. In many plants (oxalis, for instance), the change from day to night causes the leaves or flowers to close as darkness comes.

Sepal
One of the outer circle of usually green modified leaves which protect the petals and sex organs of a flower. When fused they are called a **calyx**.

Shading
Measures taken to protect plants from sunscorch, particularly in the middle of the day and in the spring when the plants are not yet accustomed to light intensity. Shading can be accomplished with curtains, blinds, awnings, tissue paper or by the arrangement of neighbouring plants.

Shallow-rooted
Plant that does not develop deep-reaching main roots or taproots but whose roots branch vigorously sideways, for example azaleas.

Sharp sand
Lime-free river or quartz sand, which is added to potting materials to improve water-permeability and to disperse fertilizer salts. It is an important component of propagating seeding mediums. Not recommended for houseplants are coloured sands or builder's sand, which contain lime.

Shoot
New growth, as a rule consisting of stem, leaves and terminal bud.

Short-day plant
Plant that needs a short day – short periods of light and long periods of darkness – for a particular period of time in order to set flowers. Examples: chrysanthemums and poinsettias. Compare **Long-day plant**.

Silicon (Si)
Chemical element that constitutes 80 per cent of the earths's surface. In plants it occurs primarily in horsetails and grasses. The silicon compound silicic acid strengthens the cell walls of plants and makes them resistant to attacks of fungus and bacteria. Broths made from horsetails (see recipe, page 52) are thus outstanding plant tonics.

Slow-release fertilizer
Fertilizer designed to give up its nutrients to the plants slowly over a long period of time.

Soaking
First-aid measure for a root ball that is completely dried out (see drawing, page 42).

GLOSSARY

Sogginess
Occurs when water cannot drain away and the potting medium becomes waterlogged. Too much water expels the oxygen from the soil, the roots suffocate and rot, and the plant dies. Always provide for good **drainage**.

Soil-based compost
Potting mixture based on the formula of seven parts loam (or soil), three parts peat and two parts sand with added **nutrients**. Nutrient quantities vary according to the function of the medium: lightly fertilized for propagation and seeding, more strongly fertilized for potting on and continued culture. Commercially available mixtures vary slightly according to manufacturer. Less commonly used for houseplants today because it is heavier than the soil-less alternatives.

Soil-less compost
Potting mixture based on **peat**. Available commercially are a weakly fertilized planting medium for propagation and seeding and a more heavily fertilized mixture for continued culture or potting on. Mixturers vary slightly according to manufacturer.

Soil warmth
A soil temperature of 20°C (68°F) or more. Important for plants that are accustomed to high soil temperatures in their native locations and which fail to thrive when their roots are cold. A requirement for **germination** for many tropical plants, warm soil can be provided by warming mats, heated propagator or soil-warming cables.

Sooty mould
A fungal disease caused by scale, aphids or whitefly (see page 55).

Sorus (pl. sori)
Cluster of spore cases (or sporangia) on the underside of certain fern leaves. Sori are located in differently shaped clusters depending on the species of fern. In some species they are covered with a special film until maturity.

Spadix
A thick or fleshy spike-like form of inflorescence (see drawing, page 15). Example: arum family.

Spathe
Large **bract** which surrounds the flower spike of members of the Araceae family. Sometimes strikingly coloured, it serves as an attractant for pollinators.

Species
A classification of an individual plant or a group of closely related plants within a **genus.** All the plants in a particular species are alike in their essential features. The species name is the second element in a botanical name and commonly says something about the plant appearance, characteristics or place of origin. Thus in *Clivia miniata*, the species name *miniata* describes a fiery-red *Clivia* or kaffir lily (from Latin: *miniatus*=minium-coloured, *minium* being red lead).

Sphagnum
Fresh sphagnum moss is much used for lining hanging baskets and is incorporated into the potting mixtures of some plants.

Spider mite
An insect pest that thrives in conditions which are too warm and dry (see page 54).

Spike
Form of inflorescence (see drawing, page 15).

Spirit-soap solution
Home remedy for control of scale and mealy bugs (see recipe, page 52).

Sporangia
Cases in which **spores** are developed. On ferns, for instance, they are arranged in clusters (see **Sorus**) on the undersides of the fronds.

Spore
Single, asexual cell without germinating or nourishing tissue, by which primitive plant life (such as ferns and fungi) can reproduce itself. Mature spores are launched from the **sporangia** to form intermediary sexual structures which in turn produce plantlets.

Stalk
Unbranching, leafless stem, which bears the flower or **inflorescence** and sometimes also **bracts**. Examples: amaryllis, strelitzia and arum lily.

Standard
Form or training in which the plant is limited to a stout single stem with a mophead of growth at the top (see drawing, page 44).

Stem
Herbaceous, branching or unbranching shoot with or without leaves.

Stem cutting
Piece of a stem, for example of dieffenbachia, cordyline or yucca that can be used for **vegetative propagation**.

Stem rot
General term for fungal infection (see page 55).

Sterile
Unfruitful or germ-free. The opposite of **fertile**.

Sterile leaves
Modified leaves that serve as collectors of humus and water to provide the plant with **nutrients**. Such leaves should not be removed. The brown leaves of the staghorn fern are one example.

Sterilize
To make germ-free, to disinfect. Commercially prepared potting mediums are sterilized either by steaming in special apparatus or with chemicals. Germ-free mediums are important both for seeding and for potting on because disease organisms can be transmitted through them.

Stigma
Part of the female organ of the flower, specifically the upper part of the **pistil** and the real organ of conception (see drawing, page 15). To attract the male pollen, it is coated with a slippery or sticky substance.

Stinging-nettle extract
Home remedy for control of aphids (see recipe, page 52).

Stolon
See **Runners**.

Storage organ
Any organ that can stockpile water and **nutrients**, such as **tubers**, **bulbs**, **pseudobulbs** and **rhizomes**.

Sub-shrub
Plant whose lower parts remain firm and woody but whose upper parts are **herbaceous**. Examples: *Columnea*, *Pelargonium* species and *Pentas lanceolata*.

subsp
Abbreviation for **subspecies**.

Subspecies
Plant with a few characteristics that are divergent from the species. Subspecies are designated by the addition of *subsp* (for *subspecies*) to their botanical name.

Succulent
Plant with fleshy, juicy leaves or stems. Examples of leaf succulents: agave, aloe and the Livingstone daisy; examples of stem succulents: cacti, column euphorbias and stapelias.

Sucker
Young plant growth that emerges from the soil close to the parent plant and springs usually from its roots.

Sulphur (S)
Chemical element that is one of the principal plant **nutrients**. Needed for synthesis of protein, vitamin B_1 and pungent oils (garlic, horseradish, mustard) and is supplied in fertilizers in the form of sulphates of potassium, magnesium, ammonium and calcium.

Sunscorch
Silvery, brown or red spots which result from incorrect culture (see page 54).

Sympodial
Stem consisting of several axes. Compare **monopodial** growth. Occurs when a shoot stops growing either because its terminal bud dies or because if develops a flower and the bud in the axil of the uppermost leaves of the stem continues the stem system.

Systemic control agent
Chemical pesticide that is sprayed or watered onto the plant and operates by entering the leaves or roots and being distributed throughout it by means of its vascular system (see **Vascular bundles**).

T

Tendril
Leafless, often spiral-form organ by which certain climbing plants support themselves. There are tendrils that spring from stems and others that spring from leaves. Stem tendrils are formed by the passion flower, for example, and grape vines; leaf tendrils are found on members of the pea family.

Terminal cutting/top cutting
Cutting that contains a terminal bud and at least two strong leaves (see drawing, page 58).

Terrarium
A small glass display case for plants that need high **humidity**; can also be called an indoor greenhouse. Larger units are called growing cabinets. Terrariums were first made in the nineteenth century. Ingeniously fashioned from cast iron and glass, they were called Wardian cases after the botanist N. B. Ward who designed the first one. Today they are technologically refined, with heating, humidifiers and provision for sufficient light and ventilation. The frames are of aluminium or rot-resistant redwood and cases are obtainable in various sizes and shapes.

Thinning out
Term used for the practice of easing congestion of young seedlings. The weakest are pulled out so that the stronger seedlings have more room to grow.

Thrips
An insect pest that thrives in dry air (see page 54).

Tomentum
Dense covering of fine hairs that protects plant parts, specifically leaves, from very bright light.

Trace element
Boron, iron, copper, manganese, molybdenum, and zinc are all trace elements. Although plants need these nutrients in only tiny amounts, lack of them can lead to disease. Also called micronutrients.

Transpiration
Release of water vapour, also called evaporation. All land plants give off water vapour, primarily through the **pores**. At warmer temperatures transpiration is increased. If the evaporated water is not replaced, the plant wilts.

Trunk
Woody, often very thick branching or unbranching main stem of a shrub or tree that does not die back in winter, formed only after several years of growth.

Tuber
Thickened, more or less fleshy part of a stem or root (see drawing, page 14). There are underground budding tubers, as with cyclamen and tuberous-rooted begonias, or above-ground ones, as with hearts entangled. All tubers are storage organs for reserve food.

Tuberous root
Tuber-like swollen root that serves as a storage area, for example in terrestrial orchids.

Tub plant
Plant of generally robust growth that requires large container for support and for root development. Tub plants come mainly from the Mediterranean regions and thus thrive splendidly when they spend summer out of doors in a protected, sunny spot. The majority of them must be overwintered in a bright location at 5 to 10°C (41 to 51°F).

U

Umbel
A form of inflorescence (see drawing, page 15).

Urn/vase
Alternative terms for bromeliads' apparatus for catching water and nutrients (see **Cup**).

V

Var.
Abbreviation of *varietas*=variety.

Variegation
Term for leaves with white or yellow flecks or stripes. These pale areas contain no green chlorophyll and thus cannot assimilate. Variegated plants must be placed in as bright a location as possible but usually cannot tolerate direct sunlight. In dark locations they begin storing more chlorophyll in their leaves, losing some of their variegation, in order to increase the areas capable of **assimilation**. Variegation can be produced through mutation, breeding or viral infections.

Variety
Hybrid variation of a plant species. May also be called a cultivar. The variety name is usually indicated by single quotation marks, for example: *Campanula isophylla* 'Mayii'.

Vascular bundles
Circulatory system of the plant, comprising structures that transport water and 'raw' or processed **nutrients** round the plant. They can also be used to carry systemic insecticides to every part of the plant.

Vegetative cone
Growth point at the end of shoots, roots and buds.

Vegetative period

Also called growth period. Limited by the seasons, in temperate zones the vegetative period begins with the increase of light in late winter and spring and ends when the days become shorter. The beginning of the vegetative period is signalled by the appearance of new growth.

Vegetative propagation

Asexual reproduction by division or rooting of stems, leaves or roots. The new plant thus obtained is identical to the mother plant genetically and in appearance.

Ventilation

Necessary measure in houseplant culture, especially in winter. Stagnant, warm, dry air promotes disease and insect infestation. Therefore ventilate often, but keep draughts and cold air away from plants.

Vermiculite

Flakes of heated and expanded magnesium, aluminium and iron silicate, used as a potting medium for cacti and as an additive for other potting mediums to increase permeability.

Virus

Disease caused by a submicroscopic entity which replicates itself within plant cells (see page 55).

Volatile oil

Fragrant, as a rule, and strong-smelling, easily dissipated material that is concentrated in glandular cells or microscopically small oil reservoirs, for example in the petals of gardenia flowers, the leaves of scented geraniums, the roots of ginger, the bark of the cinnamon tree, and the rind of the lemon.

Water

Essential for plant life. Without water plants wilt, the pores of the leaves close, **nutrients** are not transported and **photosynthesis** and **transpiration** are interrupted. The majority of our houseplants come from subtropical and tropical regions and are not adapted to the harder, more limey water often found in temperate zones. For such plants the water should be softened (see drawing, page 42).

Watering space

The distance between the top of the potting medium and the top of the container, in an average pot, should be around 2 cm (¾in). This prevents soil from washing over the edge of the pot when the plant is watered and permits a good soaking.

Water softening

A necessary measure in areas where tap water is hard or limey (see drawing, page 42).

Waxy coating

Extremely thin film or bloom with which some leaves protect themselves against evaporation of water. The immature offspring of the mealy bug are also protected by a wax covering.

Whitefly

An insect pest which spreads rapidly from plant to plant (see page 55).

White oil

A mineral product that destroys the waxy layer of an insect's outer covering and clogs its respiratory organs. Used to counteract **scale**.

Woody growth

Depositing of a complex compound called lignin in the cell walls of certain plants to make the stems stronger and more rigid.

Xerophyte

Plant that is adapted to withstand great dryness, such as cacti and other succulents; for example, euphorbias, agaves, aloes and sedum.

Yellow cards

Plastic cards coated with sticky material and coloured a particularly glaring yellow, which act as a lure for insects.

The passionflower is an assiduous climber that repays loving care with abundant and spectacularly beautiful flowers that deserve the closest scrutiny.

84

PLANT PORTRAITS

Getting plants to grow, to flower, and even to fruit are the challenges that make houseplant gardening so fascinating. The following pages tell you how to cultivate the most popular flowering and foliage plants, ferns and palms, and orchids and cacti correctly and successfully.

How to use the plant portraits

Study the following sections and you will be familiar with all the well-known houseplants and the requirements for cultivating them, as well as some of the rarer species now available. If you pay particular attention to the habit of each plant and its range of flower and leaf colours, you will discover a wealth of variety that is sure to give you many wonderful ideas for making plants more a part of your home.

Structured for clarity and comparison

All the plant portraits are structured for clarity and ease of reference so that you can find out everything you need to know about a particular plant at a glance. Since all the descriptions are arranged in the same format, plants can easily be compared with each other. And they are organized by plant type (see list at far right) in a series of chapters, where they appear in alphabetical order under their botanical names.

The botanical name is used internationally, which is why it determines the alphabetical order of the listings. When the botanical name of an entire genus is used (for example *Echevaria*, page 107), the names of several species that are appropriate for houseplant culture are given in the text below.

When a species name is used as the botanical name (for example, *Ardisia crenata*, page 94), the description refers largely to this particular species. In most cases no other species of the genus is cultivated as a houseplant.

The English or common name appears below the botanical name in large, easy-to-read type directly above the illustration. It is the name best-known to many plant lovers. Some plants have several common names. Where this is the case, alternative names are given.

The symbols

The symbols which appear below the captions to the illustrations are designed to give you instant information about the right location and such important procedures as watering and misting or whether a plant is suitable for hydroculture or is poisonous.

 The plant tolerates full sun, also midday sun.

 The plant needs a bright spot, near a window but not sunny.

 The plant will also thrive in semi-shade.

 The plant tolerates or prefers shade.

 The plant needs abundant water. Water until there is a considerable overflow in the saucer.

 Keep the plant only moderately damp. Only a few drops should appear in the saucer.

 Give little water. The saucer should remain dry.

 Mist the plant often.

 The plant is suited for hydroculture.

 The plant is poisonous

The headings

The instructions for culture are arranged under the following bold headings.

Flowering season For the flowering plants, orchids and cacti this is always the first item. It is important information if you want to know the best time to buy a flowering plant or the right flowering time for the species when a plant fails to bloom.

Family Here you will find the botanical classification.

Origin This gives the geographical region(s) in which the plant naturally occurs.

Location This is of fundamental importance for culture. Here you learn about the plant's light and warmth requirements throughout the year.

Watering, feeding The section tells you the optimum amounts of water and how often to fertilize. Important: where 'weak solution' is advised, use only one half to one third of the manufacturer's recommended quantity to 1 litre (1qt) of water.

Further culture Listed here is information about individual humidity or overwintering requirements, whether misting should be done and when a plant should be repotted. Special potting-medium requirements are also included.

Propagating This describes the quickest propagation method for the particular plant. You can find out more about the technique on pages 58–61.

Pests, diseases Those to which the plant is particularly vulnerable are listed, as are the chief potential causes of pest attack or disease. How you remedy them is described in the section First aid for your plants (pages 50–5).

Warning This indicates plants that are poisonous or cause skin irritation. Plants so designated can be harmful to susceptible adults, children and pets, and those with a death's head symbol may even be lethal if they are eaten or come into contact with the skin or the mucous membranes.

Health hazards

Some plants must be enjoyed with caution. When choosing plants for your home, keep in mind the following points if you have small children or pets.

Plants can cause allergies Classic examples are the primrose allergy, from the primin in *Primula obconica* (poison primrose), and cases of contact dermatitis through phototoxic substances, for example in *Ficus* and *Citrus* species. Various members of the Compositae family are also allergenic, especially the chrysanthemum.

Contented foliage plants present such a variety of greens that other colours are irrelevant.

Plants can cause injury Care must be taken, for example, to avoid contact with spines, thorns, sharp leaf edges or leaf tips.

Plants can cause headaches Plants with strong fragrances in flowers and leaves can be unpleasant.

Plants can contain toxic substances These can be injurious to health for people and pets and can even be lethal if they are consumed. Remember that small children put everything into their mouths, and cats and many other pets love to nibble houseplants.

Poisonous plants

Poisons appear in concentration in the following plant families:

Arum family (*Araceae*) contain a bitter plant juice and raphides, needle-shaped crystals, usually of calcium oxalate, which occur in the plant cells as a metabolic product and can pierce the skin and inject their poison.

Lily family (*Lilaceae*) can contain saponins and alkaloids as well as skin-irritating substances.

Nightshade family (*Solanaceae*) are dangerous because of their strong, powerful alkaloids.

Dogbane family (*Apocynaceae*) produce two of the most powerful poison groups, alkaloids and glycosides.

Spurge family (*Euphorbiaceae*) are furnished with toxic protein materials. The bitter milky juice has a caustic effect externally as well as internally.

What's where

FLOWERING PLANTS

They fascinate with their
multiciplity of colour and
form, and some add an
intoxicating fragrance to
their list of charms,
whereas others produce
from a rather modest
flower a decorative,
gaily coloured ornamental
fruit. Many eventually
become treasured
household friends.

88

Sales figures prove it: flowering plants are the most popular of all houseplants. Who can resist the cheerful array of spring-flowering primulas, the charm of the African violet, the elegance of the camellia or the gardenia? And many people use flowering plants to set off an occasional display of 'fireworks' against a quiet, perhaps more permanent, background, of foliage plants.

On the following pages you will meet all the beauties the flowering-plant market has to offer. Included are plants with decorative fruits; after all, a fruit is nothing more than an extension of the flower. In addition, you will also find an attractive choice of new or less common flowering plants as well as a small assortment of favourite tub plants, which at manageable pot-plant stage are easy to keep in the house.

Many beauties like browallia or the slipper flower are so-called seasonal or throw-away plants, discarded after blooming because their lifetime is limited to one year. Some, like poinsettia, chrysanthemum or cineraria, are longer lasting, but with time they either become less and less attractive or cannot be induced to bloom again without extraordinary measures. However, there are many varieties that, with loving care, grow larger and more beautiful every year, producing wonderful blooms in season. Outstanding examples include the kaffir lily, azalea, cyclamen, gardenia and camellia.

The darling of international breeders, flowering plants are continually being changed and improved. The goals are longer life and an extended flowering season, maxi or mini growth, new colours, more beautiful leaf forms, more abundant flowers and, above all, improved readiness to flower and suitability for houseplant culture.

The flowering season

Most of our flowering houseplants come from tropical or subtropical regions. Adapted to thrive in a very even climate, these inhabitants of the tropical rain forests developed the greatest variety of form and colour in their flowers.

Flower development is influenced by many factors, of which the most important is light. In general, plants with a life of more than one year bloom every vegetative year, many producing blooms of extraordinary beauty year after year. You need only think of the flower of the rose grape (see page 122) or the passionflower (see pages 84–5). But there are exceptions, like the bromeliads that bloom only once, provide for offspring that will eventually flower and then die. Or plants that need a decade or even a century until the first flowering, like the bamboos or the century plant.

The flowering season varies from species to species. With some plants the season can be changed (for example, for Mother's Day or Christmas) through horticultural manipulation. But left to themselves, plants bloom in the second year just as they did in the first. However, there are also occasions when the flowers appear unseasonally. This can happen as a result of mistakes in culture, for example, or following a severe infestation of insects. Then the survival tactics of the plant are called into play and it tries to provide for descendants very quickly before dying.

Mission accomplished for this flowering plant: its long, curved blooms and abundant nectar have attracted a hummingbird to fertilize it.

Such cases are a reminder, if one were needed, that plants do not bloom for us. We are only beneficiaries of their gigantic effort to maintain the species. In order to make the flower as seductive as possible for its particular pollinator, nature has played with colour, form and pattern, invented marvellous fragrances and unpleasant odours and designed attractive landing pads.

The right culture

Buying plants in flower is not difficult – to nurse them back when they are fading and to bring them into flower the following year, on the other hand, demands some basic plant knowledge and care in cultivation. Tropical plants from regions with consistent climatic and light conditions are brought to bloom again relatively easily; if they receive enough humidity and sufficient light during the winter, they will flower in the following vegetative year without much trouble. But with plants from other regions observation of the rest period is vital. This means

In their native habitat poinsettias develop into thick, high hedges.

mimicking living conditions in the native habitat, such as periods of dryness or reduced light, as well as possible. The culture hints in the plant portraits are designed to help you provide optimum conditions for your houseplants, whatever their needs.

Acalypha hispida
Chenille plant, red-hot cattail

Some varieties have creamy-white spikes.

The chenille plant grows wild as a bush in all tropical regions. Only the female plants of this dioecious species are offered as pot plants. It takes the common name from its flower spikes. On the market are other varieties with creamy-white flowers, such as 'Alba', and attractive hanging forms, such as *Acalypha pendula*, which has smaller, more heart-shaped leaves.

Flowering season Mid spring to mid autumn.

Family Euphorbiaceae, spurge family.

Origin Tropics.

Location Bright, but not sunny. Warm all year round; in winter never below 16°C (61°F). Avoid draughts.

Watering, feeding Keep the root ball moderately damp with soft, room-temperature water. Water sparingly from late autumn to mid winter. From late winter to late summer fertilize weekly.

Further culture Mist often. As necessary, pot on in spring using a good-quality houseplant potting medium. Cut back shoots beforehand. When young, pinch out new growth to make the plant bushier.

Propagating In spring from cuttings. A soil temperature of over 20°C (68°F) and high humidity is required for successful rooting, so use a heated propagator. Pinch back rooted young plants often.

Pests, diseases Spider mites, whitefly, aphids, and scale from hot, dry conditions.

Note Use exactly the same care for the coloured-leaved *Acalypha-Wilksiana* hybrids commonly called copper-leaf plants.

Warning All parts of the *Acalypha* species and varieties are poisonous.

Achimenes hybrids
Hot-water plant

Achimenes hybrids bloom for a long time.

This luxuriantly blooming gesneriad, which is related to the African violet and gloxinia, is available in summer in white, yellow, pink, purple and blue. Its colour range has made it consistently popular with those breeding for indoor culture. Only cultivated forms are commercially available. Characteristic are the scaly rhizomes, which look like little fir cones. The leaves are green on the upper side, reddish-tinged on the underside.

Flowering season Mid summer to early autumn.

Family Gesneriaceae, gesneriad family.

Origin Tropical central and South America.

Location From spring to autumn bright and warm (20 to 25°C/68 to 77°F). *Avoid direct sun under all circumstances.*

Watering, feeding *Do not use cold water.* While the plant is in active growth, keep slightly damp. Fertilize six weeks after the growth of the rhizome to the end of mid summer. Thereafter, water little and from early autumn on do not water at all so that the plant can rest.

Further culture Cut off withered parts and leave the rhizome in the pot until spring (or take it out and store it in peat or sand at 20°C/68°F). In late winter pot on, covering the rhizome with 2cm (¾in) of new soil. Place plant in a bright (not sunny), warm spot. Water with warm water and provide for indirect humidity (see page 43).

Propagating By division of the rhizome in spring or top cuttings in soil with a temperature above 20°C (68°F).

Pests, diseases Leaf spots from water that is too cold or splattering of leaves; rarely, aphids, mites and viruses.

Adenium
Desert rose

This specimen is grafted onto an oleander branch.

It probably owes its name to the port city of Aden in the south-west of the Arabian peninsula. Available commercially are *Adenium obesum* and *Adenium swazicum* (though rarely). The colour of the flowers ranges from white-pink to purple and lavender. These succulent plants are much more successful when grafted to the more robust oleander. This is the reason the stem is so disproportionately thick.

Flowering season Mid spring to late summer.

Family Apocynaceae, dogbane family.

Origin Southern Arabian peninsula, Uganda, Kenya, Tanzania.

Location Full sun, warm all year long. In winter keep in a dark location and cooler (around 15°C/ 59°F). In summer place outdoors in a wind-protected spot, as sunny as possible.

Watering, feeding Keep damp from mid spring to mid autumn. From late autumn to early spring water just enough to keep the roots from dying back. During the growing season use flower and cactus fertilizer alternately every 14 days when watering.

Propagating By top cuttings, grafted to oleander stems of the same thickness. Difficult: this is a task for the experienced grower.

Pests, diseases Spider mites, mealy bugs.

Warning The milky juice of the desert rose is highly poisonous. When cutting the branches, pruning or grafting, wear gloves. If you have children and pets, it is better to avoid this plant.

Aechmea
Urn plant

Aechmea fasciata *has pink bracts.*

The genus *Aechmea* consists of some 150, mostly epiphytic, species. It is usually the pink *Aechmea fasciata* that is seen on the market, but other species, like the striped *Aechmea chantinii* (with a red-gold inflorescence), are also available. Very beautiful too are *Aechmea fulgens*, with coral-pink flowers, and *Aechmea miniata*, in whose flowers both blue and red appear. The name *Aechmea* comes from the Greek (*aichme*=lance tip) and refers to the pointed bracts. The leaves are arranged in a rosette, forming a cup, and are usually very spiny.

Flowering season Late spring to mid autumn. But every rosette of leaves blooms only once.

Family Bromeliaceae, bromeliad family.

Origin Brazil.

Location Bright, but no sun. All year round not below 18°C (64°F). Tolerates central heating.

Watering, feeding Always use soft water for watering. From mid spring to mid autumn keep the root ball only moderately damp, so water into the cup. From late autumn to early spring reduce amount of water. In spring and summer add a flower fertilizer to the water every 14 days.

Further culture When no longer attractive, rosettes that have flowered should be removed. Pot on when necessary in a good-quality houseplant potting medium.

Propagating Through offsets (see drawing, page 58) or seeds. Allow new rosettes to develop to a reasonable size before potting on.

Pests, diseases Brown leaves from cold, wet conditions. Scale.

Professional tip If they will not bloom, try the apple trick (see drawing, page 45).

Aeschynanthus
Lipstick vine, basket plant

The lipstick vine astonishes with its cascades of orange or purple flowers. Obtainable are *Aeschynanthus speciosus* (orange-red),

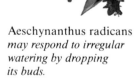

Aeschynanthus radicans *may respond to irregular watering by dropping its buds.*

Aeschynanthus radicans (syn. *Aeschynanthus pulcher*, bright red), *Aeschynanthus hildebrandii* (red), *Aeschynanthus lobbianus* (dull red and floriferous) and *Aeschynanthus tricolor* (brown-red) as well as a host of attractive hybrids. All *Aeschynanthus* species and varieties make successful hanging plants.

Flowering season
Summer. Many plants will start blooming in spring.
Family Gesneriaceae, gesneriad family.
Origin Tropical Asia.
Location Most of year keep bright but not sunny, and warm, best over 20°C (68°F). However, in winter keep cooler for four weeks (around 15°C/59°F) and almost dry. This promotes bud formation.
Watering, feeding
Keep the root ball only slightly damp. The succulent leaves can store water, a sign that the plant needs only moderate watering. From early spring to late summer feed every two weeks using a weak solution.
Propagating By soft cuttings in early summer. You can also simply lay shoots on damp seeding medium and roots will form at the leaf nodes. Warm soil is important so use a heated propagator.
Pests, diseases Rarely aphids. Bud drop from change of location, temperature fluctuation and too much or too little water.
Professional tip I hang my *Aeschynanthus* outdoors in a densely leaved tree in summer. Summer half-shade and damp humid air clearly do it good.

Allamanda cathartica
Golden trumpet

An energetic climber and stunning colour.

The *Allamanda* develops shoots several metres (yards) long in a very short space of time. Then the large, dazzling yellow flower trumpets, which range from 2 to 12cm (3 to 4½in) in length, depending on the species, open one after another. Available commercially are *Allamanda cathartica* 'Hendersonii' (orange-yellow), 'Grandiflora' (lemon yellow) and the extremely vigorous grower 'Schottii' (yellow). At its best in large window areas, conservatories and humid swimming pools, it needs something to climb on.
Flowering season Late spring to early autumn; with suitable lighting even till mid winter.
Family Apocynaceae, dogbane family.
Origin North-eastern South America, mostly Brazil.
Location Full sun. Warmth all year long, daytime temperature never below 18°C (64°F).

In winter rest period, nights 15 to 18°C (59 to 64°F). The potting medium must be warm.
Watering, feeding
From mid spring to mid autumn give plenty of water and mist often. Then reduce both. In summer fertilize weekly, in winter only in a very bright location every four weeks.
Further culture
Following flowering, plant stems can be reduced in length by about a third to encourage flowering on new growth. In late winter/early spring, pot on as necessary using a good potting mixture.
Propagating By top cuttings in spring or autumn in a soil warmth of about 25°C (77°F).
Pests, diseases
Yellowing of leaves from nutrient deficiency; mealy bugs and scale.
Warning All parts of the *Allamanda* are poisonous.

92

Anthurium
Tailflower, flamingo plant

Aphelandra
Aphelandra

Anthurium scherzerianum *variety.*

Aphelandra squarrosa *comes from Brazil.*

The true flower of the tailflower is not the coloured spathe but the 'tail' or spadix that rises out of it. On the market are *Anthurium scherzerianum* varieties with spathes of various colours, and a mostly orange-red, spiral spadis, and *Anthurium crystallinum*, which has beautifully marked leaves.

Flowering season Anthurium scherzerianum varieties bloom all year round.

Family Araceae, arum family.

Origin Central and tropical South America.

Location All year round warm and very bright, but not sunny. In winter provide heat beneath the container and high humidity.

Watering, feeding During the growth period keep evenly damp. *Never use hard or cold water. Avoid sogginess.* From early spring to early autumn, feed weekly, but use only half or a third of the quantity recommended.

Further culture Mist often in spring and summer. When completely potbound, pot on in spring, using a good houseplant potting medium, with added polystyrene granules (optional).

Propagating From seeds.

Pests, diseases Curling leaves and spider mites in direct sun and air that is too dry. Also leaf spots and root rot.

Professional tip Maintaining a moist, humid atmosphere is essential.

Best-known representative of the genus is *Aphelandra squarrosa* (zebra plant), of which some hybrids are available commercially. It has compact growth, attaining at least 76cm (30in) in height (more in a large pot), and dark-green leaves with creamy-white veins. The striking sun-yellow flower spike consists of bracts that overlap like roof tiles and last for a long time and a tiny, short-lived, bright yellow, tube-shaped flower. Anyone with a greenhouse or an enclosed flower window will have more success with this plant.

Flowering season Early summer to mid autumn (for *Aphelandra squarrosa*); but the blooming period can be altered so that plants are available in flower at other times.

Family Acanthaceae, acanthus family.

Origin Central and tropical South America.

Location Bright all year, no sun. Warm, *and in winter not below 20°C (68°F).* Provide humidity (see page 43).

Watering, feeding Use only soft, room-temperature water. Keep soil moist at all times. From early spring to late summer fertilize at least every week, twice weekly in mid summer when growing well.

Further care Mist often. Following flowering, cut back to a sound pair of leaves. In spring, pot on as necessary in good houseplant potting mixture.

Propagating From firm cuttings with two pairs of leaves, taken from shoots which develop in leaf axils. Heated propagator is essential.

Pests, diseases Aphids or scale in locations that are too warm and dry. Curling and dropping of leaves in dry air, draughts and when temperature too cool.

FLOWERING PLANTS

Ardisia crenata
Coralberry

Ardisia *berries last for many months.*

An attractive, small evergreen tree from Asia that is notable for its brilliant red berries, set off against elegant dark foliage. The berries last for many months, and the leaves are dark green and crenated along their margins. The white or pink flowers are rather insignificant. The plant grows to about 1m (39in) high in its natural habitat, but slightly less robustly when in a pot. On account of its slow rate of growth, this is a plant that is only occasionally offered by retailers.

Flowering season Late spring and early summer. The red, pea-sized berries last for six months but sometimes stay on even longer.

Family Myrsinaceae, myrsine family.

Origin South-east Asia.

Location Bright and warm all year long, but *no full sun.* In winter somewhat cooler. An east window is ideal.

Watering, feeding Keep root ball only moderately damp. From early spring to late summer use weak fertilizer every week.

Further culture Provide heat beneath the container and high humidity. Mist often. Pot on in spring as necessary in good houseplant potting mixture.

Propagating From seed at soil temperatures over 25°C (77°F) or from cuttings, which do not root easily.

Pests, diseases Scale and mealy bugs in dry centrally heated air.

Professional tip Provide high humidity during flowering season or the onset of new flowers and berries will be rather modest. A brush can be used to pollinate artificially, flower by flower, and thus promote fruiting.

Begonia Elatior hybrids
Winter-flowering begonias

Elatior hybrids, *looking like potted bouquets.*

When we speak of winter-flowering begonias today we are almost always referring to the so-called Elatior hybrids, which used to be called *Begonia × hiemalis* because originally they were winter-bloomers. In the hit parade of flowering plants they remain near the top. This is primarily due to the huge variety of colours offered and the fact that they can be bought in bloom all year round and will flower for almost a year uninterruptedly. In recent years the many wonderful colours that are available have been vastly improved, but plants are seldom offered by name. Very popular also are the slightly trailing varieties in white, red or pink from the Aphrodite strain, which look superb in hanging pots. First-year plants following propagation give best results.

Flowering season Almost all year round.

Family Begoniaceae, begonia family.

Origin Tropical South America. All begonias in trade are cultivated.

Location Bright, but no sun. Room temperature all year round not below 18°C (64°F).

Watering, feeding Keep moist at all times. *Avoid sogginess or dryness of root ball.* Fertilize every 14 days.

Further culture Potting on is not needed because further culture does not pay.

Propagating From top cuttings in mid or late spring (but also possible at other times), only from mature, healthy plants. Most successful in a heated propagator.

Pests, diseases Fungal problems may result from too high humidity. Prone to mildew.

Begonia
Cane-type begonias

Begonia glaucophylla *blooms through spring.*

Most species possess strikingly colourful foliage and attractive flowers and are noted for their durable qualities indoors. Some also thrive on shady balconies. The best-known representatives are:
● *Begonia corallina delucerna*
● *Begonia limmingheana* (syn. *B. glaucophylla*)
● *Begonia serratipetala*
● *Begonia metallica*
● *Begonia egregia*
● *Begonia coccinea* and varieties like 'Comte de Miribel'

Flowering season Dependent on species and variety.

Family Begoniaceae, begonia family.

Origin Tropical America.

Location Bright all year round. Smooth-leaved species tolerate more light and sun than species and varieties with hairy leaves. In summer 20 to 22°C (68 to 72°F), in winter somewhat cooler (not below 15°C/59°F).

Watering, feeding Always keep root ball evenly moist. *Avoid sogginess and standing in water.* Fertilize every 8 to 14 days from early spring to late summer.

Further culture Can be potted on from early spring to mid summer, and also at other times of year, if necessary. Use good houseplant potting mixture or ericaceous compost. Mix in polystyrene pieces. Following flowering, untidy growth can be trimmed.

Propagating Insert firm cuttings in peat and sand mixture, preferably in a heated propagator.

Pests, diseases Mildew can be a problem in dank conditions; also leaf and flower drop in poor light.

Professional tip There are both upright and trailing kinds that will add much to any houseplant collection.

Beloperone guttata
Shrimp plant

The shrimp plant is often considered a valuable throw-away plant for house and balcony. But this pretty subshrub from Mexico can be a welcome houseguest for many years. Its leaves are oval and slightly hairy. The flower spikes, which resemble hop blossoms, are composed of yellow-orange bracts overlapping like roof tiles, and from them the real flower protrudes like a white tongue.

Flowering season The plant bears its bracts almost all year round. However, the white flower lasts only a few days.

Family Acanthaceae, acanthus family.

Origin Mexico.

Location Outside or inside, very bright but no full sun. In summer warm, in autumn/winter enjoys 12 to 16°C (54 to 61°F) but tolerates room temperatures.

Watering, feeding In summer water well; from late summer through autumn, somewhat less. In winter keep drier still. From early spring to late summer fertilize weekly.

Further culture In spring, pot on as necessary in good houseplant potting mixture. Pinch out growing tips of young plants before potting on. This promotes the development of new shoots and compact, bushy growth. In summer only minimal tipping to retain compact shape.

Propagating From cuttings in spring in a heated propagator.

Pests, diseases Aphid attack after hot spells; leaf drop if plant pot bound or starved of nourishment.

Professional tip Try making a standard form from a rooted cutting (see page 44).

Note Similar care is required by the yellow form of *Beloperone lutea*.

Given proper care, the shrimp plant can keep its colour throughout the year.

FLOWERING PLANTS

Billbergia nutans
Queen's tears

Queen's tears is both beautiful and robust.

This bromeliad is one of the toughest houseplants we have, blooms tirelessly and develops many offsets. It develops tubular rosettes of leaves and nodding inflorescences (*nutans*=nodding) of green-purple flowers and deep-pink bracts. There are hybrids with orange bracts and other *Billbergia* species on the market.
Flowering season An accommodating plant that will bloom at any time.
Family Bromeliaceae, bromeliad family.
Origin Southern Brazil, Uruguay, Paraguay, northern Argentina.
Location Very bright but not sunny. The plants may spend the summer outside in a protected place. Tolerate room temperature all year long. *Billbergia nutans* can also be cooler in winter. Hybrids and other varieties need warmth.
Watering, feeding In summer water well. In winter in a cool location, water less; in a warm location, water more. From late spring to late summer fertilize weekly.
Further culture In summer mist often and pot on plants as necessary in good houseplant potting mixture.
Propagating From offsets.
Pests, diseases Rare.
Professional tip Queen's tears is a decorative beginner's plant that thrives despite dry centrally heated air and a not very bright location.

Browallia
Bush violet, Amethyst flower

Browallia speciosa *blooms all year round.*

Of the six known species, *Browallia speciosa* is the most widely known. The 30 to 50cm (12 to 20in) high subshrub has dark-green leaves and, arising from the leaf axils, many blue, lavender and white single flowers that appear all year round. Also familiar are *Browallia viscosa* and *Browallia grandiflora* – both summer-flowering annuals which make useful bedding plants for the garden. Their flowering season depends on the time of sowing. If used as garden plants, they are sown in late winter; for pot culture in late summer.
Flowering season *Browallia speciosa* all year long; *Browallia grandiflora* and *Browallia viscosa* from late autumn to mid winter.
Family Solanaceae, nightshade family.
Origin Tropical America.
Location Bright windowsill, avoiding strong sunlight. Keep warm (over 20°C/68°F) in summer, in winter somewhat cooler.
Watering, feeding In summer water plentifully, in winter only moderately (danger of rot). As long as the plant is in active growth, fertilize weekly.
Further culture No need to repot because the bush violet is generally cultivated as an annual.
Propagating From cuttings or seeds. Sow in late winter in a bright window and do not cover seeds. Germination will take place at 20 to 25°C (68 to 77°F) within 14 days. Place five or six young plants in a pot to create a good-looking bushy effect.
Pests, diseases Whitefly when air is too dry.
Warning Like almost all members of the nightshade family, the bush violet is poisonous.

Brunfelsia
Yesterday, today and tomorrow

Calceolaria hybrids
Slipper flower, pocketbook flower

Brunfelsia pauciflora *var.* calycina

This plant is happiest in a bright, cool position.

Some 30 species of small trees and shrubs constitute the genus *Brunfelsia. Brunfelsia pauciflora* var. *calycina* has the greatest importance as a house or summer patio plant. It develops sparlike, wide-spreading shoots that tend not to branch. The flowers of white, yellow or light to dark purple, depending on the variety, are not very long-lived, but new ones appear continually.

Flowering season Mid winter to late summer. There is also a winter-blooming variety with violet-blue flowers that have a white eye.

Family Solanaceae, nightshade family.

Origin Brazil.

Location All year round bright to semi-shaded and warm. From late autumn to mid winter keep plants cool (10 to 12°C/50 to 54°F), to promote flowers.

Watering, feeding Water with soft, warm water. Keep plants well dampened from early spring to early autumn and feed every 14 days. Then stop fertilizing and water less. *Avoid dry centrally heated air at all costs.* Mist often.

Further culture After the end of the main flowering period in early summer pot on as necessary in good houseplant potting mixture. Cut back long shoots.

Propagating By top or stem cuttings with bed temperature of 25°C (77°F). Difficult.

Pests, diseases Yellowing of leaves (chlorosis) from hard water, aphids.

Warning Like almost all the nightshade family, this plant is poisonous.

In the some 500 different species and the hybrids that have been derived from them, the inflated lower lip of the flower, which looks like a wide shoe (Latin, *calceolus* = small shoe), is the common chracteristic. This lip, especially in the hybrids, may appear in one colour, two colours or spotted in brilliant yellow, red or orange. Do not confuse these hybrids, which are offered in spring as houseplants and are also kept in conservatories as colourful eyecatchers, with the subshrub *Calceolaria integrifolia*, the slipper flower for balcony tubs and flower beds, although both are grown as annuals and thrown away after flowering.

Flowering season Mid winter to late spring.

Family Scrophulariaceae, figwort family.

Origin Tropical South America. Only cultivated forms in trade.

Location Very bright but not full sun, as cool as possible (15 to 20°C/59 to 68°F) and airy. A north window is ideal.

Watering, feeding Water well but pour off excess water after half an hour. Fertilize weekly.

Further culture Potting on not necessary because the slipper flower plant is only kept as an annual.

Propagating From seed in summer, germinating temperature 18°C (64°F). Do not cover with soil. For the non-professional, generally successful only when the young plants are given additional light (from a plant light) in autumn and winter.

Pests, diseases Susceptible to every type of pest attack.

FLOWERING PLANTS

Camellia
Camellia

Camellia japonica *'Chandleri Elegans'*

Camellia japonica *'Alba Simplex'*

Above Camellia japonica *'Hatsu Warei'*
Centre Camellia japonica *'Rubescens Major'*
Right Camellia japonica *'Oki no Numi'*

Camellias have the reputation of reacting to the tiniest mistake in cultivation by dropping their buds; it is not entirely deserved. If you provide high humidity and coolness, avoid sudden temperature changes and hard water, and do not place it near a heating unit, the camellia will bring forth magnificent flowers every year. These are plants that can be grown in the garden if the soil is fertile but do very much better when grown in containers that can be housed in the conservatory when in flower and placed in a shady part of the garden for the rest of the year,

excluding cold winter conditions. They will not do well in conventional home interiors.

For the enthusiast, there are more than 10,000 varieties, with flowers ranging in colour from pure white through countless shades of pink to pale and intense shades of red as well as bi-coloured varieties. Many of these varieties and colours are now available at local garden centres. Varieties of *Camellia sasanqua* are best for houseplant

culture. They grow slowly, develop elegant trailing branches and begin blooming in mid autumn. But single varieties of

Camellia japonica are good candidates too, for example 'Apollo', 'Silver Waves', 'Apple Blossom' and 'Maiden's Blush'.
Flowering season Mid autumn to early spring.
Family Theacea, tea family.
Origin East Asia.
Location Airy, cool and bright all year round. No direct sun. Overwinter at 6 to 8°C (32 to 46°F), if possible not over 12°C (54°F). These are plants which will tolerate wide-ranging temperatures provided they never become excessively hot. In late spring place outdoors in a semi-shady spot.
Watering, feeding *Never use hard water,* Keep root ball evenly damp. From beginning of new growth till end of mid summer provide azalea fertilizer. After this, reduce water, which will promote setting of buds.
Further culture Although plants do not require frequent potting

on, it is important when this task is undertaken to use an ericaceous mixture.
Propagating With budless terminal cuttings in late summer. A heated propagator is essential. Olive-green shoots provide the best material. Rooting occurs after about eight weeks.
Pests, diseases Aphids, sooty mildew, leaf drop from too warm overwintering or incorrect summer care. Bud drop caused by too-high temperatures or turning the plant after the budding begins, too-dry soil, sogginess or hard water.
Professional tip Buy in spring when plants are in flower. Some never do make flower.

Opposite
A wonderful showpiece for the conservatory: the camellia hybrid 'Barbara Clark' is superb in form and blooms luxuriantly.

FLOWERING PLANTS

Campanula
Bellflower

Campanula isophylla *'Mayii' is a popular variety.*

This plant is one that tolerates hard water – a rare occurrence. It is mainly *Campanula isophylla* that is offered as a pot plant, but both the white 'Alba' and the bluish-purple 'Mayii' are available. Similar care is required by *Campanula fragilis* and *Campanula pyramidalis*, whose common name is chimney bellflower.

Flowering season Early spring to mid autumn.
Family Campanulaceae, bellflower family.
Origin Mediterranean region.
Location Bright to sunny, but in summer protect from blazing midday sun. During the growth period in summer keep ventilated, best in a conservatory. In winter a cooler place around 10°C (50°F) is sufficient for 'resting'.

Watering, feeding From spring to autumn always keep moist. On hot days water well, in winter very little. From late spring to late summer apply flower fertilizer every 14 days.

Further culture Cut back in autumn after blooming; pot on in good houseplant potting mixture in spring, when necessary.

Propagating From cuttings, which root easily in a peat–sand mixture.

Pests, diseases Spider mites in too warm a winter location and dry centrally heated air. Grey mould and leaf-spot disease in too-high humidity.

Professional tip Dead flowers must be removed daily to prolong *Campanula isophylla*'s flowering capability.

Above Campanula poscharskyana
Right Campanula isophylla *'Alba'*

Capsicum annuum
Ornamental pepper

Capsicum annum *looks well on a kitchen windowsill.*

The ornamental pepper is primarily available in autumn and at Christmas time. Depending on the variety, it has round, drum-shaped or pointed oval fruits in brilliant violet, red, orange or yellow. It is a little known fact that the plant is closely related to the vegetable red pepper. The green parts of the plant are poisonous but not its extremely hot fruits, which contain the skin-irritating alkaloid capsaicin, which can be of varying strengths. As the species name indicates, the plant is an annual, and it is thrown away when the fruits shrivel.

Flowering season Spring and summer. The fruits are its true ornaments and these develop after flowering.
Family Solanaceae, nightshade family.
Origin East Asia and Central to South America.

Location Bright to sunny and airy, *if possible not over 20°C (68°F).* In poor light these plants will immediately shed their fruit. Keep plants bought in winter cool, which will prolong their attractiveness.

Watering, feeding Keep moist but not wet. Fertilize weekly during the growing period.

Further culture Potting on not required because plants are cultivated as annuals.

Propagating From seed in spring. Keep flowering plants in a very bright and protected spot outdoors to promote setting of fruit.

Pests, diseases Aphids and spider mites in too warm and dry a location and stagnant air.

Warning Like almost all the nightshade family, the ornamental pepper is poisonous. The fruits are especially tempting to children, so keep these plants out of their reach.

Catharanthus roseus
Periwinkle

The periwinkle grows bushier year by year.

The periwinkle is the exotic cousin of our blue-violet myrtle (*Vinca minor*) and used to be called *Vinca rosea*. A tropical subject that is really a shrub, it is offered as an annual pot plant but also can be planted in a decorative bed in a conservatory. Its dark-green leaves, 2.5 to 7cm (1 to 3in) long, are distinguished by a white central rib. The flowers, about 3cm (1½in) in size, are pink or white with red or yellow centres. The periwinkle has been in cultivation since 1757 and still enjoys great popularity.

Flowering season Late spring to mid autumn.
Family Apocynaceae, dogbane family.
Origin Tropics.
Location Bright but no full sun and warm; somewhat cooler in winter (around 15°C/59°F).
Watering, feeding In summer water well, but *avoid sogginess*; in winter reduce watering. From early spring to late summer fertilize every 14 days.

Further culture
Although usually grown as an annual, these are plants that can be potted on in spring in a good houseplant medium to become permanent members of a collection.
Propagating From cuttings in early spring or seeds in late winter in a heated propagator. Always put three young plants to a pot and pinch them once so that they will branch.
Pests, diseases Rare.
Professional tip If you overwinter plants, you must take care that despite the cool winter location they do not get cold roots.
Warning All parts of the periwinkle are poisonous.

Chrysanthemum indicum hybrids
Pot chrysanthemum

Chrysanthemums love a cool location.

This shrub is now available all year round as a result of light manipulation by the commercial growers. Colours range from snow white through lemon yellow, golden yellow, bronze, pink, wine red and on to purple and light violet. There are varieties with double and single flowers, bushes, subshrubs and standards.

Flowering season
Originally mid summer to mid winter; today, through horticultural manipulation, all year round.
Family Compositae, composite family.
Origin China and Japan. However, only cultivated forms are available commercially.
Location Bright and cool. Chrysanthemums will not last long in a warm room. Place overwintered plants and new young plants out of doors in late spring.
Watering, feeding Always keep root ball slightly damp. With too little water the plant will wilt immediately. Fertilize new plants and overwintered or young plants weekly during the growth period (spring to autumn).

Further culture After blooming, cut back and overwinter relatively dry at 3 to 5°C (37 to 41°F). In early spring pot on as necessary in good houseplant potting medium. Keep trimming new growth. As an alternative to overwintering: site cut-back chrysanthemums in a bright, protected spot in the garden and cover with a mulch of straw and compost before first frost to become permanent garden plants. But be warned: even with winter protection the plant is not reliably frost hardy.
Propagating In spring from cuttings.
Pests, diseases Aphids and spider mites in too warm a location.

Pot chrysanthemum as a standard.

FLOWERING PLANTS

Citrus
Miniature orange, dwarf orange

Calamondin orange (left) and a kumquat

Decorative, edible fruit, white, marvellously fragrant flowers, shiny, leathery, evergreen leaves – these characteristics have made the citrus family popular house- and tub plants for sunny patios. Of course, for culture on a windowsill or a constricted area, only the miniature members of the family, which can attain heights of 1m (39in) or at most 2m (78in), can be considered. There are numerous compact citrus plants available, the most popular of these being the calamondin orange (*Citrus mitis*).

Flowering season
Flowers and fruits appear over the course of a year, often at the same time. The fruits last for weeks or months.

Family Rutaceae, rue family.

Origin South-east Asia.

Location Very bright to sunny all year round. In summer warm and protected – best placed outdoors; in winter 15 to 18°C (59 to 64°F).

Watering, feeding
From spring to autumn water well. *Never use hard water.* In winter water sparingly. From early spring to late summer use weak fertilizer every week.

Further culture Mist often. When plant completely potbound, pot on in good houseplant potting medium. Cut back as little as possible.

Propagating By means of cuttings in a heated propagator. Difficult.

Pests, diseases Scale, mealy bugs, spider mites. Yellow leaves (chlorosis) caused by water that is too hard.

Professional tip For plants that do not go outside and therefore cannot be fertilized by insects, the pollen must be conveyed to the stigma by brush. Midday is the best time for effective pollination.

Clerodendrum
Glory-bower

The glory-bower is a vigorous climber.

Of the approximately 400 *Clerodendrum* species, only a few are under culture. The best known is *Clerodendrum thomsonae* and is called 'bleeding glory-bower' or 'bleeding-heart vine', after the snow-white calyx leaves from which its intensely red corolla peeps out. This is a vigorous climbing shrub, which in its African habitat climbs as high as 4m (13ft) by means of its twining stem. From early spring on the flowers appear in dense cymes and provide a breathtaking sight in gardens there. Houseplant forms are usually stunted with growth inhibitors and sold as shrubs.

Flowering season Early spring to early autumn.

Family Verbenaceae, verbena family.

Origin Cameroon, West Africa.

Location Very bright but *no direct sun.* Warm and humid all year round.

Watering, feeding Use only softened, room-temperature water and keep plants slightly moist. Fertilize weekly from early spring to late summer.

Further culture Provide for high humidity by misting often. Pot on in spring as necessary using good houseplant potting mixture.

Propagating From cuttings in late spring. Works only in a heated propagator.

Pests, diseases Flower and bud drop when air is too dry. Leaf spots with cold roots.

Professional tip Because the glory-bower does not tolerate heated air, it can be kept during the winter months at a cool temperature, around 12°C (54°F), and let it go through a resting period, when it loses its leaves. In spring it is cut back, potted on if necessary and placed in a warmer spot.

Clivia
Kaffir lily

The kaffir lily grows more beautiful each year.

The kaffir lily grows in damp, shady places between rocks or in the forest. It develops sword-shaped leaves from a bulbous stem and in spring a long flower stalk.
Flowering season Late winter to late spring; with appropriate cool treatment, also at Christmas.
Family Amaryllidaceae, amaryllis family.
Origin Natal province, South Africa.
Location From mid autumn to the very end of winter bright, cool (not over 12°C/54°F) and not sunny. As soon as the flower stalk appears, half-shady and warm (18 to 20°C/64 to 68°F). The plant can spend the summer out of doors.
Watering, feeding Water well in summer, but *avoid sogginess*. From mid autumn to the very end of winter maintain the resting period very strictly, keeping plants almost dry at 8 to 10°C (46 to 50°F). From early spring to mid summer fertilize every 14 days.
Further culture When new leaves grow and the flower spike develops, mist. Dust the leaves occasionally with a damp wad of cotton. Pot on young plants as necessary in good houseplant potting medium; better to leave older ones alone. Cut off dead flowers.
Propagating In spring or summer from offsets. Separate carefully. It takes from three to six years for first flowering.
Pests, diseases Scale in too warm a winter site.
Professional tip If your kaffir lily does not bloom, it may be because the resting period has been inadequate, because the amount of water has been increased too soon in the spring (the flower spike should be at least 15cm/6in high) or because of insufficient water during the main growth phase.
Warning The kaffir lily contains poisonous alkaloids.

Columnea
Goldfish plant

Few can resist the goldfish plant's cascade of fiery-red flowers; it is probably one of the showiest of all hanging plants. There are countless species and varieties under culture, such as *Columnea hirta*, *Columnea × banksii*, *Columnea gloriosa*, with the variety 'Purpurea', *Columnea microphylla*, of which there are also varieties with coloured leaves, and species hybrids like 'Stavanger'.
Flowering season The red-orange to scarlet-red, tube-shaped flowers appear at various times of year depending on the species and variety. The production of flowers is induced by a 30- to 40-day cooling period in winter at about 15°C (59°F).
Family Gesneriaceae, gesneriad family.
Origin Central America, mostly Costa Rica.
Location Bright to semi-shady. Warm all year round except during the flower-setting phase.
Watering, feeding During the growing period keep it slightly moist and fertilize weekly with a weak solution. *Avoid hard water and alkaline fertilizers.* During the winter water only enough to prevent the plant from drying out. As soon as buds are 0.5cm (¼in) long, give more water and put the plant in a warmer spot.
Further culture Mist carefully, *but not in sun and not on the flowers*. Increase water as air temperature increases. After blooming, cut back and pot on in shallow container as necessary using good houseplant potting medium.

Species hybrid 'Stavanger' is a lovely hanging plant.

Propagating From top or stem cuttings at a bed temperature of 25°C (77°F).
Pests, diseases Leaf drop from daughts. In dry centrally heated air, the stems lose their leaves.

Crassula coccinea
Rochea

Rochea flowers boast fragrance and stunning colour.

This was formerly classified under the botanical name *Rochea coccinea*, but today it is included in the genus *Crassula* (see page 155), which consists of some 300 species of succulents. The fiery-red rochea is a subshrub (although this is not at first apparent because the lower parts become woody) only as the plant matures. It grows 30 to 60cm (12 to 23in) tall and bears fragrant, brilliantly red flowers. The sturdy green branches are thickly furnished with opposite leaves, some 2cm (¾in) long.

Flowering season Late spring and early summer.
Family Crassulaceae, orpine family.
Origin South Africa.
Location Very bright to sunny, and airy. *No direct sun.* Can spend the summer out of doors in a place protected from rain. In early autumn bring in and place in a bright, cool spot (around 10°C/

50°F) until flower buds appear.
Watering, feeding In summer keep lightly damp, in winter almost dry. Apply cactus fertilizer every 14 days in summer.
Further culture After blooming cut the branches back about 10cm (4in). This allows space for new growth and new flowering shoots.
Propagating From top cuttings in early summer in sandy soil. Let cut surfaces dry for a few days before planting.
Pests, diseases Aphids, mealy bugs, mites and leaf eelworms. Straggly growth in too warm and dark a winter location. When humidity is too high, mildew is possible.

Crossandra infundibuliformis
Firecracker flower

The world-famous hybrid 'Mona Wallhed'

Of the some 50 species of the genus, only *Crossandra infundibuliformis* is available commercially. It arrived in Europe from India as early as 1817, was then ignored and became current again only in the 1950s, when a Swedish gardener had bred out its 'tropical demands'. His variety, 'Mona Wallhed', is still under cultivation today. It is clearly smaller and more compact than the original form, which in its native habitat can grow as tall as 1m (39in). The trumpet-shaped yellow, salmon or orange flowers appear in spikes on long stems, which occur at the leaf axils.
Flowering season Late spring to early autumn.
Family Acanthaceae, acanthus family.
Origin India, Sri Lanka.
Location Bright (especially in winter) to semi-shady, *no sun*. Warm all year round, in winter not below 18°C (64°F).

Watering, feeding During the growth and flowering periods water freely with soft, room-temperature water; from mid autumn to late winter more sparingly. From early spring to late summer use flower fertilizer in the water every 14 days.
Further culture Provide for high humidity, misting often, *but do not wet the leaves while doing so.* Pot on as necessary in spring in good houseplant potting mixture with added polystyrene granules. Caution: cold, wet roots are lethal. Make sure the medium is warm.
Propagating In late winter, from top cuttings, which root well in a heated propagator. Pinch back young plants frequently so they will bush nicely.
Pests, diseases Aphids, spider mites, leaf drop and curling leaves from dry centrally heated air or cold, wet roots.

Cyclamen persicum
Cyclamen, alpine violet

A specimen in the classic cyclamen colour.

Such variations are described as 'white with an eye'.

Fresh, cool air and slight dampness are the culture secrets of the cyclamen, as we know it today. It originates in mountainous forest regions, where it grows in light shadow in alkaline soil, in scree or in leafmould, so it feels happier in a cool bedroom than in a heated living room. However, where the soil is concerned, you should certainly not imitate the native conditions. The Mediterranean locations of the original form are not only quite dry in summer but also offer the corm only a compacted, alkaline soil.

The cyclamen is high on the hit parade of favourite flowering plants. Annually over 20 million plants are under cultivation. There are varieties with large or small, fringed or bordered, white, red, pink or violet flowers and with green or marbled foliage – besides the so-called fragrant cyclamen and the mini-cyclamen, the latter growing ever more popular. The breeders extol the miniature's willingness to bloom and the length of its flowering season. The important thing is never to allow its small pot to dry out, except when it is dormant. It is unfortunate that cyclamens are usually regarded as throw-away plants because they flower so regularly when cultivated over several years.

Flowering season Early autumn to mid spring.
Family Primulaceae, primrose family.
Origin Eastern Mediterranean.
Location Bright but not sunny. Airy all year round, but not too warm. Place otudoors in summer in a semi-shady spot; in winter the optimum temperature is around 15°C (59°F).
Watering, feeding Keep plants moist except in the summer dormant period. But take care: cyclamen are extraordinarily sensitive to wetness. Water the soil but *never the top of the corm*, where the leaf and flower stalks are clustered. Feed weekly before and during blooming.
Further culture Pot on in late summer (after the rest period has ended) in good houseplant potting mixture, removing most of the old soil so that the same container can be used. Up to a third of the corm must protrude from the soil. Only young seedlings may be deeper.
Propagating Possible at any season from seeds in heated propagator at 18 to 20°C (64 to 68°F). Cover seeds with soil (dark germinator). Young plants need a great deal of light so that they will bush nicely and not develop straggly growth. Therefore, it is better to sow in late winter so that the seedlings can grow in the months when there is plenty of light.
Pests, diseases Browning of roots and rotting corms caused by sogginess; aphids, spider mites and mites, especially when too warm. Grey mould with too much humidity.
Professional tip Pull out old leaves and flowers with a jerk, rather than cut them off, for the residue rots easily and botrytis may develop.

Miniature cyclamen tolerate room temperatures much better than large-flowered varieties and have the special charm of wild flowers.

Dipladenia
Dipladenia

White with orange throat: Dipladenia boliviensis

Dipladenia enchants with its purple-red, dark pink or white flowers, which appear all summer long on the thin branches. Various hybrids of *Dipladenia sanderi* and *Dipladenia splendens* are found under cultivation, for example the lushly blooming 'Rosea' (salmon pink) and 'Rubiniana' (strong rose red), which does not flower so profusely. Entirely new is *Dipladenia boliviensis*, whose white flowers have an orange throat. The dipladenia needs a sturdy frame to climb on.

Flowering season Late spring to mid autumn.

Family Apocynaceae, dogbane family.

Origin Tropical America.

Location Very bright but not sunny all year round. Very warm and humid, especially during new growth. In winter 15°C (59°F) is enough.

Watering, feeding *In principle, never use cold or hard tap water.* From early spring to late summer water regularly and feed every 8 to 14 days. Reduce amount of water after blooming. Rest period from early/mid autumn to early spring.

Further culture Mist often or provide indirect humidity (see page 43). Well-rooted young plants can be potted on in spring, adding polystyrene granules to a good houseplant potting mixture; for older plants use a sturdier, standard potting medium without the additional drainage.

Propagating In spring from stem cuttings in a heated propagator.

Pests, diseases Curled leaves from air that is too dry, leaf and root damage from sogginess, scale, mealy bugs, spider mites.

Warning All parts of the dipladenia are very poisonous.

Dipteracanthus
Ruellia

Ruellia have attractive foliage.

Of the 250 known species the only ones currently in pot-plant collections are *Dipteracanthus devosianus* (syn. *Ruellia devosiana*) with white-and-violet-striped flowers, *Dipteracanthus makoyanus* (syn. *Ruellia makoyana*) with dark pink flowers and *Dipteracanthus portellae* (syn. *Ruellia portellae*) with pink flowers. They all have velvety, unusual leaves with paler veins and are low, almost creeping subshrubs. Therefore they are particularly good as ground cover for climate-controlled plant windows and terrariums as well as for hanging plants.

Flowering season Early autumn to early winter.

Family Acanthaceae, acanthus family.

Origin Brazil.

Location Bright to semi-shaded, no sun. All year round very warm and humid. *Avoid dry centrally heated air and cold roots.*

Watering, feeding Use softened, room-temperature water. Always keep moderately damp and from early spring to late summer use a weak solution of fertilizer every two weeks.

Further culture Provide high humidity and warm base for pot by insulating from cold stone windowsills with a heated mat or polystyrene pad in winter. As necessary, pot on in a shallow container with good houseplant potting mixture and added polystyrene granules.

Propagating In spring, from top cuttings in heated propagator with a bed temperature of more than 22°C (72°F). After rooting has occurred, pinch back once or twice so the plant will branch better.

Pests, diseases Curled leaves in too-dry air; growth disturbances and root rot from soil too cold and wet; whitefly.

Echeveria
Hen-and-chickens

Echeveria derenbergii *comes from Mexico.*

Another stemless species: Echeveria pumila

The species that remain small are decorative, easy-to-care-for collector's plants with minimal space requirements. This extraordinarily varied genus comprises about 100 species, which come from the regions between Texas and the northern territories of South America. They almost all have in common the fleshy leaves arranged spirally in a rosette. Some grow stemless as heads, others form short-stemmed, branching subshrubs or bushes. The orange-yellow or orange-red inflorescences are always carried on slender stems. There are countless varieties and hybrids on the market, with green and brownish-red, often hairy or frosted leaves. The best-known are:

● *Echeveria agavoides*, with rust-red margined leaves, the variety 'Red Edge' being especially beautiful.

● *Echeveria carnicolor*, the flesh-coloured echeveria. Grows less densely and puts out runners, so that it makes a successful hanging plant.

● *Echeveria derenbergii*, with glossy green leaves and orange flowers.

● *Echeveria gibbiflora*, with purplish rosettes on stems 30 to 50cm (11½ to 20in) high. It blooms with bright-red, white-frosted flowers, which appear in autumn in lofty cymes.

● *Echeveria harmsii*, a subshrubby, decorative species, whose leaves are clustered in a tight rosette. The rust-red flowers appear in summer.

● *Echeveria nodulosa*, with interestingly marked leaves bearing a violet stripe pattern. It is only 20cm (8in) high, and blooms from early spring on with little red-brown flowers that have yellow tips.

● *Echeveria pulvinata*, with leaves that look as though they have been powdered. The white hairy covering indicates that they are used to a great deal of light. The variety 'Ruby' is distinguished by red-tinged leaf margins, which disappear when the location is too dark.

● *Echeveria setosa*, the brushy echeveria, forms flat, stemless rosettes and blooms in the spring.

Echeverias look most beautiful when planted in groupings of different subgenera and varieties.

Flowering season
Depending on species, in winter, spring or summer. Flower development is dependent on the length of the day and the temperature, which varies widely according to the particular species.

Family Crassulaceae, orpine family.

Origin South-western USA, Central and South America.

Location Full sun all year round, warm in summer, best outdoors in full sun. During rest period in winter, cool 5 to 10°C (41 to 50°F).

Watering, feeding
Little in summer; during the winter rest period *give all non-flowering echeverias almost no water at all.* Dampness kills them. From early spring to late summer during the growth period, give them cactus fertilizer weekly.

Further culture Pot on young plants yearly in cactus medium or good houseplant potting mixture; older plants only as necessary.

Propagating After blooming, by removal of side rosettes or by leaf cuttings. Allow the cuttings to dry for a short time after planting, place in sandy soil and root at a bed temperature of 20°C (68°F).

Pests, diseases Root rot and mildew from too much water. Mealy bugs and root mealy buds, usually produced by too warm a winter location.

FLOWERING PLANTS

Euphorbia millii
Crown-of-thorns

Euphorbia millii *can be trained over a hoop.*

Euphorbia millii *hybrid 'Marathon'*

The crown-of-thorns is one of the most popular representatives of the extensive genus *Euphorbia*, which comprises over 2000 known species. External appearances within the genus vary enormously, ranging from cactus-like succulents to herbs and bushes to trees. Common to all euphorbias are the rubbery, poisonous, caustic milky sap and the unisexual or bisexual simulated flowers that botanists term *cyathia*.

The crown-of-thorns, which is an extremely undemanding, persistently flowering houseplant, is unharmed by dry centrally heated air or blazing sun. In its own habitat, in central and southern Madagascar, it grows on granite and gneiss outcrops and there forms 1m- (39in-) high deciduous bushes. It develops long, thorny branches, about the thickness of a pencil, which can be trained over a hoop or espaliered. Newer varieties grow rather upright and compact and can reach a metre (3 feet) in height, making successful wall plants for the conservatory. Rosy red is the colour most commonly available, but other colours are occasionally offered. Also from Madagascar is the white- or pink-flowered *Euphorbia lophogona*, an evergreen, ever-blooming species that grows in forest undergrowth.

Crosses of the two species produce particularly vigorous, decorative plants which bloom well and have almost replaced the pure species. These so-called *Euphorbia-Lomi* hybrids (the name contains the first two letters of both the parent species) flower almost all year round in yellow, pink, red and violet, do not lose their leaves and have a slightly greater need for dampness in the potting medium. They are somewhat susceptible to mildew, however.

Flowering season Mid autumn to early spring.
Family Euphorgiaceae, spurge family.
Origin Madagascar.
Location Very bright to full sun and warm all year round. Can be set outside in summer in a flower bed in a fully sunny, wind-protected place.
Watering, feeding Water moderately, especially in winter. After it has been flowering for one month, give only enough water to prevent the root ball drying out. From early spring to late summer water somewhat more and use cactus fertilizer in the water every two weeks.
Further culture Pot on young plants every two years in cactus soil. The plant can be cut back or trimmed before the new shoots form in early summer.
Propagating From cuttings in spring. Use the cuttings left from pruning or pieces of older branches. Dip the cut surfaces in lukewarm water so that the milky juice will stop flowing, leave to dry for one day and then place in a peat–sand mixture.
Pests, diseases Leaf drop from too cool a location, too much water, or both. Mealy bug among twining branches.
Warning All parts of the crown-of-thorns are poisonous. The milky juice contains skin and mucous-membrane irritants. You can also be injured by the sharp thorns.

Above *Cream-coloured hybrid*
Right Euphorbia keysii

Euphorbia pulcherrima
Poinsettia, Christmas star

Not all poinsettias are red, as this display of cultivars demonstrates.

In its Mexican habitat the poinsettia grows as vigorously as the elder does in temperate regions. It can reach a height of more than 3m (10ft) and during its 'flowering season' in early winter it is the ornament of any tropical garden. However, as a houseplant this magnificently coloured member of the spurge family is known as a throw-away subject produced in quantity for sales at Christmas time. But continued culture does pay. Weedy-looking at first, the poinsettia later becomes woody, then develops into a pretty branching bush.

Like its cousin the crown-of-thorns (see page 108), its true flowers are insignificant. It is the bracts that make a show in creamy white, yellow, pink or brilliant red. There are single-stemmed or bushy pot plants and decorative standard forms on the market. 'Gropom' is a French hybrid with apricot bracts. 'Regina' has creamy-white 'stars' and looks very attractive when trained to standard form. 'Dorothea' grows bushy and bears pink bracts.

Flowering season Late autumn to mid winter, but with light control (short-day treatment) all year is possible.

Family Euphorbiaceae, spurge family.

Origin Mexico and Central America.

Location Bright and warm all year round. While blooming somewhat cooler so the flowers will last longer. Summering outdoors is possible in a protected situation.

Watering, feeding Water freely before blooming from late spring to late autumn. After blooming from late winter to late spring rather sparingly. From early summer to mid autumn fertilize weekly.

Further culture Cut back when plants have lost their attraction, trimming side branches back to some 10cm (4in) from the main stem. After cutting, keep warm at 18 to 20°C (64 to 68°F) and almost dry. Pot on in fresh potting mixture when new growth is evident. Water regularly again; fertilize only when plants become established. Pinch out growing tips to encourage bushy habit.

Propagating From top cuttings of new growth in summer after potting on. Stop flow of milky juice by dipping the cut places in lukewarm water. Plant cuttings firmly in small peat pots; you need a mist propagation unit to succeed.

Pests, diseases Whitefly when air is too dry; mealy bugs and scale on very old plants.

Professional tip To promote flower development and colouring of the bracts, the poinsettia must receive only 10 to 12 hours of light a day, depending on the species, from early autumn for about two months. This includes lamplight and streetlights so an unlit room at night is indicated.

Warning The milky juice can irritate eyes, skin and mucous membranes.

FLOWERING PLANTS

Eustoma grandiflorum
Prairie gentian

Prairie gentians are grown as annuals.

Until recently the prairie gentian (syn. *Lisianthus russelianus*) was available only as a cut flower. Today this biennial plant which in summer produces fragrant flower bells in cream, pink and violet, is also recognized as an attractive, easy-to-care-for houseplant. With the aid of growth inhibitors, the optimum cut-flower height of 90cm (35in) has been checked. The pot plants are low and look very pretty in shallow containers. The prairie gentian has bluish-green oval to oblong leaves; it is not kept under cultivation after it flowers.

Flowering season Mid and late summer.
Family Gentianaceae, gentian family.
Origin Colorado, Nebraska, Texas, northern Mexico.
Location Very bright, but not sunny, and warm.
Watering, feeding Keep moderately damp and feed weekly.

Further culture Potting on not necessary because of biennial culture.
Propagating From seed. Difficult for non-professionals, but intriguing. Sow the very fine seeds in early/mid summer in heated propagator. Barely cover with fine soil. Keep seedlings in bright conditions and at 15 to 18°C (59 to 64°F). Overwinter at 10°C (50°F). Once established, group three plants per 13cm- (5in-) pot. Important: the leaf rosettes must have formed before winter. Flowering begins 10 to 12 months after sowing.
Pests, diseases Not a problem.

Exacum affine
German violet, Persian violet

The German violet: plentiful and fragrant flowers

The German violet comes from the island of Socotra in the Gulf of Aden and is a biennial in its habitat. Indoors the branching herbaceous plant grows as an annual 15 to 20cm (6 to 8in) tall. It has small leaves and from summer to autumn produces a wealth of fragrant light purple or white flowers, from which project exquisite yellow anthers. It is usually discarded after it flowers. However, it you overwinter the plant at cool temperatures (at about 15°C/59°F), you can take cuttings in the spring.

Flowering season Mid summer to early autumn.
Family Gentianaceae, gentian family.
Origin Socotra, Gulf of Aden.
Location Very bright, but not full sun. Average room temperature. The plant loves fresh air – an ideal situation would be a rainproof hideaway under a balcony.

Watering, feeding Keep moderately damp all summer. If the root ball dries out, the flowers will immediately begin to deteriorate. Feed every 14 days in summer.
Further culture None.
Propagating From cuttings in spring or from seed sown in warm conditions in late winter. Do not cover seeds with earth: this is a light germinator. Prick out seedlings and pot them in good houseplant potting mixture.
Pests, diseases Not a problem.

Gardenia
Gardenia

Gardenia jasminoides and its double-flowered varieties grow more than 1m (39in) tall and bloom with creamy white, strongly fragrant flowers. The growth is shrubby and the leaves are evergreen and glossy.

Flowering season Mid summer to mid autumn.

Family Rubiaceae, madder family.

Origin Ryukyu Islands, Japan, China.

Location Very bright to sunny. Warm in summer, in winter from 15 to 18°C (59 to 64°F), but keep potting medium warm.

Watering, feeding *Never use hard, cold water.* Do not allow to dry out in summer. From early spring to late summer use a lime-free fertilizer every week. In winter water only moderately.

Further culture When the buds appear, provide high humidity (see page 43) and mist often. *Stop spraying when plants bloom.* In late winter pot on as necessary in good houseplant potting mixture.

Propagating In spring and late summer from cuttings in heated propagator.

Pests, diseases Bud and flower drop because of temperature fluctuations or too much warmth. Growth disturbances and yellowing of the leaves from cold roots and hard water.

Right
Gardenias unite fragrance and elegance, and they are equally splendid in small pots, containers or as standards.

Gloriosa rothschildiana

Glory lily, climbing lily

The glory lily is a sensational-looking vine with fiery-red and yellow flowers that can be as large as 10cm (4in) in size.

Flowering season
Early to late summer.

Family Liliaceae, lily family.

Origin Tropical Asia, Africa, Madagascar.

Location Very bright and warm for forcing and during the growing period.

Watering, feeding
Water regularly from early spring to late summer and fertilize weekly. Then gradually reduce watering and allow the plant to die back slowly.

Further culture
Overwinter tubers in the pot at about 15°C (59°F). In early spring place in pot with good houseplant potting mixture, begin watering and force at a bed temperature of 25 to 30°C (77 to 86°F). Introduce a stake or trellis for support. Mist often until buds form.

Propagating In spring from side tubers; however, each possesses only one vegetative cone.

Pests, diseases Aphids and spider mites. Failure to bloom caused by too little light and warmth in the spring.

Professional tip When buying, make sure that the walnut-shaped tubers each show a little green point (the bud).

Warning The tubers contain colchicin, which is a poison.

Left
The glory lily will bloom as sumptuously as this after a good rest period.

Haemanthus
Blood lily, African blood lily

Haemanthus multiflorus *blooms mid to late spring.*

White-flowering, thick-leaved *Haemanthus albiflos* (the shaving-brush plant) is a summer-flowering, robust houseplant. Its common name derives from the peculiar, brush-like inflorescence which is borne on a fleshy stem beside the leaves. In time the plant develops bulbous basal growth not unlike that of an onion. Red-blooming species are *Haemanthus katharinae* and *Haemanthus multiflorus.*

Flowering season
Haemanthus albiflos mid summer to mid autumn; *Haemanthus multiflorus* mid to late spring; *Haemanthus katharinae* mid summer.

Family Amaryllidaceae, amaryllis family.

Origin South Africa, tropical East Africa.

Location *Haemanthus albiflos* bright to full sun all year round. In summer warm, in winter cooler if possible 10 to 15°C (50 to 59°F). Red species very bright but not sunny, in winter not under 12°C (54°F). In summer, can be grown on a sunny balcony or patio.

Watering, feeding In summer keep *Haemanthus albiflos* moderately damp and in winter relatively dry, but only when at lower temperatures. Fertilize every four weeks and pot on as necessary. In summer water red species well and fertilize weekly. *But be careful not to overwater.* Decrease water from early autumn so that foliage can die back.

Further culture Remove dead leaves from the red species and overwinter the bulb at 12 to 14°C (54 to 57°F). Do not let the soil dry out completely.

Propagating *Haemanthus albiflos* through offsets; red species from bulbs.

Pests, diseases Troublefree.

Warning The bulbs of the entire amaryllis family contain poison.

Hibiscus rosa-sinensis
Rose of China, Chinese hibiscus

Hibiscus grows 3m (10ft) tall in its native habitat.

The trumpet-shaped flowers of this hibiscus can grow up to 15cm (6in) across and attract special attention with their prominent golden-yellow stamens. They can be double or single in yellow, orange, pink or red. The flowers of the pure species are rose red. Especially attractive is the variety 'Cooperi' with small leaves dappled with white, pink and carmine red and bearing deep pink flowers.

Flowering season
Early spring to mid autumn.

Family Malvaceae, mallow family.

Origin Tropical Asia, southern China.

Location Very bright to full sun and warm. Bud and flower drop often follow change of location and lack of light. Cooler winter temperatures, around 15°C (59°F), help promote the development of flowers. Can be sunk in a warm, sunny spot in the garden from early summer on. First carefully acclimatize it to the sun to avoid sunscorch.

Watering, feeding Water copiously and regularly until early autumn, less in winter. Bud and flower drop with dry root ball or cold, wet roots. At the beginning of new growth until the end of summer, feed weekly; in a warm, bright winter location feed once a month. Hibiscus must be nourished; otherwise it will not bloom.

Further culture In heated rooms mist often or provide for indirect humidity. Pot on young plants yearly, older plants as necessary in spring in good houseplant potting mixture. First cut back any over-long shoots.

Propagating From semi-mature top cuttings in late spring in warm conditions.

Pests, diseases Aphids, mealy bugs and spider mites in dry centrally heated air.

Hippeastrum hybrids
Amaryllis, Barbados lily

The variety 'Trixi' is very free-flowering.

'Apple Blossom' (left) and 'Fantastica' (right)

The fat bulbs of the amaryllis are on sale around Christmas time. Today there are countless varieties available, with colours ranging from snow-white through salmon, orange and pink to all possible shades of red. There are also white flowers with red margins, which look like piped ballet tutus, and hybrids with stripes of two and three colours.

The most famous hybrids are the so-called Ludwig amaryllises from Holland, for example the red-and-white-striped 'Fantastica', the deep-rose 'Dutch Belle', the fire-red 'Ludwig's Goliath' or the pink 'Fairyland'. Especially sought after are white varieties like 'Maria Goretti', 'Ludwig' Dazzler, 'Picotée' and 'Early White'. An evergreen among the amaryllises is 'Apple Blossom' in tones of pink and white, and it is sweet smelling. Mail-order houses that specialize in bulbs stock other beautiful and exciting varieties.

For those for whom the forcing of the bulb takes too long, the recent appearance of the so-called pre-pot-amaryllis is good news. These are prepared bulbs that come into bloom within five to six weeks.

Flowering season Mid winter to mid spring.
Family Amaryllidaceae, amaryllis family.
Origin Tropical and subtropical America. The only plants now offered commercially are cultivated forms.
Location Put newly bought or overwintered bulbs in a very bright, warm spot, after they have been planted in a roomy pot in good houseplant potting medium. (When planted, half the bulb must show above the soil.)

Watering, feeding At first water scarcely at all. When the growth begins to show, give more water. As a rule the flower stalk appears before the leaves, but it can also be the other way around. After blooming has finished, allow to die back and feed weekly until late summer. There must be plentiful leaf development so that the bulb can store strength for the following year. From late summer on slowly decrease water and allow foliage to die back.
Further culture When not in leaf, keep dry and warm until new growth becomes evident.
Propagating From side bulbs, which should be the size of a marble before they are removed from the mother plant. Other possibilities: by cuttings from the bulb scales or by seeds. Both take considerable effort.
Pests, diseases Leaf scorch, a fungal disease perculiar to amaryllis. It is promoted by a situation that is too cold and wet. If the fungus has not eaten too deeply into the tissue, the infected places can be cut out and dusted with charcoal, thus saving the bulb.
Professional tip The same care can be used for *Hippeastralia*, a cross between *Hippeastrum* and *Sprekelia* that produces daintier flowers and also does not grow as large.
Warning The amaryllis contains poisonous substances.

114

Hoya
Wax vine, porcelain flower

Hoya bella *blooms abundantly on a trellis . . .*

. . . on a hoop or as a hanging plant.

The genus is named after the Englishman Thomas Hoy, who from 1788 to 1809 was the head gardener to the Duke of Northumberland. Of the 200 recorded species, the best known are *Hoya bella*, from southern Burma, and *Hoya carnosa*, which is found from central China to Australia. *Hoya bella* grows without twining and remains altogether smaller and more delicate than *Hoya carnosa*, which is a vigorous climbing shrub with fleshy leaves. Both bloom in summer with sweet-smelling, porcelain-white cymes that are purplish red in the centre. *Hoya bella* grows best in an orchid basket or as a hanging plant in a climate-controlled warm, humid flower window. Also available is *Hoya carnosa* variety called 'Variegata' with yellow-and-green-striped leaves. It does not grow as vigorously as the pure species.

Rarely seen in the market is *Hoya lacunosa*, with elliptical-lanceolate leaves and button-shaped, greenish-white flowers, which develop in umbels from early spring to early summer. This uncommon hanging plant prefers semi-shade and likes warmth all year around. An even rarer member of the genus is *Hoya linearis*, from the Himalayas, which is also warmth-loving. Its pencil-thin shoots and the white inflorescences are pendulous. The flowers of *Hoya multiflora* are produced in yellow, upright clusters amid dark green foliage. Given good cultivation and regular potting on, it will develop into a fairly large plant that will need warm, shady, moist conditions to do well.

Flowering season Late spring to early autumn.
Family Asclepiadaceae, milkweed family.
Origin Southern Burma, Central China to Australia.
Location Very bright to full sun (no midday sun). Keep warm in summer (18 to 22°C/64 to 73°F), in winter a few degrees cooler (14 to 18°C/57 to 64°F). The warmer temperatures suffice for *Hoya bella*.
Watering, feeding In summer water moderately, in winter even less. During the growing season feed every two weeks. But beware: fertilizing too well will produce vigorous shoots and leaves at the expense of flowers. Plants that look too lush will be reluctant to flower, and it may be necessary to change from a high-nitrogen to a high-potassium fertilizer. I have seen owners who do little in the way of care and never move the plants produce the most vigorously blooming hoyas.
Further culture Both species tolerate dry indoor air. Nevertheless, mist regularly when new growth begins. In spring pot on as necessary in good houseplant potting mixture with added polystyrene granules and sand. Cut back shoots that are too long.
Propagating Through top or stem cuttings in a heated propagator.
Pests, diseases Mealy bugs. Aphids from hot, dry conditions. Leaf drop and dying back of stems from too much water and cold roots. Flower and bud drop from too dark a location or change of position.
Professional tip With *Hoya carnosa* leave the short peduncle or stalk after the flower has finished blooming. The new flower will form there.

FLOWERING PLANTS

Hydrangea macrophylla
Hydrangea

Hypocyrta glabra (syn. *Nematanthus glabra*)
Clog plant

Pot hydrangeas are ideal plants for cool locations.

Hypocyrta glabr*a begins to trail as it grows larger.*

The hydrangea's large, white, pink, red or blue panicles of umbels consist of vestigial sterile single flowers, surrounded by larger, more decorative coloured sepals. Recently the plant has enjoyed new popularity. A blue colour can be obtained from certain red and pink hydrangeas by watering the soil with aluminium sulphate or alum.

Flowering season Hydrangeas are sold in bloom from early to late spring, but the species' normal flowering season is in early and mid summer.

Family Saxifragaceae, saxifrage family.

Origin Japan.

Location Bright to semi-shade, no full sun. All year, not too warm, in summer best outside in the garden in a cool, shady place. In winter it is satisfied with 4 to 8°C (39 to 46°F). Since the hdyrangea loses its leaves, the overwintering spot can be dark. Beginning in late winter, return it to a warmer, brighter place.

Watering, feeding In spring, summer and autumn, water freely. (*Hydrangea* means 'swigger of water'.) In winter water only enough to keep the root ball from drying out. *Never use alkaline water.*
Throughout summer, use rhododendron fertilizer in the water every 14 days.

Further culture After flowering it can be cut back. Transplant in spring. White, pink and red varieties need moderately acid soil, blue varieties very acid (azalea) soil.

Propagating From top cuttings with two pairs of firm leaves.

Pests, diseases Spider mites, aphids from a location that is too warm and dry.

The German name for this plant means 'little kissing mouths', a reference to the orange flowers: the puffy corona petals look like a mouth pursed for a kiss. The clog plant is a low subshrub that produces leathery, almost succulent leaves, indicating it can manage better in dry air than most of its tropical relatives. You may well find other species in the better retail outlets but *Hypocyrta glabra* is by far the best choice, being a splendid hanging plant.

Flowering season The plants, which are very much in demand commercially, are offered in bloom from late summer till spring.

Family Gesneriaceae, gesneriad family.

Origin Brazil.

Location Very bright, but not full sun; can do well in poor light. In summer can also hang in a shady position out of doors, provided not too cold. Throughout winter maintain at 12 to 15°C (54 to 59°F) to promote bud formation.

Watering, feeding From spring to autumn keep only slightly damp, in winter keep almost dry. From early spring to late summer feed every two weeks with weak solution.

Further culture Pot on in spring as necessary, using good houseplant potting mixture. Trim to shape after flowering, which will promote the growth of new shoots and a bushier habit.

Propagating By firm, young top cuttings in bed temperatures around 20°C (68°F).

Pests, diseases Not a problem.

Impatiens
Busy Lizzie, balsam, jewelweed, snapweed

Impatiens-New Guinea *hybrids in shades of pink: grouped in containers, they look magnificent.*

Busy Lizzie (*Impatiens walleriana*), from tropical East Africa, is one of the most popular pot plants for houses, balconies and gardens and is available in countless shades from white to pink, orange, red and purple. There are also pale pink varieties with a white eye like 'Accent Bright Eyes' and white-and-red-striped ones like 'Starbright' as well as the smaller varieties which grow only 15cm (6in) tall and offer a wealth of colour choices.

More recently *Impatiens*–New Guinea hybrids have been established, and these have *Impatiens hawkeri* in their ancestry. Attractive varieties include the bronzy-green-leaved, fire-red-flowered 'Tango' and the variegated-leaved variety 'Exotica'. From Sri Lanka comes *Impatiens repens*, a yellow-flowered creeping species with reddish stems, which looks very attractive in a hanging pot.

Flowering season They all bloom in summer and autumn; *Impatiens walleriana* all year long.
Family Balsaminaceae, balsam family.
Origin Tropical East Africa, Sri Lanka, India, New Guinea. Most commercially available plants are cultivars.
Location Bright to semi-shade, New Guinea hybrids also sunny. Room temperature all year round. *Impatiens walleriana* even cooler in winter (12 to 15°C/54 to 59°F). In darker locations, all species and varieties can stand cooler temperatures.
Watering, feeding Water regularly in summer, in winter less or the stems will rot. From early spring to late summer/early autumn feed weekly, at best only half the standard strength.

Further culture Clip Busy Lizzie now and again: they tend to straggle. In spring pot on as necessary in good houseplant potting medium. However, it is better to take root cuttings and overwinter these because the plants quickly become unsightly.

Propagating Very easy with top cuttings. In spring *Impatiens walleriana* also from seed, which is obtainable everywhere.
Pests, diseases Aphids, spider mites.

Above Impatiens walleriana *'Weiss'*
Below Impatiens walleriana *'Lachspastell'*

Impatiens walleriana *'Rotstern'*

Impatiens walleriana *'Orange'*

FLOWERING PLANTS

Ixora coccinea
Ixora

Ixora hybrid in one of the newer salmon shades

The ixora is an evergreen, scarlet-red flowering bush, which is happiest in a humid flower window. It has leathery glossy leaves, 5 to 10cm (2 to 4in) long. In summer the flowers are produced in lush racemes of umbels on the branches. With good culture the plant can attain 1m (39in) in a pot. Hybrids in other colours are also now available, for instance in dark orange, salmon and tinged with bright orange.

Flowering season Late spring to early autumn.

Family Rubiaceae, madder family.

Origin India.

Location All year round bright to semi-shady, warm and humid. The roots must never become cold.

Watering, feeding The plant, like the coffee tree and the gardenia, which are related to it, *will not tolerate hard, cold water*. In summer keep evenly damp, in winter water more sparingly. From early spring to late summer feed with a weak solution every two weeks.

Further culture Mist the ixora often in the house. As necessary pot on in spring in good houseplant potting mixture.

Propagating In spring from top cuttings at bed temperatures of at least 25°C (77°F) and high humidity (does not always succeed). Pinch out growing tips so new plants will branch nicely.

Pests, diseases Curled leaves in a sunny location. Blanched leaves (chlorosis) from water that is too hard or too cold and cold roots. Flower or leaf drop from abrupt changes in temperature or location. Scale, particularly from warm air.

Jacobinia
King's crown

Jacobinia carnea: an extraordinary tropical beauty

Of the numerous *Jacobinia* species, the important houseplants are *Jacobinia carnea* and *Jacobinia pauciflora*. *Jacobinia carnea* produces dark rose-red flowers, which are clumped in dense longish-to-round heads. After several years of cultivation it can grow to over 1m (39in) tall. *Jacobinia pauciflora* is a beautifully bushy evergreen shrub which grows to 30 to 60cm (12 to 23in) tall and bears flowers that are red at base and orange at tip.

Flowering season *Jacobinia carnea* from early to late summer; *Jacobinia pauciflora* from early to late winter.

Family Acanthaceae, acanthus family.

Origin Brazil.

Location *Jacobinia carnea* all year round bright, no sun. Warm in summer, in winter not below 16°C (61°F). Loves high humidity and therefore is ideal in a climate-controlled flower window. *Jacobinia pauciflora* bright to sunny all year round, outside in summer, in winter cool at 15°C (59°F).

Watering, feeding Keep both varieties moderately damp, but never let the root ball dry out. In winter water less. Feed every 14 days from early spring to late summer.

Further culture Cut back plants by half in spring and pot on as necessary in good houseplant potting mixture.

Propagating From cuttings of young shoots taken in late spring in a heated propagator 20 to 22°C (68 to 72°F). Pinch back two or three times.

Pests, diseases Spider mites, aphids and curled leaf tips from dry air. Leaf drop from dried-out root ball.

Note The white-flowered *Whitfeldia*, which is a relative, is cultivated the same way as *Jacobinia carnea*.

Jasminum
Jasmine

Jasminum polyanthum *has a powerful scent.*

The best-known house and summer balcony plant in this genus is *Jasminum officinale*, especially the large-flowered variety 'Grandiflorum'. *Jasminum polyanthum* has pink buds and white flowers. All species develop long climbing shoots.
Flowering season *Jasminum officinale* and *Jasminum polyanthum* early summer to early autumn.
Family Oleaceae, oleander family.
Origin China, Iran to Kashmir, Sri Lanka.
Location *Jasminum officinale* and *Jasminum polyanthum* all year round very bright, airy and cool. On balcony, several hours of full sun. In winter below 10°C (50°F) if possible, otherwise no flower development.
Watering, feeding *Never use cold, hard water.* In summer water regularly, in winter keep only slightly damp. In summer feed every 14 days.
Further culture Pot on as needed in good houseplant potting mixture. If lower stems lose their leaves, the plant can be cut back, but it will form very few flowers the year after.
Propagating In spring and summer from semi-woody top or stem cuttings at bed temperature of 20°C (68°F). Pinch back young plants several times.
Pests, diseases Aphids can be troublesome. Leaf drop may be a problem with *Jasminum officinale* but in spring the plant will usually put out new growth.
Warning The strong scent of jasmine flowers can cause headaches and migraine.

Jatropha podagrica
Tartogo, bottle plant

A succulent with a bottle-shaped stem

Coming from regions with periods of drought, the tartogo always carries its own water supply so it is the ideal plant for people who often forget to water. The unusual-looking succulent, 30 to 60cm (12 to 23in) tall, is from Central America and has shield-shaped, three- to five-lobed leaves about 20cm (8in) across. The inflorescences are vermilion red and often develop before the long-stemmed leaves but can also appear simultaneously with them in early summer.
Flowering season Early spring to mid summer, with good culture almost all year round.
Family Euphorbiaceae, spurge family.
Origin Nicaragua, Guatemala, Costa Rica.
Location Full sun and warm the year round, in winter not below 16°C (61°F).
Watering, feeding Water little. After the leaves fall in the autumn, water very sparingly. As soon as new flowers and leaves develop in early spring, slowly begin giving more water. In summer apply cactus fertilizer once a month.
Further culture Pot on as needed using cactus potting mixture.
Propagating From seeds that have been freshly gathered. However, the flowers must have been articifially pollinated beforehand. Ideal germinating temperature is 20 to 25°C (68 to 77°F).
Pests, diseases Rare.
Warning Although the name *Jatropha* freely translates as 'medicine' (Greek: *iatros*=doctor, *trophe*=food), all parts of this spurge are poisonous.

The tartogo is deciduous, always dropping its leaves in the autumn. Water it even more sparingly than during its growing period.

FLOWERING PLANTS

Kalanchoe
Flaming Katie, Palm-Beach bells

These plants look best when arranged in groups.

Flaming Katie (*Kalanchoe blossfeldiana*) is near the very top of the popularity chart of flowering plants: millions of them are sold every year. Breeders are continually working on this easy-to-care-for plant and there is now a wide colour range, from yellow, orange, through pink and red to violet. These little plants with succulent leaves are available in bloom all year round since growers learned to fool them by limiting their light supply. The original form, which in its natural habitat in the Tsarantanana mountains of northern Madagascar grows as a subshrub to a height of 30cm (12in), produces its vermilion-red flowers in mid-winter.

Flaming Katie was first recorded by the Frenchman Perrier de la Bâthie. He took it back to Paris, where it bloomed for the first time in 1927. The tongue-twisting genus name *Kalanchoe* is said to be of Chinese origin. The species name recalls a German seed dealer, Blossfeld.

Of the more than 200 *Kalanchoe* species, the most familiar houseplant is still the one with flowers of rose-coloured bells (see photographs page 30 and below) descended from *Kalanchoe manginii*. Also familiar are the baby-bearing plants *Kalanchoe pinnata*, *Kalanchoe daigremontiana* and

Kalanchoe manginii:
a delight for the hanging basket

Kalanchoe tubiflora, which produce already-rooted plantlets on the leaves; these fall off and grow wherever there is a little soil.

Flowering season
Kalanchoe blossfeldiana late winter to late spring; *Kalanchoe manginii* late winter to early spring.
Family Crassulaceae, orpine family.
Origin Madagascar.
Location Bright and sunny, warm in summer, cooler in winter:

Kalanchoe blossfeldiana at least 15°C (59°F), the other species 10 to 14°C (50 to 57°F).
Watering, feeding In summer water only moderately, keep plants almost dry in winter. From early spring to late summer use cactus fertilizer every four weeks. Feed *Kalanchoe blossfeldiana* every 14 days with a flower fertilizer.
Further culture Pot on as necessary in good houseplant potting mixture. All kalanchoes are short-day plants. The flowers develop when the plants receive only eight to ten hours of light daily for four to six weeks.
Propagating In spring or summer by cuttings for *Kalanchoe blossfeldiana* or with baby plantlets from the other species.
Pests, diseases Aphids, mealy bugs, mildew from too much warmth and dampness.

Leptospermum scoparium
Tea tree, New Zealand tea tree, manuka

The relationship to myrtle is unmistakable.

The tea tree is a native of Australia and New Zealand. It is available either as a bushy pot plant or in charming standard forms. Of the some 50 known species, this one is the most important horticulturally. In its native habitat it grows both as a bush 30cm (12in) tall and as a 10m- (33ft-) high tree, and it begins blooming when still a young plant. The varieties offered today come with red, rose-coloured and carmine-red single or double flowers. The evergreen leaves are green or bronze-red and likewise variable in form, but mostly narrow with sharp points.

Flowering season Late spring and early summer.

Family Myrtaceae, myrtle family.

Origin Australia, New Zealand.

Location Very bright to full sun all year round. In summer warm, in winter cool (4 to 10°C/39 to 50°F).

Watering, feeding In summer water freely with soft water. When the root ball dries out, the needles drop. Like all the myrtle family it cannot tolerate lime. In winter water only enough to keep the root ball from drying out. From early spring to late summer feed every 14 days.

Further culture In spring pot on in good houseplant potting mixture as necessary. Cut back slightly after blooming, before overwintering or in early spring so that the plant retains its shape and will grow bushier.

Propagating From vegetative cuttings (use firm young shoots) in spring or from semi-woody cuttings in late summer. The cuttings will root in sand or in a sand/peat mixture in four to six weeks. Cover with a plastic bag (see page 59).

Pests, diseases Rare.

Lotus berthelotii
Parrot's beak, winged pea, coral-gem

The parrot's beak needs a moist potting medium.

Parrot's beak is a splendid hanging plant that is often available in the spring. It is a shrub and in the ground it develops woody, creeping or trailing branches with fine, silvery-haired leaves up to 2cm (¾in) long. The flowers occur in bunches on the stems, are a little more than 3cm (1¼in) long and are usually scarlet red (see page 31). The variety 'Gold Flush' has yellow flowers.

Flowering season Early and mid spring.

Family Leguminosae, legume family.

Origin Cape Verde and Canary Islands.

Location Bright to sunny all year round, in summer 20°C (68°F), in winter not warmer than 10°C (50°F). From early summer also in a protected spot outdoors with full sun or dappled sunlight. In autumn bring in before first night frost.

Watering, feeding Keep evenly damp but *never waterlogged*. In winter water less. Leaves will drop immediately if root ball dries out. Feed every 14 days from late winter to mid autumn. The plants need frequent feeding.

Further culture Pot on as necessary in good houseplant potting mixture after blooming.

Propagating From cuttings, which root easily in spring and early summer at bed temperatures of 20 to 25°C (68 to 77°F).

Pests, diseases Aphids.

121

Medinilla magnifica
Rose grape

The rose grape is not only the most beautiful of a genus consisting of some 400 species but one of the most splendid of all flowering plants. It grows in the tropical forests of its native Philippines as a shrub over 2m (79in) high with thick, squared branches and dark-green, leathery leaves up to 30cm (12in) long. Its rose-red, elegantly pendulous panicles of flowers are composed of numerous single flowers suspended below a canopy of bright pink bracts and can be up to 40cm (16in) long. Since the rose grape is very difficult to propagate, it is one of the most expensive houseplants available.

Flowering season Mid spring to mid summer.

Family Melastomataceae, melastoma family.

Origin Island of Luzon in the Philippines.

Location Bright but no sun and warm, over 20°C (68°F). Best in a humid flower window. In winter keep cooler for two months (16°C/61°F). This rest period promotes the development of flowers.

Watering, feeding Always keep moist. *Never use cold or hard water.* During the rest period water very little. As soon as buds show, increase water and raise temperature. From early spring to late summer feed weekly.

Further culture Mist in dry weather to increase humidity. As necessary

pot on in spring in good houseplant potting mixture with added polystyrene granules. Cut back straggly-looking plants to old wood.

Propagating By top cuttings at soil temperatures of 25 to 30°C (77 to 86°F). Difficult.

Pests, diseases Failure to thrive because air too dry or roots too cold.

Professional tip Do not move once it has set buds.

Note Two relatives of the rose grape are *Bertolonia* and *Sonerila*.

● Bertolonias are small, creeping herbs from South America, which are also useful as ground cover. For example × *Bertolonia houtteana* has very beautiful leaves. Olive-green and broadly oval, they bear purple-pink veins and spots. Bertolonias need year-long air temperatures of 20°C (68°F) and bed warmth, will not tolerate hard, cold water and do not like to be misted. The potting medium can be any good houseplant potting mixture with added polystyrene granules.

● *Sonerila* is its Asiatic counterpart. It is thought to be a parent of the × *Bertolonia houtteana. Sonerila magaritacea* 'Argentea' is sometimes offered as a houseplant, but is not generally available. This plant, which grows to some 30cm (12in) tall, is a very difficult indoor subject that will need the protection of a heated growing cabinet. The leaves are marked with silver-green on the upper side. The small flowers are pink and furnished with three sepals and three stamens.

Opposite
Medinilla magnifica:
*the pink 'petals' are
in fact bracts.*

Nertera granadensis
Bead plant, coral moss

The berries of the bead plant last for months.

The bead plant is only a few centimetres (inches) tall and spreads like a carpet of grass or moss. *Nerteros* is Greek and can be translated as 'low'. The most beautiful thing about this subject is its orange-red, pea-sized berries, which develop from rather insignificant, greenish star-shaped flowers. A perennial creeping plant, it can be cultivated very successfully for years.

Flowering season Spring. The berries last from late summer into the winter.

Family Rubiaceae, madder family.

Origin Mountain regions of Central to South America. New Zealand and Tasmania.

Location Bright but not sunny all year round, but keep as cool and fresh as possible. In winter not below 12°C (54°F). From early spring on somewhat warmer.

Watering, feeding All summer keep moist, from autumn to spring water less. From early spring to late summer fertilize every four weeks with a weak solution. Otherwise the foliage will grow too lush and obscure the decorative berries.

Further culture Mist occasionally, except during the flowering season. Pot on as necessary in good houseplant potting mixture.

Propagating By division after the fruits drop.

Pests, diseases Aphids if growth is too lush.

FLOWERING PLANTS

Passiflora
Passionflower

Passiflora caerulea *needs cool overwintering.*

Passiflora violacea *needs more warmth.*

There are over 400 passionflower species, but the robust blue passionflower (*Passiflora caerulea*) is the best known as a houseplant. In mild climates and with winter protection it can even be planted outdoors against a house wall. Needing more warmth are *Passiflora edulis*, *Passiflora racemosa*, *Passiflora violacea* and the giant granadilla, *Passiflora quadrangularis*.

Common to all is the exquisite flower. Jesuit missionaries in South America were the first to draw parallels between parts of the plant and the passion of Christ. It was the Jesuits who named the genus *Passiflora* (from Latin: *passio*=suffering, *flos*=flower). The hand-shaped leaves are said to represent the hands of His persecutors, the tendrils the lash, the ten petals the disciples (minus Judas and Peter or Thomas), the circle of purple-blue filaments the crown of thorns, the five anthers the wounds, the three stigmas the nails in the cross, and the central column the stake to which Christ was bound during the flagellation.

All *Passiflora* species are assiduous climbers that develop 4.5m (15ft) shoots and grow best on a trellis or frame. The plants trained on hoops that are frequently offered commercially are usually susceptible to attacks of spider mites and whitefly because the leaves are crowded too closely together, allowing only poor air circulation.

Flowering season *Passiflora caerulea* and *Passiflora edulis* early summer to end summer/ early autumn; *Passiflora quadrangularis* late spring to mid summer; *Passiflora racemosa* late spring to early autumn; *Passiflora violacea* late summer and early autumn.

Family Passifloraceae, passionflower family.

Origin Tropical America.

Location Bright to sunny all year round and airy. In summer warm, in winter cooler. *Passiflora caerulea* and *Passiflora edulis* around 10°C (50°F). This rest period promotes the development of flowers. *Passiflora racemosa* and *Passiflora quadrangularis* can be kept in a warm, humid flower window all year round. *Passiflora caerulea*, *Passiflora violacea* and *Passiflora edulis* may also spend the summer out of doors.

Watering, feeding Water well in summer, in winter only enough to prevent the root ball drying out. Feed weekly from early spring to late summer.

Further culture In spring, before potting on in good houseplant potting mixture, cut back to two or three shoots. Add compost to the potting mixture. Pot on older plants seldom, younger ones yearly.

Propagating From slightly woody top cuttings at a bed temperature of 22°C (72°F). In contrast to the mother plant, overwinter the rooted cuttings the first year in a warm, bright location. Passionflowers can also be propagated very easily from seed, for example from the fruit of *Passiflora edulis* (see pages 64–5) or *Passiflora mollissima*.

Pests, diseases Should be sprayed in spring and summer to control sucking and chewing insects such as aphids. Spider mites and thrips.

Tip Prune in spring to encourage compact new growth.

Pelargonium domesticum hybrids
Geranium, Regal pelargonium

Geraniums are in flower for much of the year.

The single flowers of *Pelargonium domesticum* hybrids are exotically spotted or striped and can be up to 5cm (2in) across. They appear in dense clusters in different colours from white, through pink and red down to a deep violet, often with a blotch of darker colour at the base of each petal. The spring-green leaves have toothed margins. Geraniums usually develop a single stalk, form woody stems and become about 40cm (16in) tall. Recently varieties with daintier flowers and leaves have come onto the market.
Flowering season From mid spring to early summer. The season is controlled by temperature and day length, however, so plants can be bought in flower all year round.
Family Geraniaceae, geranium family.
Origin South Africa. Only hybrid forms are commercially available.
Location All year round very bright to full sun and airy. From early summer on a protected balcony outside. In summer warm, in winter at 10 to 15°C (50 to 59°F).
Watering, feeding From early spring to late summer water well, but *absolutely avoid sogginess*. Feed weekly. Reduce water in autumn and water only seldom in winter.
Further culture In spring cut back shoots and pot on in good houseplant potting mixture with added sand. As soon as the new growth shows, put plants in a warmer place and water more.
Propagating From top cuttings, best in late summer, in a peat–sand mixture. Pot on as soon as the root ball gets larger and pinch back.
Pests, diseases Whitefly and aphids. Grey mould and fungal infections from too damp and dark a location and lack of fresh air.

Pentas lanceolata
Star-cluster, Egyptian star-cluster

Star-cluster is available in pink, salmon and red.

Of the many species that inhabit tropical and subtropical Africa and Madagascar, only *Pentas lanceolata* is under culture. It is a popular garden plant in tropical countries and has been raised in greenhouses in more temperate climates for more than a hundred years. The subshrub that is seen in houseplant culture is 30 to 60cm (12 to 23in) tall, has an upright to prone growth habit and blooms with terminal cymes in white, pink, mauve and carmine red. The small single flowers consist of 20 tubes about 3cm (1¼in) long. The leaves are oval to elliptical and hairy.
Flowering season Early autumn to mid winter.
Family Rubiaceae, madder family.
Origin Tropical Africa, Arabian peninsula.
Location Very bright but not sunny all year round. In summer warm and airy; suits a sunny balcony; in winter cool, around 12 to 15°C (54 to 59°F).
Watering, feeding Use only softened, room-temperature water. Water when dry to the touch. *Avoid sogginess*. After flowering keep drier until new growth shows. Feed with weak solution every 14 days.
Further culture In spring pot on as necessary in good houseplant potting mixture.
Propagating From top cuttings in a heated propagator. Keep pinching back young plants so they will branch nicely, pot on twice and then feed every 14 days after the second repotting.
Pests, diseases Yellow leaves caused by sogginess, cold roots and water that is too hard. Mildew in too much shade.
Professional tip Prune regularly when not in bud.

Wet or very dry roots mean death for the star-cluster. This warm-blooded beauty ornaments gardens on the slopes of Mount Kilimanjaro.

FLOWERING PLANTS

Primula
Primrose

Primula malacoides *(left)* and Primula obconica

Of the some 500 primrose species the following have importance as houseplants:

● *Primula malacoides*, the fairy or baby primrose. As an annual, it is thrown away when it finishes blooming.

● *Primula obconica*, the poison primrose. It grows to a height of 25cm (10in), bears dense clusters of white, pink, red or light violet flowers and can be further cultivated.

● *Primula vulgaris* (syn. *Primula acaulis*), the English primrose, is offered commercially in white, cream, yellow, orange, pink, red, purple, violet and blue.

Flowering season Winter and spring; but *Primula obconica* all year in cooler climates.

Family Primulaceae, primrose family.

Origin *Primula vulgaris* western and southern

Europe; the other species come from China. Only hybrid forms are commercially available.

Location Bright but not sunny. Cool, especially before flowering season (10 to 15°C/50 to 59°F). The plants will tolerate a heated room for only a very short time. Suitable for balconies in summer.

Watering, feeding Always keep slightly moist, *but avoid sogginess*. During the flowering season fertilize with a weak concentration every 14 days.

Further culture Plant *Primula vulgaris* in the garden after it finishes blooming. *Primula obconica* can be potted on after flowering.

Propagating From seed, usually in summer.

Pests, diseases Yellow leaves from too warm a site, too much fertilizer, dryness, sogginess or hard water.

Reinwardtia indica
Yellow flax, linum

The yellow flax flowers in winter.

The yellow flax is among the more recent pot plants to have conquered the market. As a winter-bloomer, it is a wonderful addition to the cool conservatory. The most attractive feature of this subshrub, which grows about 1m (39in) tall, are its brilliant golden-yellow flower trumpets, which appear in great numbers. Its genus name it owes to the Dutch botanist Caspar Georg Carl Reinwardt, who founded the Bogor Botanical Garden in Jakarta in the last century and wrote a book about vegetation of the Indonesian archipelago: the plant is a native of the mountains of northern Indonesia.

Flowering season Late autumn to early spring.

Family Linaceae, flax family.

Origin Northern Indonesia.

Location Very bright and airy, but not full sun. In summer outdoors as well, in a semi-shady •

spot. In winter under 10 to 12°C (50 to 54°F).

Watering, feeding In summer during the growing season keep moderately damp and feed every 14 days with a weak solution. In winter water when dry to the touch.

Further culture In summer trim the shoots often so that the subshrub develops a nice bushy growth and forms many shoots, on which flowers will appear during the winter.

Propagating From top cuttings in spring. Keep the roots cool. No bottom warmth is necessary.

Pests, diseases Aphids, snails.

English primroses: a beautiful spring greeting

Rhododendron simsii (syn. *Azalea indica*) hybrids
Florist's azalea, Indian azalea

Rhododendron simsii *with single flowers*

A double-flowered variety

One of our most important flowering houseplants, *Rhododendron simsii* is evergreen and available in many different colours, from white through pink to deep red. Double forms and bicoloured shades are also available.

Flowering season
From autumn through to early spring.

Family Ericaceae, heath family.

Origin Central China, Japan.

Location Fresh, cool, airy, bright to semi-shady, no sun. From late spring give it a semi-shady place outdoors. The dappled shade of an overhanging tree would be ideal. In autumn and winter keep *Rhododendron simsii* hybrids at 5 to 12°C (41 to 54°F) to ripen the buds. As soon as they begin to swell, place in a warmer situation (around 18°C/64°F).

Watering, feeding Use only soft water. Azaleas will not tolerate lime.

Immerse the plant pot in water until all the air bubbles have escaped. Plants may also be watered from the top using a watering can, but thorough watering is important. *Never allow the root ball to dry out, but avoid sogginess at all costs.* In summer water well – to maintain in good condition you may have to water thoroughly as often as twice a week. For bud formation in the autumn, keep plant somewhat drier. After blooming until late summer feed with a weak solution of ericaceous fertilizer every 14 days.

Further culture
Regularly remove dead flowers. Using an ericaceous potting mixture, plants can be potted on into slightly larger containers in early spring. Lightly trim over new growth in early and mid summer for a dense, compact shape. After potting on, it is important that they should have a

cool summer location out of doors where they can enjoy lightly shaded conditions.

Propagating By top cuttings at a bed temperature of 20 to 25°C (68 to 77°F). Difficult, done only by specialist nurseries.

Pests, diseases Galls on foliage, a rare condition remedied by gently removing the growth. In more temperate areas plants may be susceptible to many problems, such as petal blight and spider mite.

Professional tip These are plants that are sometimes used for bonsai culture, but they are generally grown in this fashion by those who are experienced in the cultivation of bonsai and not by the beginner, who would find both care and maintenance and the training of plants somewhat beyond their skills. Even when grown conventionally, these are

plants many beginners find difficult to manage The most common reasons for failure are that plants are not adequately watered, that they are inadequately fed, and that potting is neglected.

FLOWERING PLANTS

Rosa chinensis
China rose

Modern pot roses, including a miniature form

Roses are among the best-loved of all the flowering plants. So that rose-lovers who do not garden may also enjoy them, breeders have created numerous dwarf varieties that are charming miniature editions of the garden roses. Best known are the descendants of the Chinese rose (*Rosa chinensis*) like 'Minima' (red-flowered). They grow to be 25 to 40cm (10 to 16in) tall and, depending on the hybrid, are double or single and in a wide range of colours. Recognized varieties include *Rosa* 'Yellow Doll' and 'Baby Darling' (both yellow), 'Starina' (vermilion) and 'Cinderella' (pink). Like all roses, miniatures are summer-flowering, lose their leaves in autumn and like to be over-wintered in the cold.

Flowering season Summer and autumn.
Family Rosaceae, rose family.

Origin China. Only hybrid forms are commercially available.
Location Very bright to sunny and airy. Best kept out of doors in summer in a bright spot, out of full sun. Keep cool in winter.
Watering, feeding From spring to autumn keep evenly moist. In cold winter areas water only enough to keep the root ball from drying out. From early spring to mid summer feed with foliar fertilizer every 14 days. Then stop to allow the wood to ripen.
Further culture Overwinter in a cool but frost-free place. In late winter pot on in good potting mixture, cut back and keep in a brighter but still cool spot.
Propagating From seeds, cuttings, grafting.
Pests, diseases Aphids, spider mites, mildew and, in humid climates, black spot.

Saintpaulia ionantha
African violets

Saintpaulia ionantha hybrids: a ruffled variety

There are African violets in many variations with single or double, wavy or ruffled flowers in white and shades of pink, red, purple and blue, as well as two-coloured flowers and miniatures.

Flowering season Plants bloom several times throughout the year, following rest periods of several weeks.
Family Gesneriaceae, gesneriad family.
Origin Tanzania.
Location Bright to semi-shady. No sun. Room temperature all year round, in summer 20°C (68°F) or over, in winter not under 18°C (64°F). Cold roots are poorly tolerated.
Watering, feeding Always keep moist with room-temperature, soft water. *Never water from top.* Water that is too cold or too warm on leaves or flowers will produce ugly spots. Always pour off superfluous water. *Sogginess is lethal.* If central heating is used in winter, provide for indirect humidity (see page 43). In spring and summer use weak fertilizer weekly.
Further culture Always remove faded flowers. In spring pot on as necessary in houseplant potting mixture.
Propagating From leaf cuttings at a bed temperature of over 20°C (68°F).
Pests, diseases Aphids, mealy bugs and thrips. Grey mould from cold, wet roots. Crown rot from watering over top of plant.
Professional tip An assortment of African violets could be expected to have flowers all year.

Single-flowered miniature Saintpaulias

Schizanthus
Butterfly flower, poor man's orchid

Scutellaria
Skullcap

The butterfly flower is easily grown from seed.

The flowers of the butterfly flower appear in great profusion. They are white, pink, yellow, salmon, carmine red or violet and may be mottled or blazed, encouraging the comparison with the orchids. This plant is popular as a balcony, hanging and garden subject because it blooms vigorously until late summer in cooler areas, but it is also an excellent pot plant for the windowsill. After flowering, it is thrown away: as an annual it can easily be grown from seed for the following year.

Flowering season Spring to late summer.

Family Solanaceae, nightshade family.

Origin Chile. Only cultivars commercially available.

Location Plants in bloom in very bright, airy and warm conditions, part to full sun. Young plants sunny in winter, airy and cool (around 10°C/50°F).

Watering, feeding Always keep moist and feed weekly.

Further culture None, because it is an annual.

Propagating From seed (readily available) between late autumn and mid spring. Germinating temperature: 16 to 18°C (61 to 64°F). Plant several young plants to a 12-cm (5-in) pot in good houseplant potting mixture. Cultivate cool and bright.

Pests, diseases Rare. A location in full sun behind window glass can result in sunscorch.

Professional tip If you sow in autumn, you will have spring-flowering plants; if sowing in late spring, the young plants will not bloom until early autumn.

Skullcap is a light-hungry mountain beauty.

Like the alpine skullcap (*Scutellaria alpina*), the tropical skullcap (*Scutellaria costaricana*) is a mountain plant and accustomed to a great deal of light. The attractive, somewhat woody plant grows some 0.5m (20in) high and in summer produces striking terminal spikes of fiery red, short-lipped flowers. Commercial growers treat them with a growth inhibitor to ensure a compact appearance.

Flowering season Late spring to mid summer.

Family Labiatae, mint family.

Origin Costa Rica.

Location Very bright and airy all year round, but no sun. In summer around 20°C (68°F); in winter no cooler than 15°C (59°F). Important: *the bed temperature should never fall below the air temperature*.

Watering, feeding Keep moist. From early spring to late summer feed weekly with a weak solution.

Further culture Every two years in autumn pot on in good houseplant potting mixture after cutting back. Better results are obtained by producing new plants in autumn, which will then bloom the following year.

Propagating By top or stem cuttings in autumn (spring in Australia and New Zealand). They root quickly at bed temperatures of 20 to 25°C (68 to 77°F). Put several plants into one pot to produce a bushy effect. *Do not pinch back*. The inflorescences form only at the ends of shoots.

Pests, diseases Spider mites in too warm and dry a location, especially in summer.

Light wanted. When grown as houseplants, tropical mountain plants like the skullcap change their habit and grow tall in the search for light.

Senecio cruentus (syn. *Cineraria cruenta*) *hybrids*
Cineraria

Annual cinerarias in many bright colours: a cheerful 'throw-away' subject

With 2000 to 3000 species, the cinerarias are the largest and most varied genus of the composite family. The *Senecio cruentus* hybrids, which came originally from the cool, damp mountains of the Canary Islands, have, with their apparently inexhaustible range of colours, become especially popular as pot plants. They are on sale in the spring and are thrown away when they finish blooming because further culture does not pay.

Flowering season Mid winter to late spring.

Family Compositae, composite family.

Origin Canary Islands. Only hybrid forms are commercially available.

Location Bright, airy, cool (16 to 18°C/61 to 64°F). Do not place plants close together.

Watering, feeding Water well. If possible, provide for indirect humidity (see page 43). It is important that the roots should never dry out, and it will encourage beneficial humid conditions if the plant is placed on a bed of clay granules or gravel. This is a plant that develops an extensive root system, and it is advisable to feed young plants with a high-nitrogen fertilizer, switching to a high-potash fertilizer as they come into flower. Regular feeding will ensure that plants retain their bright green leaf colouring.

Further culture Potting on is not necessary since the plants are bought only for and because of their flowers.

Propagating From seed in autumn. Overwinter young plants in bright and cool (9 to 12°C/48 to 54°F) situation.

Pests, diseases Every type of pest. As a precaution, stick an insecticide pin in the soil.

Professional tip The cineraria is what may be termed a 'cheap and cheerful' temporary houseplant because it is quickly brought to maturity and is available in a wealth of different colours. However, when purchasing it is important to choose plants growing in pots with a diameter of at least 13cm (5in) because plants in smaller pots are difficult to maintain. Incidentally, in the cactus and succulent houses of many botanical gardens there are numerous *Senecio* species. Take a look sometime. It is surprising how varied this genus is and how little most of them resemble the cineraria, despite a close relationship.

Purple cineraria with white eye

Sinningia hybrids
Gloxinia

Single-flowered gloxinias: modern varieties with sturdier leaves

The *Sinningia* and its relatives are indigenous to tropical South and Central America. Some 50 different species are recorded there, which – with the exception of two rhizomatous species – all form tubers but have quite inconspicuous flowers. The ancestor of our modern *Sinningia* hybrids is *Sinningia speciosa*. It grows in southern Brazil on damp, rocky slopes, producing dainty, violet-blue flower bells. In 1815 the plant was taken to England.

The first large-flowered forms developed when *Sinningia regina* was used for hybridizing. This species, brought to Europe in 1903, was notable especially for its brown-red, velvety hairy leaves with striking white veins. The nodding flowers are lavender and have a pale-yellow, purple-spotted central stripe. From these two species and others such as *Sinningia guttata*, *Sinningia helleri* and *Sinningia villosa* came numerous hybrids.

Over the years the hybridists have greatly improved these flowering plants by developing varieties both with large flowers and a wider range of colours. Work has also been done on the development of plants with softer and more pliable leaves. The latter is important because the brittle leaves of these plants were very easily damaged by careless handling.

Flowering season Early spring to late summer.

Family Gesneriaceae, gesneriad family.

Origin Tropical South and Central America. However, only hybrid forms are commercially available.

Location Warm and humid, bright but not sunny.

Watering, feeding Keep slightly moist with soft, room-temperature water. Fertilize weekly while in active growth.

Further culture Do not mist; preferably provide for humidity (see page 43). *Do not wet the leaves.* Following flowering, the foliage will begin to die back, which is a signal to reduce, and eventually cease, watering. The tuber can be stored in dry, warm conditions until started into growth again the following season by potting in good houseplant potting mixture and forcing in a warm, bright, humid situation.

Propagating From seed. Expensive for the non-professional because artificial light is necessary from late autumn to late winter.

Pests, diseases Curling of leaves, aphids.

Note The red-flowered *Sinningia cardinalis* (syn. *Rechsteineria cardinalis*) is cultivated in exactly the same way. But forcing the tuber is easier.

Professional tip It is important when purchasing to ensure that foliage is in good condition and that plants are amply provided with flowers and flower buds.

FLOWERING PLANTS

Solanum
Nightshades

Solanum melongena, *the annual eggplant hybrid*

Solanum peudocapsicum, *the Jerusalem cherry*

Three popular species of the genus *Solanum* thrive splendidly as houseplants and therefore enjoy great popularity: the Jerusalem cherry (*Solanum pseudocapsicum*), the eggplant (*Solanum melongena*), an annual, and the false Jerusalem cherry (*Solanum capsicastrum*), which also exists in a variegated form. The greenish-white flowers look very like potato flowers. The yellow, orange or brilliant red berries of the Jerusalem cherry last, if the temperature is not too high, from autumn far into the winter. Many people throw the plants away when the fruits drop, which is a mistake because the evergreen, twiggy bushes can be cultivated further if you overwinter them correctly.

Flowering season Late spring to early summer; the fruits keep from October to March.

Family Solanaceae, nightshade family.

Origin Madeira, Brazil, Uruguay.

Location Bright to sunny and airy. In summer out of doors as well. Overwinter at 10 to 15°C (50 to 59°F), but can be grown on a balcony through winter in warm and temperate areas. In poor light berries will shed alarmingly.

Watering, feeding In spring and summer water freely, in autumn and winter only enough to keep the root ball from drying out. From early spring to late summer feed every 14 days.

Further culture Mist often in a warm winter location – otherwise danger of aphids. Pot on in spring if necessary after reducing the size of the root ball slightly and cutting the plant back. Use good houseplant potting mixture and a pot only a little larger than the former one.

Propagating From self-harvested seeds. Remove the flesh of the fruit, let

seeds dry and sow in spring. Trim young plants twice so that they will become bushy.

Pests, diseases Aphids, spider mites and whitefly in a location that is too warm.

Professional tip Some even more interesting *Solanum* species are sometimes available, for example:

● *Solanum aviculare*, the kangaroo apple, a bush from New Zealand and Australia that bears blue-violet flowers throughout the warm weather.

● *Solanum jasminoides*, the potato vine, a fast-growing climber for the cool conservatory. It blooms from late winter on until almost summer bearing whitish-blue flowers, and with good nourishment can produce shoots up to 1m (39in) long.

● *Solanum rantonnetii*, in English-speaking regions known as the 'blue potato bush'. It produces blue-

violet single flowers 3cm (1¼in) across from mid summer to mid autumn (in perfect locations almost all year round). The shrub, which originates in South America, grows vigorously and can be trained into many different forms.

● *Solanum wenlandii*, also called potato vine or giant potato creeper. This is a warmth-loving evergreen vine with hooked thorns and is considered the most beautiful climber in the family. The violet flowers, 6cm (3in) across, give pleasure from mid summer until late autumn. The leaves may be as long as 25cm (10in).

Warning All parts of the Jerusalem cherry and the *Solanum* species listed under the previous heading are poisonous.

Spathiphyllum
White sails, spathe flower

There are large and miniature forms of spathe flower.

Forty or more species of white sails are recorded growing naturally in tropical America. The most important variety in the range now offered as houseplants is *Spathiphyllum* 'Mauna Loa', which is one of our most reliable and attractive flowering subjects. White sails, incidentally one of the best plants for hydroculture, possesses evergreen, undivided, glossy leaves which sprout directly from soil level and form attractive tufts of soft greenery. The flower may appear at any time during the year and consists of a spiked cream-coloured spadix and a white or greeny-white spathe. *S. clevelandii*, or peace lily, is similar in appearance.

Flowering season Year round.

Family Araceae, arum family.

Origin Colombia, Venezuela.

Location Bright to semi-shady; astonishingly adaptable to light variations. Room temperature all year round 18 to 25°C (64 to 77°F), in winter not under 16°C (61°F).

Watering, feeding In spring and summer water generously with softened, room-temperature water and keep humidity high, reducing the amount in autumn and keep plants on the dry side over winter. From early spring to late summer feed every week.

Further culture On warm days mist or provide for indirect humidity (see page 43). In late spring pot on as necessary using good houseplant potting mixture.

Propagating By division when potting on.

Pests, diseases Not a problem.

Stephanotis floribunda
Stephanotis, Madagascar jasmine

Stephanotis *does not like to be moved.*

In its native habitat the stephanotis grows as an evergreen climbing shrub with long runners. But it is also a popular houseplant. The leaves are dark green and glossily leathery, and the flowers are snow-white, waxy stars. Given controlled artificial light, stephanotis can be induced to flower at any time, but it is best to obtain naturally grown, summer-flowering plants when purchasing.

Flowering season Early summer to early autumn. In winter with artificial light.

Family Asclepiadaceae, milkweed family.

Origin Madagascar.

Location Very bright and airy, but not sunny. In summer warm at 20 to 25°C (68 to 77°F), in winter cool at 12 to 14°C (54 to 57°F). Does not tolerate frost, wet and cold winter conditions, and hates change of position, especially after buds set, so make a light mark (see page 45).

Watering, feeding Water freely from early spring to late summer with room-temperature, soft water. *The root ball must never dry out*, but it is important to reduce the amount of water over the winter months. Plants should be fed while in active growth.

Further culture Mist often in summer. Pot on only as necessary in spring in good houseplant potting mixture.

Propagating From seed or stem cuttings but plants are slow to develop. Cut these from spring to summer and root in a heated propagator.

Pests, diseases Mealy bugs, spider mites, aphids and scale in hot and dry conditions. Yellow leaves from hard water or lack of light. Bud and flower drop from draughts or changes in available light and water.

The white star flowers of the stephanotis are among the most fragrant of all flowering plants.

133

FLOWERING PLANTS

Streptocarpus
Cape primrose

Streptocarpus *hybrid with a striped throat*

Streptocarpus
wendlandii *has only one
giant leaf, whose underside
is purplish red.*

In 1824 a botanist brought the first Cape primrose to Europe. Since then innumerable hybrids have been developed with elegant orchid-like flowers in white, pink, red, violet and blue, some of which have a striped throat or ruffled margins. Small-flowered species are also available, such as the blue to lavender-flowered *Streptocarpus saxorum* (see photograph page 30), which is very pretty as a hanging plant. There is also the splendid old variety 'Constant Nymph', which is available in both blue and white forms, an excellent plant for cool, light, airy locations.

Flowering season Late spring to early autumn.
Family Gesneriaceae, gesneriad family.
Origin South Africa, tropical Africa, Madagascar, Thailand and Burma.

Location Bright to semi-shady, but not sunny. Room temperature all year round. For the small-flowered hybrids the room temperature can go down to 15°C (59°F) in winter.
Watering, feeding Use room-temperature, soft water. Keep plants moist, in winter water somewhat less. From early spring to late summer feed every 14 days with a weak solution but *never fertilize a dry root ball.*
Further culture Provide humidity. In spring pot on as necessary in good houseplant potting mixture.
Propagating Among the easiest of plants to propagate from sections of leaves. Almost any piece will root in warm, shaded conditions at any time.
Pests, diseases Aphids, spider mites and thrips from air that is too dry. Brown leaf margins from too wet or too dry culture.

Tillandsia
Tillandsia

Tillandsia cyanea, *showing its 'cuttlefish' bract*

With over 400 species, *Tillandsia* is the largest and richest genus in the family of bromeliads. Mostly tillandsias live epiphytically on trees, rocks or other available supports. There are green and grey species. On the grey ones the narrow to grass-like leaves are thick with silver-grey absorption scales that can capture water vapour. Most tillandsias need relatively little space. Plants are sold attached to tree branches, or glued to stone, wood or shell ornaments. The latter is, on the whole, an unnatural method of culture that the keen plant lover may find unacceptable.

Flowering season Depending on species, late winter, spring or summer.
Family Bromeliaceae, bromeliad family.
Origin Tropical and subtropical America.
Location Grey tillandsias need light all year, in summer sunny and warm, best out of doors in the fresh air. In winter 10 to 15°C (50 to 59°F). Green tillandsias warm and bright all year round, but not sunny; ideal location is a warm, humid flower window, shady balcony, or atrium.
Watering, feeding In summer mist daily with lime-free water, in winter once or twice weekly. In summer feed by adding a weak solution to the spray water every 14 days.
Further culture Provide for indirect humidity (see page 43).
Propagating By offsets, which are separated only when they are a reasonable size and then bound on a branch.
Pests, diseases Trouble free.
Professional tip Tillandsias can look particularly interesting when a selection of the many different types are grouped together.

Vriesea
Vriesea

Zantedeschia
Calla, calla lily, arum lily

Vriesea splendens is the best-known species.

The calla needs a rest period if it is to bloom.

The vrieseas offered as houseplants are mostly cultivated hybrids. Both green- and variegated-leaved forms are available.

The best-known species is *Vriesea splendens*, the flaming sword. It produces leaf rosettes about 50cm (20in) tall, the leaves crossed with striking brownish-red horizontal stripes, and sports an orange-red, flat flower spike. There are also green-leaved hybrids with dark-red inflorescences or crosses of *Vriesea carinata* (meaning 'lobster claws') and *Vriesea psittacina* ('parrot'), which have spikes in several colours. Vrieseas can be cultivated bound to epiphyte supports or in small pots with a well-aerated potting mixture.

Flowering season Vriesea hybrids are sold in bloom throughout the year.

Family Bromeliaceae, bromeliad family.

Origin Brazil.

Location Bright to semi-shady. Warm and humid all year round. Soil temperature over 18°C (64°F).

Watering, feeding Always keep slightly moist with room-temperature, soft water. Put water in the cup and on the root ball. In summer feed with a weak solution every 14 days.

Further culture Tolerant plants that rarely require potting on, but when they do use an orchid potting mixture.

Propagating By offsets, which must be a reasonable size before being separated from the mother plant. But vrieseas do not develop offsets as easily as other bromeliads. When detached, the rooted rosette should be planted in orchid potting mixture.

Pests, diseases No problems.

The most popular house-plant calla, *Zantedeschia aethiopica*, comes from South Africa's swamp regions, a habitat that dries out in summer. There it grows as a clump plant some 80cm (31in) tall, which has either a partial or total rest period, and a sturdy, fleshy root stock. The juicy, green, glossy leaves are carried on upright stems and the inflorescence consists of a white covering leaf (the spathe) and the yellow spadix. Tubers of the pink-flowering *Zantedeschia rehmannii* and the yellow-flowered *Zantedeschia elliottiana* are also available.

Flowering season Spring to early summer.

Family Araceae, arum family.

Origin South Africa.

Location Full sun to semi-shady. Warm in summer, cool in winter. Place outside in summer.

Watering, feeding Indoors, keep completely dry for two months after blooming (late spring and early summer), conforming with the dry summer season in its native location. Afterwards shake out the root ball, pot on in good houseplant potting mixture and slowly increase the amount of water. The plants need a great deal of humidity during this growing period. Before the new flowers develop, decrease the amount of water a little and water freely again when flowering begins. From mid summer until flowering fertilize weekly.

Further culture None.

Propagating In mid summer by division of root stock after the rest period.

Pests, diseases Spider mites and aphids in hot, dry conditions.

Professional tip In favourable climatic conditions and protected spots the calla can be planted outdoors.

RARITIES

Uncommon flowering plants: a small selection of attractive novelties and rarities for those who enjoy the challenge of the unusual.

Pavonia multiflora
Pavonia

Evergreen bush, 2m (6ft) high. The flowers have purple-red bracts and a somewhat darker corolla; the stigma is pink, and the stamens are blue. (Not grown in Australia and New Zealand.)

Flowering season Year round, in right conditions. **Family** Malvaceae, mallow family. **Origin** Brazil. **Location** All year round bright and warm, in winter not under 15°C (59°F). **Watering, feeding** Keep only moderately moist with soft water. From early spring to late summer feed weekly with a weak solution. **Further culture** The plants need high humidity. Mist often. In spring pot on as necessary in good houseplant potting mixture. Cut back after flowering. **Propagating** From top cuttings. Difficult.

A half-open pavonia blossom with purple-red calyx, pink stigmas and blue anthers

Globba
Globba

Ginger-like plants with rhizomatous roots, large, oblong-lanceolate leaves and pendulous panicles of flowers. About 100 species are recognized, all having the characteristic, very unusual flowers. *Globba winitii* is the species most commonly offered as a houseplant, and it has rose-pink bracts and a bright yellow corolla; other species can also be cream-coloured. Besides *Globba winitii*, *Globba atrosanguinea*, from Borneo, and *Globba marantina*, which comes from the South Sea islands, are also available. (Globba plants are not grown in Australia and New Zealand.) **Professional tip** Anyone lucky enough to get hold of a curcuma or

hidden lily (*Curcuma roscoeana*) can cultivate it just like the globba. **Flowering season** Mid summer to late autumn. **Family** Zingiberaceae, ginger family. **Origin** Thailand. **Location** Very bright, but not full sun. All year round 20 to 23°C (68 to 73°F). **Watering, feeding** Water moderately. From early spring to late summer feed with weak solution. **Further culture** Provide high humidity. Leaves wilt in early/mid winter, but do not let rhizomes dry out. In spring pot on in good houseplant potting mixture and force again. **Propagating** By division.

Eranthemum pulchellum
Blue sage

Small bush with dark-green leaves and sturdy blue flower spikes. Usually cultivated as an annual; it is a wonderful winter bloomer.

Flowering season November to February. **Family** Acanthaceae, acanthus family. **Origin** India. **Location** Bright but not sunny. In summer 18 to 23°C (64 to 73°F), in winter not below 16°C (61°F). **Watering, feeding** Keep moderately damp all year round. **Further culture** Pot on in early spring as necessary in good houseplant potting mixture. **Propagating** From top cuttings after blooming at bed temperatures of 20 to 25°C (68 to 77°F).

Oxalis adenophylla
Wood sorrel, oxalis

Clumps of grey-green leaves that fold up in the evening as if for sleep. The

pink flowers are carried on stems some 5cm (2in) long. Some oxalis species are weeds in Australia and N.Z. but there are non-invasive species sold for flowering pot plants for balcony or patio.
Flowering season Early spring.
Family Oxalidaceae, oxalis family.
Origin Chile, Argentina.

Location Bright to full sun and cool all year round. **Watering, feeding** Keep evenly moist during the growing season and fertilize weekly. **Further culture** Plants die back in autumn and sprout again after a rest period. **Propagating** By bulbils.

Smithiantha hybrids
Temple bells

The temple-bells, whose genus is now named after the nineteenth-century English botanical artist Matilda Smith, was formerly known as *Naegelia multiflora*. The modern hybrids are descendants of *Smithiantha multiflora* and *Smithiantha zebrina*. They have soft, brown-patterned leaves and orange-red flowers. The small plants renew themselves from scaly rhizomes.
Flowering season Summer to early autumn. **Family** Gesneriaceae, gesneriad family. **Origin** Southern Mexico. **Location** Bright and warm. **Watering, feeding** Keep slightly moist with soft water from early spring to mid autumn. Feed every 14 days with weak solution. In winter keep plants completely dry. **Further culture** Provide indirect humidity

(see page 43). Leaves begin to wilt in mid autumn. Dry the rhizome in the old pot and overwinter cool (around 12°C/54°F). In spring pot on in good houseplant potting mixture and then water. Force in plastic bag (see page 59). **Propagating** From seed or division of the rhizome.

Anigozanthos flavidus
Kangaroo-paw

Bushy plant with lanceolate leaves, which in summer produces unusual, fuzzy, felt-like flowers.

Flowering season Late spring to late summer.
Family Haemodoraceae, bloodwort family. **Origin** Western Australia.
Location Very bright all year round. Kangaroo-paws do not tolerate wet, humid summers. In summer warm (outside if possible), in winter cool (10 to 15°C/50 to 59°F). **Watering, feeding** Water well in summer. From early spring to late summer feed every week with weak solution. In winter keep dry. **Further culture** As necessary pot on in spring in good houseplant potting mixture. **Propagating** By division of older plants or from seed.
Professional tip The kangaroo-paw needs an extraordinary amount of light and in a bad summer will scarcely bloom at all. It also has a tendency to lose its compact growth habit, especially in a dark spot, because plants are treated with growth inhibitors when raised for sale. If you cannot get plants of *Anigozanthos flavidus*, you can raise its relative, *Anigozanthos manglesii*, from seed.

TUB PLANTS

Splendid flowering plants that soon outgrow the windowsill, love the fresh summer air out of doors and need a cool position in winter.

Abutilon hybrids
Flowering maple, parlour maple

Shrub with green- or greenish-gold-flecked foliage. Plants offered commercially are all crosses of different species, except for *Abutilon*

megapotamicum and *Abutilon pictum.* Excellent dwarf varieties are available for containers.
Flowering season All year round.
Family Malvaceae, mallow family.
Origin Central and South America.
Location In summer out of doors, bright to semi-shady, bring into house in early autumn and overwinter bright and cool (12 to 14°C/54 to 57°F).
Watering, feeding Water freely from early spring to late summer and feed twice weekly. From early autumn to late winter keep the root ball merely damp. **Further culture** In spring pot in good houseplant potting mixture after cutting back by two thirds.
Propagating From tender cuttings in spring or half-woody ones in late summer.

Chamelaucium uncinatum
Geraldton wax flower

Small evergreen shrub with needle-fine leaves and small dark-pink or white flowers.
Flowering season Early to mid spring. **Family** Myrtaceae, myrtle family. **Origin** Western Australia.
Location In summer full sun, warm and airy. Overwinter from early autumn bright and cool (around 10°C/50°F). **Watering, feeding** Keep moderately moist, less

water in winter. Sogginess makes the flowers drop. From early spring to late summer feed every 14 days. **Further culture** After blooming cut back shoots. Pot on in spring as necessary in good houseplant potting mixture.
Propagating From soft cuttings at a bed temperature of 25°C (77°F).

Cytisus × racemosus
Broom

Evergreen shrub with small, three-part leaves and brilliant yellow racemes of flowers. Available commercially are bushy pot plants that, with good care, can broaden and grow as tall as 1m (39in), and there are attractive standard forms as well. The broom, like the campanula (see page 100), is one of the few houseplants that does not require softened water.
Flowering season Late winter to late spring. **Family** Leguminosae, legume family. **Origin** Canary Islands, Madeira.
Location Outdoors in summer in cool to temperate areas, in full sun to bright, and warm; bring indoors in early/mid autumn and overwinter bright and cool (8 to 10°C/46 to 50°F) so that the flowers can develop.

Watering, feeding Keep moist all year round. In summer water more, in winter less. From early spring to late summer feed weekly, in winter monthly. **Further culture** Pot on young plants every year after blooming in good houseplant potting mixture. Cutting back after blooming prevents loss of leaves. **Professional tip** Keep in a bright, cool spot (but no full sun) while flowering.
Warning Broom, like other *Cytisus* species, contains toxic materials.

138

Bougainvillea
Paper flower

Vines with strikingly coloured bracts
in cream-white, pink, red or purple.
Obtainable as a pot plant trained on a
hoop, a bush or a standard. Species
include *Bougainvillea glabra*, the
common purple variety, and the
vigorous grower *Bougainvillea
spectabilis*, which has thorns and likes
to spread.
Flowering season Mid spring to
early summer. **Family** Nyctaginaceae,
bougainvillea family. **Origin** Brazil.
Location In summer place outdoors
in a sunny to very bright, warm and
protected spot. From early autumn on,
bring inside and keep bright and cool
(10 to 14°C/68 to 77°F). **Watering,
feeding** From start of active growth
until late summer, water freely and
feed weekly. Then keep drier. From
late autumn water little, and after
foliage drop, do not water at all.
Further culture Cut back in early
spring and pot on in good houseplant
potting mixture. Mist on sunny
days. **Propagating** Difficult.

Callistemon citrinus
Crimson bottlebrush

Evergreen shrub with grey-green
lanceolate leaves and long,
bottlebrush-like flower spikes about
10cm (4in) long, in which the red
filaments of the stamens are especially
prominent. The commonest species,
Callistemon citrinus (syn. *Metrosideros
citrina* or *Callistemon lanceolatus*), will
grow to a height of about 3m (10ft) in
its native habitat and even in a pot
will become an impressive plant
relatively quickly. Dwarf *Callistemon*
varieties are popular container plants
for a sunny balcony or patio.
Flowering season Early to mid
summer. **Family** Myrtaceae, myrtle

family. **Origin** Southern Australia,
New Caldeonia. **Location** Place
outdoors in summer in full sun or in a
very bright, warm spot. From early
autumn bring inside and overwinter
cool and bright (6 to 8°C/43 to
46°F). **Watering, feeding** Water in
summer with soft water and fertilize
weekly. **Further culture** Pot on in
spring as necessary in good

houseplant potting mixture or an
ericaceous mixture.
Propagating From top cuttings
from late summer to mid autumn at a
bed temperature of 20 to 25°C (68 to
77°F).

*The garden plant
Campanula
poscharskyana can
make an enchanting
hanging plant for the
summer months.*

Campanula poscharskyana
Campanula

About 15cm (6in) high, densely bushy,
cushiony garden plant with thousands
of sky-blue bells in short clusters and
heart-shaped leaves. Produces runners
and makes a beautiful hanging plant.
Flowering season All summer and
into autumn.
Family Campanulaceae, bellflower
family. **Origin** Dalmatia.
Location Sun to semi-shade.
Watering, feeding In summer
water freely. The plant loves very hard
water. Feed weekly. **Further
culture** After flowering, plant in the
garden to overwinter in a cool, bright
spot with little
water. **Propagating** From runners
in the garden in summer.

139

FOLIAGE PLANTS

Foliage plants play an important role in any houseplant collection. They look striking alone or as the most natural background for colourful groupings of flowering plants.

The popular division of plants into foliage and flowering categories is really very superficial. Some, for instance, are considered foliage plants simply because their leaves have more decorative impact than their often modest or insignificant flowers. In fact almost all foliage plants are actually flowering plants, which, in their native regions, regularly produce flowers and fruits. They may never bloom as houseplants because in their natural habitats they become very tall trees, and in pots they always remain in the juvenile form, never maturing enough to flower. Exceptions include the sago palm, the Norfolk Island pine and the Monterey cypress, all plants are older in evolutionary terms than the flowering plants and already in existence for many millions of years when they evolved.

The foliage-plant collection on pages 142–93 will acquaint you with the most beautiful and best-known species and varieties currently available on houseplants, along with some bizarre rarities and interesting novelties in the marketplace. Ferns and palms, which really also belong in the foliage-plant category, are deliberately excluded here. They have their own, separate chapters because they are very different plants, both botanically and in cultivation.

Foliage plants are wonderfully suited for decorating living spaces. Their immense variety of shapes and leaf sizes, structures and colorations offer almost infinite possibilities. They can cascade down from columns or pedestals, hang from the ceiling, climb on room dividers or serve as a living curtain in a window. Especially eye-catching are those plants that with good culture develop into stately indoor trees.

Equally important is the positive effect that green plants have on us. Green is the colour human beings need most. Its nature is peaceful, it

The giant leaves of the anthurium are light-traps. Using these vast surface areas, the plant tries to capture as much of the light filtering down through the foliage canopy of the rainforest as possible.

banishes depression and it has a relaxing effect. This is not surprising when you know that the lenses of our eyes do not have to adjust for green as they do for other colours.

The most popular foliage plants are, according to statistics, the *Yucca*, *Aglaonema*, the weeping fig, the grape ivy, the philodendron, the dracaena and the various forms of umbrella tree and maranta. All are discussed here, but those who look for the unusual will certainly find pleasure in such uncommon plants as the string-of-beads, a succulent *Senecio* species (see page 193) or in the ornamental leaves of the *Anthurium* (above) or the *Alocasia* (left).

The right plant

Our foliage plants come from every possible plant family. Certain families – such as the arum, begonia, aralia, bromeliad, grape and maranta families (see photograph, pages 34–5) – give us an especially large number of representatives. The extraordinary variety of growth and leaf forms is immediately evident. There are upright forms, creeping and climbing ones, herbaceous, shrubby or tree-like growers, evergreen and deciduous plants, as well as grasses,

epiphytes, succulents and insect-eating plants. Leaf shape and size varies from needle-fine to violin-sized. Depending on the species, leaves can be thin or thick, fleshy or hard, leathery or velvety-soft, and hairy or waxy. Exciting leaf patterns and colours also document how inventive nature is. (But remember some leaf decoration, called variegation, is brought about by human intervention.)

The right culture

The leaves are the life focus of the plant, the place where photosynthesis and respiration take place. Keep a constant watch on them. They are usually the first to indicate disease or insect attack.

In its natural habitat the Ficus benjamina *develops sturdy air roots, which it sends to the ground like powerful guy ropes.*

Remember when you are watering – apart from any individual care instructions – that a plant with lush foliage always needs more water than one with only light foliage because it has a larger evaporation area.

FOLIAGE PLANTS

Acorus gramineus
Grassy-leaved sweet flag

Yellow-striped sweet flag 'Argenteostriatus'

The grassy-leaved sweet flag, a swamp plant, looks very like grass (as its species name indicates: *gramineus*=grasslike). It belongs to the same family as the Swiss cheese plant (see page 172) and the philodendron (see pages 178–9) and is a very close relative of the sweet flag (*Acorus calamus*), an ancient medicinal herb. The commercial growers offer white- and yellow-striped varieties with sedge-like leaves about 50cm (20in) long, like 'Argenteostriatus' and 'Aureovariegatus'. Especially pretty is the variety 'Pusillus', which at only 10cm (4in) tall is a true dwarf. All have a creeping root-stock and are decorative plants for small or large water gardens in the house, conservatory or balcony.

Family Araceae, arum family.

Origin Japan, China, Thailand, India.

Location Bright to semi-shady, not sunny, but airy. Cool (0°C/32°F) in winter, if possible not warmer than (16°C/61°F). The plants love the fresh air of summer in a bright, cool, damp place in the garden and are happiest in the swampy margins of a garden pond. Sink the pot and retrieve it in autumn.

Watering, feeding Water well. *Being a swamp plant, the grassy-leaved sweet flag must never be allowed to dry out.* It is best to stand the pot in a water-filled saucer. From spring to autumn feed every 14 days, in winter every six to eight weeks.

Further culture Pot on in spring as needed in good houseplant potting mixture.

Propagating By division of root stock in spring.

Pests, diseases Spider mites and thrips, poor growth and leaf damage in a winter location that is too warm and dry.

Aeonium
Aeonium

Aeonium arboreum, *the 'little rosette tree'*

The name *Aeonium* (from Greek: *aionios*=eternal, outlasting) indicates that this plant is a skilled survivor. In fact, in its native habitat, the aeonium uses its juicy leaves as a water reservoir to survive in times of drought. The leaves are arranged in rosettes and in the best known species, *Aeonium arboreum*, are carried on bare stems about 1m (39in) high so that the plant looks like a little rosette tree. The variety 'Atropurpureum' has wine-red leaves in summer, but in winter these become green from lack of light. The effect created by *Aeonium tabuliforme* is very unusual. It develops plate-shaped rosettes, from 15 to 30cm (6 to 12in) wide, consisting of 100 to 200 individual leaves. Aeoniums rarely bloom when cultivated as houseplants.

Family Crassulaceae, orpine family.

Origin Canary Islands, Morocco.

Location Bright to full sun. For summer can be sunk in the garden in a spot protected from rain. In winter maintain 10 to 16°C (50 to 61°F).

Watering, feeding Water sparingly, *but never let the leaves shrivel with dryness.* In winter water very seldom. From late spring to early autumn add cactus fertilizer to water every 14 days.

Further culture Pot on in spring as necessary in cactus mixture or a good houseplant potting medium.

Propagating By leaf rosettes or single leaves. Allow the cut surface to dry before planting. *Aeonium tabuliforme* by seed only.

Pests, diseases Mealy bugs.

142

Aglaonema
Aglaonema

'Silver Queen' is almost without chlorophyll.

The silver designs on the leaves are the distinguishing characteristic of the aglaonemas. The most common species is *Aglaonema commutatum* with silver-green striped, spotted or dotted varieties like 'Silver King', 'Silver Queen', 'San Remo' and 'Pseudobracteatum'. The plants develop small trunks 50cm (20in) high with herbaceous, broadly oval leaves; they sometimes bloom and, after flowering, develop red berry fruits. *Aglaonema costatum* remains small. Its trunk branches bushily at the base.

Family Araceae, arum family.
Origin South-east Asia.
Location Shady to semi-shady. Warm all year round, in winter not below 16°C (61°F).
Watering, feeding Water with soft, room-temperature water, in spring/summer more, in autumn/winter somewhat less. From early spring to late summer feed every 14 days with weak solution.
Further culture Provide for warm potting mixture and indirect humidity (see page 43). Pot on young plants every year, older ones only as necessary in good houseplant potting mixture.
Propagating By division of clumps at potting on in a heated propagator. Difficult.
Pests, diseases Growth disturbances and brown leaf margins from water that is too hard and cold, and cold roots.
Warning The plants contain substances that irritate skin and mucous membranes. The berries are poisonous.

Alocasia
Elephant's-ear plant

Foliage beauty for the flower window

The elephant's-ear plant is widely regarded as one of the most beautiful of all foliage subjects. Only a few of the approximately 70 species in the genus are available as houseplants. *Alocasia lowii* from Borneo has dark olive-green leaves up to 40cm (16in) long with the large veins in white. In *Alocasia sanderiana* from Mindanao (Philippines) the dark olive-green leaves gleam metallically and are decorated with silvery white veins and leaf margins. They are best raised in a heated greenhouse or an enclosed plant window because they demand high temperature, humidity and a lot of space.

Family Araceae, arum family.
Origin South-east Asia.
Location Semi-shady to shady. Most of the year above 20°C (68°F), in winter somewhat cooler, but never below 17°C (63°F).
Watering, feeding Use only soft, room-temperature water. In spring, summer and autumn keep moist, *but avoid sogginess*. Water only sparingly in winter rest period. From early spring to late summer feed with weak solution every 14 days.
Further culture Provide for high humidity. Pot on every two years at the end of winter in a good houseplant potting mixture with added polystyrene granules.
Propagating By division of rhizomes at potting on. Protect cut surfaces from infections with dusting of fungicide. Grow in heated propagator.
Pests, diseases Rotting of rhizomes in too cold or too wet soil.
Warning Wet plants can cause skin irritations when handling.

143

FOLIAGE PLANTS

Aloe
Aloe

Aloe variegata, *the partridge-breasted aloe*

The partridge-breasted aloe, *Aloe variegata*, is a popular plant all over the world. It has white-spotted, succulent, triangular leaves, which are arranged to overlap each other like roof tiles, and it grows to be 30cm (12in) tall at the most. The candelabra aloe (*Aloe arborescens*) is a well-known, problem-free house and tub plant. Aloes are drought and salt-air tolerant. Many a child's scraped knee has been healed with its juices. It grows higher and more spreading, often developing a branching stem that is bare at the bottom, and has green leaves that are spiny at the edges. The *Aloe barbadensis* (syn. *Aloe vera*), the medicinal aloe, is also good for healing purposes. Today this species is marketed in pots as a 'new' cosmetic plant. The juice of its succulent leaves is said to soothe burns, promote healing, and improve skin and hair. No *Aloe* species can be expected to bloom until it reaches maturity and rarely indoors.

Family Liliaceae, lily family.
Origin South Africa.
Location Full sun. In summer warm, in winter cool 6 to 10°C (43 to 50°F). Loves a summer sojourn in a rain-protected, sunny spot out of doors.

Watering, feeding
From spring to autumn keep moderately moist, in winter water seldom. *Avoid sogginess at all costs.* During the summer feed every two weeks, adding a weak solution of cactus fertilizer when watering.
Further culture Pot on in spring as necessary in good houseplant potting mixture with added sand.
Propagating From side growths, which are separated, allowed to dry and then planted in sandy soil.
Pests, diseases Root lice and mealy bugs.

Ampelopsis brevipedunculata
Ampelopsis, Chinese grape

Ampelopsis *loves the freshness of summer outdoors.*

Commercial growers sometimes call the ampelopsis *Vitis heterophylla variegata* because of its grapelike leaves. The correct botanical name is nevertheless *Ampelopsis brevipedunculata*. In garden centres you most often encounter the small-leaved hybrid form *Ampelopsis brevipedunculata* var. *maximowiczii* 'Elegans'. It is a charming vine and hanging plant with red stems and green-, white- or pink-marbled leaves, which it loses in autumn if the location is too dark or the temperature too low. Bright conservatories are therefore the ideal location for this vigorous climbing shrub. There in a short time it will creep over walls, posts and trellises. The green-leafed species is much more vigorous and ideal for patio, balcony or courtyard walls where quick cover is needed.

Family Vitaceae, grape family.
Origin Eastern China.
Location Bright (but not full sun) to semi-shady. In winter as bright as possible. Only moderately warm all year round, preferably briskly cool. Overwinter at about 5 to 12°C (41 to 54°F). Loves a summer sojourn out of doors.
Watering, feeding
Water freely in summer, less in winter. After the leaves fall, keep almost dry during cool overwintering. From early spring to early autumn feed every 14 days.
Further culture Prune to control in winter while dormant. Pot on plants each spring in good houseplant potting mixture. In spring plants may be trimmed to shape.
Propagating By top or stem cuttings in summer.
Pests, diseases Spider mites and thrips after overwintering too warm.

Ananas
Pineapple

You need space for the ornamental pineapple.

Plants available include *Ananas comosus* var. *variegatus* with green-yellow-white-striped leaves, *Ananas comosus* var. *aureovariegatus* with pink-tinged leaves, and *Ananas bracteatus*, which has a vivid red tuft of bracts over the fruit. They all form typical bromeliad rosettes of spiny-toothed leaves up to 1m (39in) long and, with a diameter of 1m (39in), need a great deal of space. On the other hand the dwarf pineapple, *Ananas nanus*, develops rosettes that are only 20cm (8in) across. There are also dwarf forms of *Ananas bracteatus* and varieties with smooth leaf margins. Important: pineapple rosettes that have bloomed and fruited die out. Pineapples grown indoors rarely fruit – grow for foliage effect.
Family Bromeliaceae, bromeliad family.
Origin Tropical Central and South America.

Location Bright, in winter also sunny. Warm (over 20°C/68°F) all year round, in winter not under 18°C (64°F).
Watering, feeding In summer water freely with soft, room-temperature water, in winter more sparingly. From late spring to early autumn feed with weak solution every 14 days.
Further culture The pineapple tolerates dry air. Every two years in summer pot on in good houseplant potting mixture.
Propagating By offsets; only separate when they are a reasonable size. Or cut off the tuft of leaves at the top of the pineapple and root it in a good seeding mixture with added sand. Put a plastic bag over it (see page 59) and place in a warm, bright spot.
Pests, diseases Rarely.
Warning The leaf margins are dangerously sharp and pointed. Risk of cuts.

Araucaria heterophylla
Norfolk Island pine

This pine is a very popular indoor tree.

The discoverers of the Norfolk Island pine were Captain Cook and the no less famous British botanist Sir Joseph Banks. There are about 18 known species, but only this one is suitable for culture in the home. In its South Pacific habitat the Norfolk Island pine grows to a height of 60m (197ft). It appeals primarily because of its symmetrically arranged, horizontally projecting 'tiers' of branches.
Family Araucariaceae, araucaria family.
Origin Norfolk Island.
Location Bright, well lit position near a window. Turn pot regularly to maintain even growth. Ideal on a balcony or patio, and popular brought indoors as a Christmas tree. In summer 18 to 22°C (64 to 72°F), also outdoors in a semi-shady spot with good air circulation; in winter cool, at least 5°C (41°F).

Watering, feeding In spring, summer and autumn, keep moderately moist; in winter water sparingly. From early spring to late summer feed while in active growth.
Further culture Provide high humidity with misting. Pot on every two or three years at most with a good houseplant potting mixture.
Propagating Can grow from seed but very difficult. Better to buy small seed-grown plant and grow it on.
Pests, diseases Drooping and degenerating branches as well as needle drop in too warm a location with poor air circulation, poor light, too much water in winter or too little water in the growing season.
Professional tip I have been very successful using a fertilizer for ericaceous plants on my Norfolk Island pine.

The Norfolk Island pine enjoys fresh, cool sea breezes in its native habitat so it is beneficial to mist the houseplant frequently.

Asparagus
Asparagus

Of the *Asparagus* 'ferns' utilized as indoor plants the two most popular are *Asparagus setaceus* (syn. *Asparagus plumosus*), with delicate green foliage on slender, upright stems, and *Asparagus densiflorus sprengeri*. The latter, usually sold as *Asparagus sprengeri*, has needle leaves and is very tolerant.

Family Liliaceae, lily family.

Origin Africa, Asia.

Location Very bright, but not sunny; the variety 'Sprengeri' also full sun. Room temperature year round at 20°C (68°F); *in winter not under 10°C (50°F)*.

Watering, feeding Keep moist in summer, in winter water little. Feed weekly from early spring to late summer.

Further culture When completely potbound, pot in good houseplant potting mixture.

Propagating By division or from seed in spring at bed temperatures of 20 to 25°C (68 to 77°F). When sowing, cover seeds with a thin layer of houseplant seeding mixture (dark germinators).

Pests, diseases Rarely a problem.

Warning The berries are poisonous to humans but attractive to birds who spread the plant in this way.

Left
From top to bottom
Asparagus setaceous *'Pyramidalis',* Asparagus acutifolius, Asparagus densiflorus *'Meyeri',* Asparagus densiflorus *and* Asparagus falcatus

Aspidistra elatior
Cast-iron plant

The cast-iron plant thrives anywhere.

This plant is aptly named for it is very robust and can thrive even with the little light that staircases, hallways and offices have to offer. It comes from the cool, shady mountain forests of Japan, grows to be 1m (39in) tall and continually increases its width by means of its horizontally spreading rhizomes. The evergreen leaves are 70 to 80cm (27 to 31in) long and 10cm (4in) wide. They shoot up directly from the rhizome, rolled in a horn-like shape, and in the variety 'Variegata' they have yellow or white stripes. The insignificant, grey-violet flowers emerge at ground level.

Family Liliaceae, lily family.

Origin China, Japan.

Location Bright to shady, never sunny. Fresh and cool all year, in winter not under 10°C (50°F). However, the cast-iron plant also tolerates warmer temperatures and dry indoor air. Variegated leaf varieties need a well lit position to maintain variegation. The plants love a summer sojourn out of doors.

Watering, feeding Keep moderately moist, in winter almost dry. *Avoid sogginess at all costs.* From early spring to late summer feed every two weeks.

Further culture Pot on in spring, but only when completely rootbound.

Propagating By division of the rhizomes, best in early/mid spring when potting on. They become very congested and you may have to use a saw to separate older plants into sections.

Pests, diseases Root rot from standing water, leaf burn from blazing sunshine. Scale and spider mites in too warm a location.

Professional tip Fertilize the coloured-leaved variety 'Variegata' less. If fed too much, the leaves turn green.

Beaucarnea recurvata
Ponytail plant

The thickened stem serves as a water reservoir.

Anyone who has seen the ponytail plant in its Mexican home is impressed. There it grows to a height of 8 to 10m (26 to 33ft), and is a many-branched shrub with down-curving, grey-green leaves almost 2m (79in) long. But the most bizarre feature is the base of its stem. It can swell to a wide ball 1m (39in) in diameter and looks – as does the stem – scaly, like an elephant's foot. This extraordinary structure serves the plant as a water reservoir against dry spells. Naturally as a houseplant it does not begin to reach the height it achieves in its native environment, but with good culture it can grow to be 1m (39in) tall in a pot or tub and develop leaves that are 60cm (23in) long.

Family Agavaceae, agave family.

Origin Mexico.

Location Bright to full sun and good air circulation. Can be grown on a balcony or patio, or in a well lit position indoors near a window. In summer put outside in a place protected from rain. In winter keep bright and cool but not under 10°C (50°F).

Watering, feeding In summer water moderately, in winter keep nearly dry. *Avoid standing in water at all costs*; it is lethal. From late spring to mid autumn, fertilize every four weeks.

Further culture Pot on every two or three years in good houseplant potting mixture. Provide good drainage.

Propagating By seed or side shoots, which sometimes appear.

Pests, diseases Spider mites and scale from too warm and dry a location.

FOLIAGE PLANTS

Begonia
Begonia, leaf begonia

Left to right Begonia masoniana, Begonia boweri *hybrids,* Begonia *'Cleopatra' and several* Begoniarex

The classic leaf begonias are the Rex hybrids with their extensive range of varieties. Their development goes back to the year 1858, when *Begonia rex* was first imported into Europe and initiated a flurry of hybridizing that still persists today. *Begonia rex* could be crossed surprisingly well with other species, for instance with *Begonia diadema*, whose genes are still recognizable today. Rex begonias with diadema blood are identified by deeply lobed, toothed, longish leaves, whereas the classic Rex begonias have almost completely smooth-edged, more rounded leaves. Bizarre oddities among the Rex begonias are 'Comtesse Louise Erdody', with its snail-shaped, rolled leaf base, as well as the purple-red-margined 'Bettina Rothschild', which attracts further attention with fiery-red new growth.

Frequently seen on the market besides Rex begonias are *Begonia boweri*, *Begonia* 'Cleopatra' and *Begonia masoniana*, which bears the black marking of an 'iron cross' on its spring-green leaves and is popularly known as the iron-cross begonia.

There are many unusual and beautiful leaf begonias available. Angel wing begonias, for example, with their tall, bamboo-like stems, showy leaves and cascades of long-lasting flowers, are ideal for part shade on balconies, patios and courtyards.

Other hybrids are available too, and a variety of especially attractive rare species from specialist begonia nurseries. Recommended are: *Begonia imperialis* 'Speculata', with green, irregular brown-bordered leaves, and *Begonia heracleifolia* var. *nigricans*, the star begonia, with hand-shaped, black-splotched leaves and light bristles on the undersides. Then there are the red-black-leaved *Begonia* 'Halina', the fern-leaved *Begonia foliosa*, *Begonia goegoensis*, with shield-shaped, almost circular dark-green leaves and brilliant red-leaf undersides, *Begonia* 'Sabi' with its enchanting silver-washed foliage and *Begonia* 'Thrush' with pink spots on the uppersides of its leaves.

Family Begoniaceae, begonia family.

Origin Tropical and subtropical regions.

Location Bright but not sunny. Warm all year round, winter temperature not under 16°C (61°F).

Watering, feeding Use only soft, room-temperature water. Keep moderately moist all year round, but never allow to dry out. *Avoid sogginess and root ball dryness at all costs.* Fertilize with weak solution every 14 days from early spring to early autumn.

Further culture Provide for indirect humidity (see page 43). *Never mist the leaves – causes leaf spots.* Pot on only when thoroughly potbound in spring, using good houseplant potting mixture with added polystyrene granules. If necessary, trim root ball.

Propagating From leaf or root cuttings or by division of rhizomes in a heated propagator at a bed temperature of 24°C (75°F).

Pests, diseases Nematodes, mildew and root rot from bad location or errors in culture. Leaf drop in autumn will as a rule be compensated for by new growth in spring.

Professional tip With rex begonias the leaves will become smaller if the plant needs potting on or if culture is indifferent.

Brachychiton rupestris
Queensland bottle tree

The characteristic trunk of the bottle tree

The bottle tree belongs to the same family as the cacao and cola trees. Of the 11 recognized species, the best known is *Brachychiton rupestris* from Queensland. There it grows to a height of 6 to 15m (20 to 49ft) and develops a striking bottle-shaped trunk, which can have a diameter of more than 3m (10ft) at maturity. The grey-green leaves can be simple or compound on the same plant. In a pot, the effect of the thickened trunk base, which is often twisted, is interestingly bizarre. As in the *Beaucarnea* (see photograph, page 147), it serves as a water reservoir for times of drought. *Brachychiton rupestris* is also sold as a bonsai.
Family Sterculiaceae, sterculia family.
Origin Eastern Australia.
Location Very bright to full sun. In summer 18 to 20°C (64 to 68°F), from June on can be placed

outdoors in a tub on a sunny balcony or patio that is protected from rain. In winter no cooler than 10°C (50°F). If grown as bonsai, filtered sunlight, and should only have short periods indoors.
Watering, feeding Water little, keeping rather dry. *Avoid sogginess at all costs.* From early spring to early autumn feed with weak solution every four weeks.
Further culture Pot on in spring when completely potbound in good houseplant potting mixture with some sand added to improve drainage.
Propagating From top cuttings and from seed.
Pests, diseases Spider mites and scale in too warm and dry a location. 'Keeling over' of plant from too much water.

Caladium
Angel's wings, mother-in-law plant

Caladiums *also have red and pink variegations.*

The caladiums obtainable commercially are, generally speaking, crosses and are called *Caladium* bicolour or *Schomburgkii* hybrids. There are snow-white, pink and red-flecked or marbled varieties. The coloured-leaved types are often bought as tuberous root stocks, from which the magnificent leaves develop in summer, dying back again in the autumn.
Family Araceae, arum family.
Origin Tropical America, especially Brazil.
Location Bright to semi-shade, no sun. Constantly warm soil and air temperatures over 20°C (68°F). Likes humidity.
Watering, feeding Keep plants that are actively growing moist from spring to late summer; then stop watering so that the leaves can slowly dry out. Feed weekly from early

spring until leaves die naturally.
Further culture Provide for high humidity (see indirect humidity, page 43). To overwinter, leave tubers in the old potting mixture until growth starts (or remove and place in peat) and store at 18°C (64°F). In mid/late winter lay tubers in good new houseplant potting mixture. Place the pot in a bright spot and keep moist and warm (air and soil temperatures (25 to 26°C/77 to 79°F).
Propagating By separation of side tubers after development of some leaves. Or with larger plants by division of tuber after overwintering, as soon as the new growth is 15cm (6in) long.
Pests, diseases Aphids on new growth from too-dry air.
Warning Contains irritants to skin and mucous membranes.

Divide only after new growth shows is the rule for anyone who wants to propagate the caladium. The reason: before the new growth, the eyes on the tuber are very difficult to recognize so you may cut into them.

FOLIAGE PLANTS

Calathea
Calathea

Calathea zebrina, *one of many recognized species*

Terrariums or warm, humid greenhouses are favourite places for this inhabitant of the tropical rain forests. Thanks to the breeders, however, there are also calatheas that get along very well in the home without such protection. *Calathea makoyana* is a prime example and one of the easiest to grow. It has oval leaves with olive-green spots on a cream-coloured ground and grows to a height of 1m (39in). *Calathea lancifolia* has oblong leaves 30cm (12in) long, carried on stems 10 to 30cm (4 to 12in) in length. Silver-white leaf blades with green margins decorate the foliage of *Calathea picturata* 'Argentea'; brightly coloured lines parallel to the side veins distinguish *Calathea ornata* 'Roseo-Lineata', whereas *Calathea zebrina* is marked with light green.
Family *Marantaceae,* maranta family.

Origin Tropical America.
Location Bright to semi-shady all year round, no sun. Days 20°C (68°F), nights not under 16°C (61°F). When soil temperature is not warm enough, growth is impeded; in too dark a spot the leaf coloration is impaired.
Watering, feeding Keep moderately moist with soft, room-temperature water. Feed every 14 days with weak solution from early spring to late summer.
Further culture Provide high humidity with misting. Pot on yearly in summer.
Propagating By division of root stock.
Pests, diseases Spider mites, scale and rolled leaves from centrally heated air.
Professional tip *Calathea crocata*, a beauty with saffron-yellow inflorescences, is more commonly available now and worth looking for.

Ceropegia woodii
Hearts entangled, rosary vine

Hearts entangled is decorative and undemanding.

Of 160 known species, only *Ceropegia woodii* plays a role as a houseplant. It is a succulent drought-beater with fleshy leaves and a tuberous root stock. Its thread-like shoots, up to 2m (79in) long, are furnished at intervals with small, heart-shaped leaves with silvery markings. This trailing growth makes it one of the prettiest hanging plants available. In summer little round tubers appear in the leaf axils; these quickly develop roots upon contact with the earth. The small flowers consist of a flesh-coloured tubular corolla, which ends in five dark-brown points, giving the flower the appearance of a little umbrella or a lamp.
Family Asclepiadaceae, milkweed family.
Origin Southern Africa.
Location Very bright to full sun. In summer warm, in winter cooler, but not under 12°C

(54°F). Average indoor temperatures are also tolerated.
Watering, feeding Keep slightly moist all year round, water only seldom in a cool winter location. From early spring to late summer feed with weak solution every four weeks.
Further culture Pot on in spring every two or three years in a cactus potting medium.
Propagating From small tubers that form on the leaf axils or from stem cuttings. Allow cut surfaces to dry before planting.
Pests, diseases Rare.
Style tip Several plants hanging from the frame of a light window create a decorative and easy-care 'plant curtain'.

150

Chlorophytum comosum

Spider plant, spider ivy

The spider plant, *Chlorophytum comosum*, forms thick clumps of rosettes, arching shoots with small white flowers and many offsets. It thrives everywhere. The original form is green-leaved, but the striped varieties are better known.

Family Liliaceae, lily family.

Origin South Africa.

Location Sunny, bright or semi-shade. Room temperature all year around. Put out of doors for the summer.

Watering, feeding Keep moist all year round. *Never allow the soil to dry out*, but never overwater either. The roots rot easily. Feed weekly from early spring to late summer.

Further culture Mist plant now and then in warm and dry conditions. As soon as the roots rise above the edge of the container, pot on in good houseplant potting mixture.

Propagating Any time from offsets.

Pests, diseases Aphids in too warm and dry a location. Brown leaf tips from starvation and indicates that the plant should be potted on.

Right
Spider plants are easy to care for and quickly produce masses of offsets.

FOLIAGE PLANTS

Cissus
Grape ivy

Cissus antarctica *'Ellen Danica'*

The following species have proven themselves for houseplant culture. *Cissus antarctica*, the kangaroo vine, is a strong climber and produces shoots over 3m (10ft) long bearing firm, glossy-green simple leaves with saw-toothed edges. *Cissus rhomboidia*, the grape ivy, is one of our most tolerant indoor plants. Its most beautiful variety, 'Ellen Danica', is distinguished by its serrated leaves, which sometimes have reddish hairs, and it grows more compactly than the species plant. Both species are outstanding vines and hanging plants and suitable for covering trellises and room dividers. *Cissus discolor* and *Cissus amazonica* are suitable for warm, humid situations – flower windows or well lit bathrooms, but equally difficult to manage.
Family Vitaceae, grape family.
Origin Tropics.

Location Bright to semi-shady, no sun. For *Cissus antarctica* and *Cissus rhomboidia* year-round temperatures of between 16 and 20°C (61 and 68°F) are recommended but in winter can tolerate around 10°C (50°F); for *Cissus discolor* and *Cissus amazonica* over 20°C (68°F) all year round.
Watering, feeding Keep moist. In cooler temperatures water less. Feed weekly from early spring to late summer.
Further culture Pot on young plants every spring, mature ones only as necessary in good houseplant potting mixture. Bare shoots can be cut back anytime.
Propagating From top and stem cuttings in heated propagator.
Pests, diseases Leaf drop, leaf spots from poor location and culture. Mildew and other fungal diseases from too wet a potting mixture in winter.

Clusia rosea
Balsam apple

Clusia is an attractive, glossy-leaved evergreen.

Although the balsam apple is supposed to have been imported into Europe by 1692, it is counted among the new introductions to the houseplant market. It belongs to a genus of epiphytic trees or shrubs and in its native habitat is found on and between rocks. Its branches are thick, and its twisted leaves evergreen and leathery, with lengths of 20 to 30cm (8 to 12in) not unusual. Its rose-coloured, fragrant blossoms resemble large camellias. They are filled with golden-yellow stamens, and the seed capsule that develops from them may be as large as a golf ball. Unfortunately the flowers seldom appear in pot culture. But on the grounds of its attractive leaves alone the balsam apple, which has many similarities to the rubber plant, is a handsome plant with great decorative value.

Family Guttiferae, garcinia family.
Origin Tropical and subtropical America.
Location Bright to semi-shady, no sun. Warm all year round, even in winter not below 18°C (64°F). From early summer can be set outdoors in a warm place protected from sun.
Watering, feeding Always keep moderately moist. Use soft, room-temperature water. During growing season feed with weak solution every 14 days.
Further culture Mist often. As necessary pot on in spring in good houseplant potting mixture.
Propagating From top cuttings in heated propagator at bed temperatures between 25 and 30°C (77 and 86°F).
Pests, diseases Rare.

Codiaeum (syn. *Croton*)
Joseph's coat

The exuberantly coloured leaves need bright light.

There are countless variations of the only species under cultivation at present, *Codiaeum variegatum* var. *pictum*, though these plants are seldom offered by name. The leathery leaves can be large or small, simple or lobed, strap-like or spiralling like a corkscrew. The colour palette ranges from green through yellow, orange and red to purple-red and hints of blackish-green. Colour patterns include spots, veining, mottling and stripes. Since the leaves begin to colour only when mature, you often see foliage of different colours on the same plant.

Family Euphorbiaceae, spurge family.

Origin South-east Asia.

Location Bright but not sunny. Without enough light, the strong colours fade. Warm all year round and as humid as possible. *Avoid draughts, cold roots and temperatures below 16°C (61°F).*

Watering, feeding In spring/summer keep moist. From early autumn to late winter water less. From early spring to late summer feed weekly.

Further culture Mist often or provide for indirect humidity (see page 43). Pot on young plants every two years, older ones only as necessary in good houseplant potting mixture.

Propagating In mid winter to early spring from top and stem cuttings at 25 to 30°C (77 to 86°F). Dip cut places in charcoal powder so that the white milky juice will not leak out. Air layering is another possibility.

Pests, diseases Scale, spider mites in too-dry air. Leaf drop and bare stems from poor culture.

Warning The milky juice is irritating to eyes, skin and mucous membranes.

Codonanthe crassifolia
Codonanthe

The codonanthe *needs high humidity.*

The codonanthe has trailing, woody, reddish-tinged shoots and makes a pretty hanging plant, which does best in a climate-controlled flower window. The leaves are opposite, leathery and slightly succulent, as the species name acknowledges (from Latin: *crassus*=thick; *folium*=leaf). The trumpet-shaped flowers are white with red markings inside.

Family Gesneriaceae, gesneriad family.

Origin Tropical America.

Location Very bright but not sunny all year round, and warm, preferably over 20°C (68°F). In winter keep cooler for four weeks (around 15°C/ 59°F) and almost dry. This promotes bud development.

Watering, feeding Keep root ball only slightly moist. From early spring to late summer feed with weak solution every two weeks.

Further culture Mist frequently. Pot on in late winter/early spring or after flowering in good houseplant potting mixture, mixed with polystyrene granules for better soil aeration.

Propagating Cuttings (with at least three pairs of leaves) from firm young shoots in early summer. Simply stick the cuttings into damp seeding mixture. But the propagating medium must be kept warm. Large plants can also be divided.

Pests, diseases Aphids, bud drop from change of location, temperature swings, too much or too little water.

FOLIAGE PLANTS

Coleus blumei hybrids
Flame nettle

In a sunny spot the leaves do glow like a flame.

The flame nettle is one of the most rewarding and colourful houseplants around. All the plants available are cultivars, and an astonishing multiplicity of colours is on offer. Leaf blades are bordered, veined, marbled, blazed and striped with white, cream, green, various shades of red, pink and violet, each different from the next. The plant is a sub-shrub, has a square stem like the stinging nettle and grows about 50cm (20in) tall. Its insignificant blue flowers resemble those of sage. Another species, the small-leaved *Coleus pumilus*, is particularly low-growing. It trails and is a wonderful hanging plant with its red-white, green-bordered leaves.

Family Labiatae, mint family.

Origin Tropical Asia and Africa. Only hybrid forms are commercially available.

Location Full sun all year round, otherwise loses colour and compact growth. Part shade in hot to tropical areas. In winter room temperature should never fall below 8°C (46°F).

Watering, feeding In summer water freely, otherwise the leaves wilt. In winter keep only moderately moist. Feed every 8 to 14 days from early spring to late summer.

Further culture Cut back hard in spring and pot on as necessary in good houseplant potting mixture.

Propagating From top cuttings (they root in water or potting medium) or by seed (in heated propagator). Trim young plants several times so that they will bush nicely.

Pests, diseases Spider mites in too dry a winter location. Whitefly.

Professional tip The flame nettle uses a lot of energy when producing flowers and leads to smaller leaves so pinch out buds.

Cordyline
Cordyline

Cordyline 'Kiwi': compact growth and exotic colouring

The well-known species *Cordyline fruticosa* and its varieties have long-stemmed, broadly lanceolate, reddish leaves and grow about 1m (39in) high; *Cordyline australis* and *Cordyline indivisa*, on the other hand, have small leaves, which are red-striped in some varieties.

Family Liliaceae, lily family.

Origin Tropical Asia, Australia and New Zealand.

Location *Cordyline fruticosa* bright but not sunny, warm and humid all year. An enclosed flower window is ideal. *Cordyline australis* and *Cordyline indivisa* full sun. In summer place outside, in winter cool temperatures of 5 to 10°C (41 to 50°F).

Watering, feeding Keep *Cordyline fruticosa* slightly moist all year round. *Avoid sogginess* or the fleshy roots will rot. Water the other species moderately in summer, in winter seldom. From early spring to late summer feed every 14 days with weak solution.

Further culture Mist plants often or provide for indirect humidity (see page 43). In spring pot on as necessary in good houseplant potting mixture.

Propagating *Cordyline fruticosa* mostly from top cuttings with six to ten leaves but also from stem pieces with three to six leaf scars laid horizontally on the potting medium; the latter can be divided after growth begins. *Cordyline australis* and *Cordyline indivisa* from seed from January to March.

Pests, diseases Spider mites, scale, thrips in dry, heated air; for *Cordyline australis* and *Cordyline indivisa* also from too warm a winter location.

154

Corynocarpus laevigatus
Corynocarpus

Smooth, glossy leaves like a rubber tree

This evergreen shrub, with its rounded oval, dark-green leaves, is a splendid decorative plant for bright, not too warm areas. Of the four or five species in the genus, *Corynocarpus laevigatus* is the only one under culture. Its species name probably relates to the smooth, rubber-plant-like character of the leaves (Latin: *laevigatus* = smooth). The genus name on the other hand refers to the form of the fruit (Greek: *koryne* = club, *karpos* = fruit). In nature the corynocaprus has oblong fruit, whose orange stones are very poisonous. The flowers and fruits never appear on the houseplant, however. (The corynocarpus is not grown in Australia.)
Family Corynocarpaceae, corynocarpus family.
Origin New Zealand.
Location All year round very bright. In summer around 20°C (68°F), in spring/winter 5 to 10°C (41 to 50°F). The plant loves to be out of doors in summer.
Watering, feeding Keep moderately moist all year. Water less in cool winter location. From early spring to late summer feed every 14 days.
Further culture Pot on as necessary in spring in good houseplant potting mixture.
Propagating In mid/late winter or end summer/early autumn by stem or top cuttings in bed temperatures around 20°C (68°F). Clip young plants often so that they will branch nicely.
Pests, diseases Scale and spider mites in too warm and dry a location.
Warning The seeds of the corynocarpus are very poisonous.

Crassula argentea
Money plant, silver jade plant

Crassula argentea: *a tolerant evergreen succulent*

Of the more than 300 known *Crassula* species, *Crassula argentea* has become a very familiar houseplant, and there is also an attractive variegated form. Both develop round to oval, succulent, glossy leaves and make neat tree-like bushes 1m (39in) or more in height and breadth. The money plant can, with good culture, live for many years and produces small red or white flowers.
Family Crassulaceae, orpine family.
Origin South Africa.
Location Bright to full sun, but not directly in front of a window with full midday sun. Warm in summer, even outside in a bright, sunny, sheltered position. In winter cool if possible (around 10°C/50°F).
Watering, feeding Keep moderately moist in summer if inside, give somewhat more water outdoors; in winter keep almost dry. In summer months feed weekly with cactus fertilizer.
Further culture Pot on as necessary in spring or summer in a good cactus potting medium, using heavy clay pots to help stabilize the plant.
Propagating From top cuttings with three or four leaves, which root easily in a good seeding mixture. Allow cut surfaces to dry for a few days.
Pests, diseases Mealy bugs from too warm a situation. Root mealy bugs. When overwintering too warm, leaf drop and loss of compact appearance.
Professional tip The sickle plant, *Crassula falcata*, and other *Crassula* species are cared for in the same way.

The money plant needs a stable, heavy pot as it grows older so it is worthwhile investing in a handsome container for a mature specimen.

FOLIAGE PLANTS

Cryptanthus
Earth star

The earth star is a typical ground bromeliad.

The dry thorn forest region of Brazil is the home of the earth star. Accordingly it is provided with tough leaves that can withstand dry air. In contrast to most of the epiphytic bromeliads, it roots in the ground. Soil culture is therefore the correct way to cultivate the plant, although it is sometimes offered for sale bound to an epiphyte support, where it will usually dry up. Best known are *Cryptanthus bivittatus*, with white- or pink-striped wavy leaves, and *Cryptanthus acaulis* with grey-scaled pink or brownish leaves, which can be up to 8 to 20cm (3 to 8in) long. The earth star forms flat, star-shaped rosettes, in whose centre hides an insignificant white flower; hence the genus name (from Greek: *kryptos* = hidden, *anthos* = flower).

Family Bromeliaceae, bromeliad family.
Origin Brazil.
Location Bright to semi-shade, in winter sunny too. Warm, all year round, between 20 to 22°C (68 to 72°F). Ideal are flower windows, bottle gardens and terrariums.

Watering, feeding Keep moist. From early spring to late summer feed every 14 days with weak solution.

Further culture Provide high humidity. In a window in summer, mist daily; in winter, every two weeks. Pot on as necessary in good houseplant potting mixture.

Propagating From offsets, which should be well-formed before they are separated from the parent plant. Use orchid compost for this exercise and secure rosettes firmly in the pot.

Ctenanthe
Ctenanthe

An unusual plant for the connoisseur

There are about ten species in the genus, all of which are natives of the Brazilian rain forest. Of these, *Ctenanthe oppenheimiana* and *Ctenanthe lubbersiana* have proven to be the best houseplants. The ideal place for these members of the maranta family is, inevitably, the warm, humid flower window. Ctenanthes are foliage beauties and develop leaves up to 40cm (16in) long, which are spotted or striped on the upper side. *Ctenanthe oppenheimiana*, as well as its varieties 'Variegata' and 'Tricolor', can be recognized by the red stems and undersides of the leaves. The latter makes mounds of lush foliage, whereas *Ctenanthe lubbersiana* is of more upright habit.

Family Marantaceae, maranta family.
Origin Brazil.
Location Bright, but not sunny. In too dark a spot it loses its beautiful leaf markings. Warm all year round, more than 20°C (68°F), even in winter never under 18°C (64°F). Soil warmth is very important.

Watering, feeding Keep moist at all times with soft, room-temperature water. Feed every 14 days during the growing season with a weak solution.

Further culture Mist plants often and provide for indirect humidity (see page 43). In spring or early summer pot on with good houseplant potting mixture with added polystyrene granules.

Propagating *Ctenanthe oppenheimiana* by division. *Ctenanthe lubbersiana* by cutting off the tuft of leaves at the end of the stem. Rooting takes place only in warm soil and humid air.

Pests, diseases Rolled leaves from sun damage and too-dry air. Root rot from cold winter conditions. Spider mites.

Cupressus macrocarpa
Monterey cypress

The Monterey cypress grows very quickly.

The Monterey cypress, a non-winter-hardy conifer from California, has quickly established itself as a popular houseplant. One reason for its success is that the pyramid-shaped evergreen can be trimmed into very beautiful, decorative miniature standards. Pruning back is unavoidable indoors because the cypress species grow very quickly and try hard to attain their genetically programmed size. The variety 'Goldcrest', which has attractive golden needles, is most often seen on the market.
Family Cupressaceae, cypress family.
Origin Southern California.
Location Bright to semi-shady. In summer best outdoors in a bright but not sunny spot. Warm summer temperatures and cool winter temperatures (5 to 10°C/41 to 50°F) are ideal. The ideal location is an unheated conservatory.
Watering, feeding In summer keep moist; in winter in lower temperatures water less, when warmer water more. *Avoid either dried-out root ball or sogginess.* From early spring to early autumn feed every four weeks at the most, otherwise the Monterey cypress will grow even faster.
Further culture Pot on as necessary in spring or autumn in good houseplant potting mixture.
Propagating By top cuttings in summer in a heated propagator. Difficult.
Pests, diseases Spider mites in too warm a winter location.

Cycas revoluta
Sago palm, Japanese sago palm

A large sago palm is very expensive.

The attractive sago palm is one of the oldest plants on earth and has a very distinctive appearance. It grows extremely slowly – developing a new leaf crown every one or two years – so large specimens can be very expensive. The leathery fronds, which grow out of a central decorative stem, produce a very pleasing effect. Specimens offered commercially are exclusively young plants of *Cycas revoluta*.
Family Cycadaceae, cycad family.
Origin South-east Asia, Japan.
Location Bright, no sun. In summer warm – older specimens can go outdoors – in winter cool (around 12 to 15°C/54 to 59°F).
Watering, feeding Keep moist in summer, in winter water less. Allow soil to dry between waterings but it must never dry out completely. *At all costs avoid sogginess.* Fertilize with weak solution every week from early spring to late summer.
Further culture Pot on every two to five years in good houseplant potting mixture with added sand.
Propagating From seed at room temperatures of 30°C (86°F). Difficult and lengthy.
Pests, diseases Mealy bugs in too warm a winter location with poor air circulation. Scale.
Warning Cases of animal poisoning have been reported, especially in Australia.

Cyperus
Umbrella plant

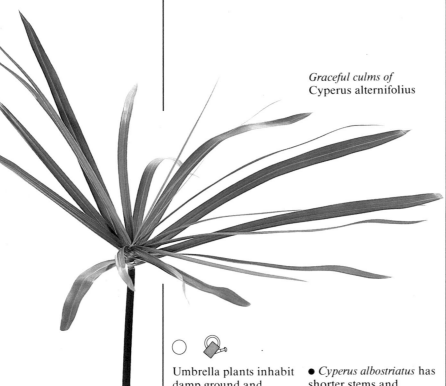

Graceful culms of
Cyperus alternifolius

Cyperus albostriatus *does not need standing water.*

○ 🪣

Umbrella plants inhabit damp ground and swamps in their natural habitat, and as houseplants, too, they like to have wet roots. The characteristic mark of most of the *Cyperus* species is an umbrella-like head of leaves. The insignificant little umbellate flowers appear almost all year round. There are some 600 species, of which *Cyperus alternifolius*, its white variety 'Variegatus', the subspecies *flabelliformis*, *Cyperus albostriatus*, *Cyperus gracilis* and *Cyperus haspan* are important as houseplants.
● *Cyperus alternifolius* grows to be more than 1m (39in) tall and has finely grooved striped stems, on the end of each of which sits a dense head of about 25cm- (10in-) long leaves, with an unremarkable brown flower in the middle. The white variety becomes green with increasing age and with too much nourishment.

● *Cyperus albostriatus* has shorter stems and broader leaves with rough edges. It is often sold, incorrectly, under the name of *Cyperus diffusus*.
● *Cyperus gracilis*, the dwarf *Cyperus*, grows only 30cm (12in) high.
● *Cyperus haspan* looks like a little papyrus plant and becomes 30 to 50cm (12 to 20in) tall.
● *Cyperus papyrus*, the true papyrus plant, provides a particularly exotic effect. It attains a height of more than 2m (6ft), develops an elegant head of loosely drooping, threadlike leaves and has a large, hundred-rayed umbellate flower. Now and then it is sold as a fully grown plant, but you can also raise it from seed yourself.
Family Cyperaceae, sedge family.
Origin Tropical and subtropical regions.
Location Bright to sunny, warm all year round. All – with the exception of *Cyperus*

albostriatus – may be placed outdoors at the end of late spring where they make good tub plants. In winter keep somewhat cooler.
Watering, feeding Keep very wet in a warm, bright location. The saucer should be full constantly. The exception is *Cyperus albostriatus*. This broader-leaved species does not require 'foot baths'; it is enough to keep the root ball moist. With the other species, remove 'foot baths' at winter temperatures 12 to 15°C (54 to 59°F). For pot culture feed every one or two weeks from mid spring to late summer with a weak solution.
Further culture In heated areas in winter, provide for indirect humidity (see page 43) and give the plants a shower often. If necessary, pot on in the spring in good houseplant potting mixture.

Propagating By division of plants or by cutting off an 'umbrella' with a 5cm (2in) stem. Shorten leaves by one third and root in room-temperature water (see drawing page 60). Another way to propagate is by seed. Seeds are available for *Cyperus alternifolius*, *Cyperus esculentus* and *Cyperus papyrus*. Do not cover and put in a very light place – *Cyperus* are light germinators.
Pests, diseases Brown leaf tips from dry air or hard or acid water, torn leaves from too cool a situation. Spider mites, thrips and mealy bugs also from dry air.
Professional tip Fertilize specimens planted in water pools or aquariums seldom and only in very small amounts. Otherwise there is a danger of developing surplus salts in the water.

Dieffenbachia
Leopard lily, dumb cane

One of the numerous leopard lily hybrids

The leopard lily is the darling of the international hybridizers. Best known are the *Dieffenbachia–Amoena* hybrid 'Tropic Snow' with large, 60cm- (23in-) long green leaves with an attractive central variegation, *Dieffenbachia* 'Camilla' with compact creamy-white leaves with thin margins of green and central veins of the same colour, or the less vigorous *Dieffenbachia maculata* with white-and-green spotted leaves.
Family Araceae, arum family.
Origin Tropical America.
Location Bright to semi-shade, never sunny. In a location that is too dark the variegated leaves turn green. Keep warm all year round, in winter never under 8°C (46°F). *Avoid draughts and fluctuations of temperature.*
Watering, feeding Keep moist year-round with soft, room-temperature water. In winter water more sparingly. In summer fertilize weekly with weak solution.
Further culture Provide for indirect humidity (see page 43) or mist often. Pot on every two years in spring in good houseplant potting mixture with added polystyrene granules. Cut back older plants that have lost their leaves for new growth.
Propagating By top cuttings or pieces of stem in heated propagator with a bed temperature of 25°C (77°F). Place pieces of stem horizontally on the surface of the potting medium with the eyes facing upward.
Pests, diseases Spider mites, thrips and aphids from dry centrally heated air. Root rot from wet soil and fungal diseases from poor location.
Warning All parts of the plant are poisonous. Its juice is irritating to skin and mucous membranes.

Dizygotheca
False aralia

Dizygotheca elegantissima: *delicate filigree foliage*

The false aralia is a native of the exotic South Sea Islands, where it develops into evergreen bushes or trees.
Dizygotheca elegantissima is – as its species name indicates – a very elegant plant with its filigree-like foliage. As a rule it grows from a central stem and even indoors it can reach a height of almost 2m (6ft). The seven to eleven narrow, long simple leaves are arranged like the fingers of a hand on a thin stem. In the juvenile stage they are reddish and delicate, later dark olive-green and somewhat broader and coarser. Only recently available commercially: *Dizygotheca veitchii* 'Castor'.
Family Araliaceae, aralia family.
Origin South Sea Islands.
Location Bright, but not sunny. Year-round soil and air temperature warm, over 20°C (68°F). Ideal is a warm, humid flower window. *Avoid draughts*, or the leaves will drop.
Watering, feeding Keep moist with softened, room-temperature water. *No sogginess or dryness*; both are lethal for the plant. In winter water less. From early spring to late summer feed every 14 days.
Further culture Mist often. Pot on young plants every two years in good houseplant potting mixture, older plants only as necessary.
Propagating From seed, which must be very fresh. Difficult.
Pests, diseases Spider mites and scale in a winter location with dry air and too little light. Leaf drop in too wet or cool a location, dried leaf tips from low humidity or dried root ball.

Dizygotheca veitchii *'Castor'*

Dracaena

Bushy-forming Dracaena surculosa *'Florida Beauty'*

The fragrant Dracaena fragrans *'Massangeana'*

Although dracaenas in their native habitats and in maturity look very

1 Dracaena draco
2 Dracaena deremensis *sp.*
3 Dracaena surculosa 'Florida Beauty'
4 Dracaena fragrans 'Massangeana'
5 Dracaena deremensis 'Warneckii'
6 Dracaena marginata 'Tricolor'
7 Dracaena 'Volkaertii'
8 Dracaena marginata
9 Dracaena congesta
10 Dracaena deremensis
11 Dracaena deremensis 'Souvenir de Schriever'

similar to palms, they are no more related to that plant family than are the yuccas. They are also frequently confused with the *cordyline* (see page 154). Unfortunately, the best distinguishing feature is the roots. Dracaenas have orange-yellow, smooth roots, whereas those of the *Cordyline* species are white and thickened like clubs. Dracaenas are among the most popular and frequently propagated foliage plants and there are numerous species and varieties on the market.

● *Dracaena marginata* may be the best known. It forms heads of very narrow, arching leaves, with a dull-red margin or, as in the variety 'Tricolor', striped with green and cream.

● *Dracaena fragrans*, the fragrant dracaena, is also frequently cultivated. It has broad, greenish-yellow or green-and-white-striped leaves.

● *Dracaena deremensis* has blue-green leaves with decorative white edges.

● *Dracaena sanderiana* is striped with whitish-yellow or silver grey.

● *Dracaena reflexa* is also sold as *Pleomele reflexa*, of which the most beautiful form is *Pleomele reflexa* 'Variegata' with rich, creamy yellow colouring. It is commonly known as 'Song of India'.

Family Liliaceae, lily family.

Origin Subtropical and tropical regions.

Location Bright to semi-shady but not full sun. Coloured-leaved varieties basically as bright as possible so that the leaves will not turn green. Warm all year round, 18 to 25°C (64 to 77°F).

Watering, feeding Keep slightly moist at all times. *Avoid sogginess and ball dryness* or the leaves will drop. Feed every two weeks from early spring to late summer.

Further culture Mist often. Pot on every two years in good houseplant potting mixture. Cutting back possible at any time.

Propagating The coloured varieties can only be propagated vegetatively, that is from top or stem cuttings in a heated propagator at a bed temperature of 25°C (77°F). Others may be propagated from the thickened roots that develop on mature plants.

Pests, diseases Mealy bugs. Browned leaf edges from dry centrally heated air. Dried up leaf tips from incorrect watering.

Professional tip Dracaenas naturally shed their lower leaves as they grow and this should not give rise for concern.

Epipremnum pinnatum
(syn. *Scindapsus aureus*)
Devil's ivy, pothos

Devil's ivy is decorative and undemanding.

In ideal conditions this plant becomes very vigorous and is ideal for covering a trellised wall in a conservatory. *Epipremnum pinnatum* 'Aureum' is almost the only variety available in the market. But it is frequently sold under its old name, *Scindapsus aureus*. The juvenile form develops heart-shaped, green-and-gold-patterned leaves, which with age can be considerably larger and lobed.

Family Araceae, arum family.

Origin Solomon Islands.

Location Light, semi-shady to shady. But in too dark a location very long intervals develop between leaves and they turn green and remain small. Room temperature and warmer all year round, in winter not under 16°C (61°F).

Watering, feeding Keep moist. From early spring to late summer feed weekly.

Further culture Pot on every two years in good houseplant potting mixture. Cutting back possible at any time.

Propagating From top or stem cuttings, which also root in water. Put several young plants in one pot.

Pests, diseases Root rot and leaf drop in too damp or too dark a location.

Professional tip If you want to grow devil's ivy on a trellis or wall, you will do better with hydroculture because you can then avoid the need for potting on.

Warning Contains irritants to skin and mucous membranes.

Euonymus japonica
Spindle tree

The species and (left) a variety 'Aureovariegata'

The European spindle tree (*Euonymus europea*) – the winter-hardy species of the genus *Euonymus* – is a well-known and useful garden plant. For house culture and the cool conservatory, only the Japanese species, *Euonymus japonica*, is suitable. In its native setting it grows to a height of 8m (26ft) but as a houseplant it can only attain 1m (39in) in a pot or tub, sometimes a little more. The leaves of the evergreen shrub are oval, slightly toothed and glossily leathery. There are numerous coloured-leaved varieties. They all are available as houseplants, but they retain their beauty only if they are treated like tub plants, that is placed out of doors from early summer and kept quite cool over the winter.

Family Celastraceae, staff-tree family.

Origin Japan, Korea, Ryukyu Islands.

Location Bright to semi-shade, in winter even sunny, so that it does not lose the leaf colouring. From early spring to late summer around 18°C (64°F), from mid autumn to late winter no higher than 10°C (50°F). Provide more warmth for higher humidity. Summer outdoors.

Watering, feeding From early spring to early autumn water freely and feed every 14 days. Then water less and do not fertilize.

Further culture In spring pot on as necessary in good houseplant potting mixture. Cutting back or trimming for shape can be done at the same time.

Propagating By top cuttings from late summer to early autumn in heated propagator at bed temperatures between 20 and 25°C (68 and 77°F).

Pests, diseases Scale, leaf drop and mildew in too warm a winter location.

Euphorbia
Spurge

Euphorbia pseudocactus: *often confused with cactus*

The spurge family, the fourth largest of the plant families, also includes cactus-like, leafless succulents. They are bizarre, undemanding plants, not a few of which look enough like cacti to be confusing. Those most commonly seen on the market are: *Euphorbia pseudocactus, Euphorbia erythraeae, Euphorbia balsamifera* and *Euphorbia grandicornis.*
Family Euphorbiaceae, spurge family.
Origin Africa.
Location Bright to full sun. Warm in summer, in winter 15 to 18°C (59 to 64°F). Can be summered out of doors in a rain-protected spot.
Watering, feeding In spring and summer water sparingly, in autumn and winter very seldom indeed. Best to water from the bottom. Feed from mid spring to early autumn with cactus fertilizer in weak solution.

Further culture As necessary pot on in spring in cactus potting mixture.
Propagating Depending on species, from seed or cuttings. Hold cut surfaces under lukewarm water (stops flow of milky juice and keeps it from gumming up the cut surfaces). Allow cut areas to dry before planting.
Pests, diseases Rare.
Warning Euphorbias are poisonous to humans and animals. The milky juice contains irritants to skin and mucous membranes. Do not allow juice to get into eyes and be careful about open cuts or scratches. With some species you can receive injury from the thorns.

Euphorbia tirucalli *thrives in hydroculture.*

Fatshedera lizei
Tree ivy, aralia ivy

Fatshedera lizei *can tolerate some shade.*

The botanical name of the tree ivy indicates that it is not an established genus but a cross of the *Fatsia japonica* and English ivy (*Hedera helix*). The tree ivy grows about 1.5m (59in) tall and forms upright stems with mostly three- to five-lobed, dark-green glossy leaves. The variety 'Variegata' has beautiful white leaves and is a little less vigorous in its upward growth.
Family Araliaceae, aralia family.
Origin None, since it is an entirely hybrid form.
Location Bright to semi-shady, the variety 'Variegata' always bright, or the coloured leaves will turn green. Room temperature all year round, well-grown specimens even somewhat cooler. Keep the plants cooler in winter (they will tolerate as low as 10°C/50°F), in warmer winter quarters provide for humidity.

Watering, feeding From spring to autumn keep moist, in winter in a cool spot water little; in a heated area give more water and mist often. From late spring to late summer feed every 14 days.
Further culture Pot on young plants every spring, older ones only when completely potbound, in good houseplant potting mixture. Cut back stems by a quarter so that the plant will bush out.
Propagating In late summer from mature top or stem cuttings, which root in water or potting medium, or by air layering.
Pests, diseases Spider mites and scale in location with too much warmth and dry air.
Note The much larger and very popular Japanese fatsia, *Fatsia japonica,* has similar requirements, but it needs somewhat more water.

163

Ficus
Fig

White and green variegated creeping fig

Ficus pumila, *the creeping fig*

Currently the most popular *Ficus* is the small-leaved weeping fig (*Ficus benjamina*). Like that old favourite the rubber plant (*Ficus elastica*), it grows to ceiling height and is obtainable in many green- and coloured-leaved varieties.

● *Ficus lyrata*, the fiddle-leaf fig, gets its common name from the shape of the mature leaf, which is distinctly like that of a violin.

● *Ficus retusa* has leaves similar to the weeping fig and is preferred for bonsai training.

● *Ficus deltoidea* grows slowly and remains small. It is also a favourite bonsai plant.

● *Ficus pumila*, the creeping fig, and its variegated variety 'Sonyn' are gorgeous hanging plants.

● *Ficus buxifolia*, the box-leaf rubber plant, is a fast-growing shrub with almost triangular leaves and copper-coloured stems.

● *Ficus aspera* 'Parcelli', a small, warmth-loving shrub from Polynesia, has projecting branches with short-stemmed, large, white-and-green-marbled leaves that feel rough.

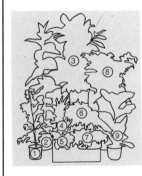

Opposite
1 Ficus diversifolia
2 Ficus elastica *'Tricolor'*
3 Ficus benghalensis
4 Ficus pumila
5 Ficus pumila *'Sonny'*
6 Ficus benjamina
  'Exotica'
7 Ficus radicans
  'Variegata'
8 Ficus benjamina
9 Ficus lyrata

● *Ficus benghalensis*, the Indian banyan tree, is a large spreading tree 20m (66ft) or more high and as wide, with a massive buttressed trunk, aerial roots from lower branches, and beautifully shaped leathery leaves.

● *Ficus rubiginosa*, the rusty fig, likes it rather cooler. In its Australian habitat it grows as a 4m-(13ft-) tall, branching shrub. There its branches bow to the ground, take root, grow up again, soon covering a large area. Best-known is the variety 'Vareigata'. *Ficus rubiginosa* grows slowly and likes a cool, bright location in winter. Suitable for bonsai.

Family Moraceae, mulberry family.
Origin Tropics and subtropics.
Location Very bright, but not sunny. Room temperature all year round, but green-leaved plants can be cooler too. Important: warm soil and humidity.

Watering, feeding
Water moderately in spring and summer, still more sparingly in autumn and winter. *Avoid sogginess* or leaves will drop. Feed every 14 days in summer.
Further culture Mist often. Pot on as necessary in spring in good houseplant potting mixture. With most species, cutting back and trimming will lead to branching.
Propagating By cuttings in heated propagator at 21°C (70°F) or by air layering.
Pests, diseases Scale, spider mites and thrips in dry centrally heated air. Leaf drop in winter as a result of too cool and damp a winter location.

165

Fittonia verschaffeltii
Snakeskin plant, mosaic plant

Silver-veined Fittonia argyroneura *'Nana'*

The Englishwomen Elizabeth and Mary Fitton stand sponsors for the botanical name of this charming, small foliage plant. There are several varieties in culture, such as the silver-veined 'Argyroneura' or the red-veined 'Pearcei'. Both have leaves about 7cm (3in) long and are proven ground covers for warm, humid flower windows, terrariums, greenhouses or warm beds in a conservatory. The silver-green variety 'Minima' with its particularly small leaves was developed for bottle gardens and mini-greenhouses. Snakeskin plants, whose ancestors came from the tropical rain forests of South America, need humidifers on the windowsill.
Family Acanthaceae, acanthus family.
Origin Colombia to Boliva.
Location Bright to shady, no sun. Room temperature and warmer all year round. Even in winter never keep the snakeskin plant below 18°C (64°F). *No draughts or the leaves will drop.*
Watering, feeding Keep moist with soft, room-temperature water. Feed with weak solution every 14 days from mid spring to mid autumn.
Further culture Provide for high humidity. Mist often. Pot on only as necessary in shallow containers in spring in good houseplant potting mixture with added polystyrene granules.
Propagating In spring from top cuttings in heated propagator. Frequent pinching back makes the plants bushier.
Pests, diseases No problem.
Professional tip These plants will overwinter better if placed in a heated growing cabinet.

Grevillea robusta
Silky oak

Grevillea robusta *is a marvellous indoor tree.*

This easy-care plant with its silvery-green pinnate leaflets is more reminiscent of a fern than an oak. *Grevillea robusta*, which – as the species name indicates – is strong and solid, actually in its natural habitat in Australia grows as a tree 50m (164ft) tall and is used for lining avenues. It is a vigorous plant even when its roots are confined to a container, and a height of 2m (6ft) can be expected in the course of two years so it is best placed in a roomy conservatory. Unfortunately, the splendid flowers typical of the protea family never appear in pot culture.
Family Proteaceae, protea family.
Origin Australia.
Location Very bright, in winter even sunny. Good air circulation all year round and fresh-cool rather than warm. The plants can be placed in a shady spot in summer. In winter if possible keep no warmer than 15°C (59°F) or ugly lanky growth will result.
Watering, feeding In summer water well, in winter more sparingly. From early spring to mid autumn feed weekly.
Further culture Pot on as necessary in spring in good houseplant potting mixture. Plants that have grown too tall may be cut back hard in spring, but they then lose their tree-like form and become bushy instead.
Propagating From seed, which must be fresh. The *Grevillea* is considered a poor germinator. Professional gardeners usually sow them in heated sawdust. In late summer a semi-mature stem cutting may be taken, but it often needs months to root.
Pests, diseases Blanching leaves incidate an unbalanced supply of nutrients. Aphids and whitefly.

Guzmania
Guzmania

One of the numerous guzmania hybrids

The name of this genus, of which some 100 species are identified, derives from the name of a Spanish apothecary, Guzman. Some of these species have been modified horticulturally and today great numbers of them are in cultivation. The beauty of guzmanias is in their strikingly coloured bracts. Of the countless hybrids and selections that are available commercially, *Guzmania lingulata* is the best known. It attracts interest with green leaf rosettes some 50cm (20in) in diameter, from whose centre appear brilliant red young leaves that shine like satin. The flower itself is not so spectacular as in other *Guzmania* species or varieties. Guzmanias can be bound to epiphyte supports or cultivated in pots.
Family Bromeliaceae, bromeliad family.
Origin Tropical central and South America.

Location Bright to semi-shady. Warm all year round, more than 20°C (68°F), and humid. Best kept in a flower window or greenhouse.
Watering, feeding Water with soft, room-temperature water in the leaf cup and on the potting medium. In summer keep cup filled, in winter water less. From early spring to late summer every 14 days use a weak solution of fertilizer when watering or misting.
Further culture Provide for indirect humidity (see page 43). Potting on not necessary since mother plant dies after blooming.
Propagating From offsets, which must be a reasonable size before they are separated from the mother plant. Pot in orchid potting medium. Seeds may also be sown.
Pests, diseases Scale and root mealy bugs.

Gynura
Gynura
Velvet plant

The purple-red foliage of the velvet plant is unique.

The purple, furry leaves of the velvet plant, *Gynura aurantiaca*, are the charm of this tropical subshrub. It is native to the mountain forests of Java, growing upright at first and later climbing to reach a height of 0.5 to 1m (20 to 39in). *Gynura aurantiaca* was introduced to Belgium in 1880. Newer in the trade is *Gynura scandens* from tropical East Africa. Its leaves are also purple-haired, but in contrast to the Java gynura are coarsely toothed. Both are extraordinarily attractive, hanging plants. The small orange flowers, which appear in summer, have an unpleasant smell and should be removed as soon as they appear.
Family Compositae, composite family.
Origin Java, East Africa.
Location Very bright, in winter sunny also, but avoid midday sun. In too dark a spot the leaves lose their coloration and long spaces will develop between the leaf pairs. Room temperature all year round between 18 and 20°C (64 and 68°F); can tolerate high temperatures in summer.
Watering, feeding Water somewhat more in spring and summer, in autumn and winter water sparingly. In summer only, feed weekly with weak solution.
Further culture Provide for indirect humidity (see page 43), but *do not spray directly on the plants*. In spring pot on in good houseplant potting mixture. After two years replace with self-raised young plants because older plants usually grow unsightly. Trim back continually so that they will keep branching.
Propagating In spring or autumn from cuttings, which root without any problems.
Pests, diseases Aphids.

Young gynura plants are easier to overwinter than older ones. If you do not have an ideal winter location, you are better off taking cuttings in the autumn.

FOLIAGE PLANTS

Haworthia
Wart plant, star cactus, cushion aloe

Haworthias are gems for the succulent collector.

Wart plants are small, succulent foliage plants that are coming very much into fashion again. They originate in South Africa, where as a rule they hide in bushes or under boulders. *Haworthia truncata* even creeps into the ground up to the tips of its leaves. The principal species under culture are *Haworthia fasciata*, with horizontally striped rosette leaves, and *Haworthia glabrata*, whose leaves are densely set with tiny pearl-like white tubercles. The flowers appear on long stems and are rather dull. Other, more unusual species, such as *Haworthia attenuata*, *Haworthia limifolia* and *Haworthia reinwardtii*, can be obtained from a cactus specialist.

Family Liliaceae, lily family.

Origin South Africa.

Location Bright, but not full sun. The wart plant loves the fresh air of summer in a place protected from rain. Keep warm in summer, in winter preferably around 10 to 15°C (50 to 59°F). But it will also tolerate room temperature (around 18°C/64°F).

Watering, feeding In spring and summer water little, in autumn and winter only sporadically. *Avoid sogginess without fail.* From early spring to late summer feed with cactus fertilizer every four weeks.

Further culture Pot on every two years in spring or summer in a good cactus potting mixture.

Propagating From seed and from side shoots, which arise from the axils of the lower leaves. Take off side shoots, allow to dry and then plant.

Pests, diseases Rare.

Note The similar-looking gasteria is cultivated exactly the same way except that it will stand more sun.

Hedera
Ivy

Now a gardener's favourite, the varieties developed for use indoors and outdoors can scarcely be counted. The large-leaved 'Gloire de Marengo' is sold in many parts of the world as *Hedera canariensis* and has very attractive green and white variegation. Given a framework to which it can be attached, it will cover a wall in a cool conservatory situation. Among the finest of the small-leaved ivies, those with golden-yellow and green variegation are particularly attractive. These can be encouraged to climb or trail and are also very effective when used as ground cover or at the base of taller plants. All varieties make excellent hanging plants.

Family Araliaceae, aralia family.

Origin Europe, Asia, North Africa. Only hybrid forms are commercially available.

Location Bright to semi-shady. Room temperature all year round; in winter cooler also, but coloured-leaved varieties not below 15°C (59°F). The greener the leaves, the shadier and cooler the location can be; the more leaf colour, the more sun and warmth needed.

Watering, feeding Use room-temperature water. In spring, summer and autumn keep moist, in winter watering somewhat less. From early spring to late summer feed weekly with weak solution.

Further culture Provide for indirect humidity (see page 43) in heated rooms and mist often. Pot on yearly in good houseplant potting mixture.

Propagating From top cuttings, which root easily in water or soil. Or by layering (see drawing, page 61). Always put several young plants in one pot to create a bushy effect.

Pests, diseases Scale from heated air. Spider mites from wintering too warm.

Professional tip When winter location is too warm and too dark, ivy develops weak stems, which are better cut back in the spring.

Warning The berries are very poisonous, but they form only on older plants that are planted outdoors or in a conservatory.

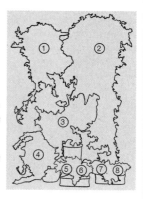

Opposite
1 'Ingrid'
2 'Eva'
3 'Gold Child'
4 'Gertrud Strauss'
5 'Gold Child' sport
6 'Schäfer'
7 'Königers Auslese'
8 'Calico'

FOLIAGE PLANTS

Hypoestes sanguinolenta
Polka-dot plant

Polka-dot plants are wonderful ground cover.

The genus name of this pretty little pot plant comes from the Greek (*hypo*=under; *hestenai*= place) and is a reference, perhaps, to its usefulness as a ground cover. In its Madagascar habitat the polka-dot grows as a decorative shrub 50cm (20in) tall. The leaves are covered with red or pink dots or spots of varying size or are variegated white and green. As a houseplant it is herbaceous and will become drawn and thin if it does not get enough light. In a very bright position, it may flower. The brilliant pink variety 'Flandria' is an immensely popular small foliage plant.

Family Acanthaceae, acanthus family.
Origin Madagascar.
Location Very bright, no sun. Warm and humid all year round, in summer around 20 to 23°C (68 to 73°F), in winter not under 18°C (64°F), best in an enclosed flower window.

Watering, feeding Keep root ball only moderately moist all year round. From early spring to late summer feed every 14 days with a weak solution.

Further culture Provide for high humidity and keep the soil temperature up. Pot on in spring in good houseplant potting mixture with added polystyrene pieces. In good light when growing well the tips should be removed to encourage a bushy habit.

Propagating From top cuttings at bed warmth of 25 to 30°C (77 to 86°F). Keep trimming back young plants so that they will branch. Seeding possible too.

Pests, diseases Seldom.
Professional tip To maintain clean and attractive plants, take cuttings regularly.

Iresine
Bloodleaf

Iresine herbstii *becomes bushy in time.*

If you want a bright spot of red on your windowsill, then the bloodleaf is exactly the plant for you. Its leaves look as if they have been dipped a couple of times into the paintpot labelled wine red. Two of the entire 70 species are popular annuals, either as houseplants or for the garden: *Iresine herbstii*, with roundish leaves, and *Iresine lindenii*, with pointed oval leaves. In the variety 'Aureoreticulata' only the stems and principal veins are dark red, whereas the leaf surfaces are variegated with green and gold. All of them grow no taller than 30cm (12in) in a pot and in a few months develop into a dense bush.

Family Amaranthaceae, amaranth family.
Origin South America.
Location In the house as bright as possible all year round, outside sunny as well. In a dark location the bloodleaf turns very dark red. Keep warm and airy, in winter not under 15°C (59°F).

Watering, feeding Water well in summer, otherwise only moderately. Dry centrally heated air is poorly tolerated. Feed weekly from early spring to late summer.

Further culture Potting on is not necessary. It is better to start new plants every year.

Propagating From top cuttings, which root easily in water or soil. Trim young plants several times so they branch nicely.

Pests, diseases Rare, occasionally aphids.
Professional tip The bloodleaf looks especially dramatic in a red or black cachepot. In a location with cross-light, its colour glows like burgundy.

Leea quineensis
Leea

The red-leaved variety 'Burgundy'

The famous Scottish gardener James Lee gave his name to this beautiful foliage plant, which was brought to England in 1880. After a long period of neglect, it is now being offered for sale once more. The only genus in the family, there are 70 recorded species, which grow as small shrubs in the tropical forests of southern Asia. It is primarily *Leea quineensis* and its red-leaved variety 'Burgundy' that are available as houseplants. The species sometimes develops umbrella-like cymes, a little reminiscent of grape flowers. In fact, the grape family is closely related.

Family Leeaceae, leea family.

Origin Southern Asia.

Location Bright, no sun. Ideally more than 20°C (68°F) all year round, in winter never below 16°C (61°F). The plant loves high humidity and is therefore best kept in an enclosed flower window.

Watering, feeding Keep moderately moist, but *avoid dry root ball or sogginess* otherwise the leaves will suddenly drop. From early spring to late summer feed with weak solution every 14 days.

Further culture Mist often. In spring pot on as necessary in good houseplant potting mixture with added polystyrene granules for drainage.

Propagating From seed, top or stem cuttings in a heated propagator. Difficult.

Pests, diseases Aphids, spider mites from dry, centrally heated air.

Professional tip The sugar droplets which the plant secretes through its leaves are characteristic of the species and a sign that the plant is feeling well.

Maranta
Prayer plant

Maranta kerchoviana

The genus *Maranta* numbers 23 species with tuberous roots and decorative foliage, all natives of the tropical rainforest. *Maranta kerchoviana* (the prayer plant) with dark spots on an emerald-green background is the best known houseplant. The prayer plant is so called because at night it folds its leaves together, like hands in prayer. Also popular is *Maranta erythroneura*, whose emerald-green leaves are characterized by intricate patterns and red lateral veins. All marantas are wonderful bushy plants for tropical windows and ideal for grouping with other indoor plants.

Family Marantaceae, maranta family.

Origin Tropical South America.

Location Bright, no sun, very warm all year round, never under 18°C (64°F).

Watering, feeding In summer water freely, in winter more sparingly. Feed every 14 days with weak solution from mid spring to late summer.

Further culture On the windowsill mist daily with soft water or provide for indirect humidity (see page 43). Pot on as necessary in spring in good houseplant potting mixture with added polystyrene granules.

Propagating By division at time of potting on in spring or by top cuttings.

Pests, diseases Leaf-margin necrosis from too cool a location. Spider mites when air is too dry. Bleached-out leaves from too much light.

Professional tip New leaves are horn-like as they develop and unfurl, but mature curled leaves are a sign that culture is too dry.

Maranta cuttings root relatively quickly in the 'greenhouse' climate provided by a transparent plastic bag.

FOLIAGE PLANTS

Monstera deliciosa
Swiss-cheese plant, fruit-salad plant

Monstera deliciosa *develops strong aerial roots.*

Beautiful perforated leaves and imposing stature have made the Swiss-cheese plant one of our most popular foliage subjects. With good care, this attractive plant will develop into a robust specimen with numerous aerial roots so it needs a trellis or a sturdy epiphyte support. The rounded juvenile leaves, and later the perforated mature leaves, are dark green, glossy and leathery. Older specimens will sometimes bloom, bearing a spadix surrounded by a lovely, creamy-white spathe; from the spadix develops a hard, dull-green fruit that smells like a pineapple. The fruit, which is edible, must be very mushy to get the real taste; it has all the flavours of a fruit salad – hence another of its common names, the fruit-salad plant. Besides the green-leaved kinds, the smaller-growing variety 'Borsigiana' and the white form 'Variegata' are also available.

Family Araceae, arum family.

Origin Mexico.

Location Bright but not sunny (thrives also in shade). All year round between 18 and 22°C (64 and 72°F). Loves high humidity and warm soil.

Watering, feeding Keep slightly moist all year round. From early spring to late summer feed with weak solution every 14 days.

Further culture Wash the leaves every now and again so that the plant can 'breathe'. Mist often. As necessary, carefully pot on in a good houseplant potting mixture. *Do not injure aerial roots or cut them off.*

Propagating From top cuttings in heated propagator or by air layering. The vast majority of commercially available plants are grown from seed.

Pests, diseases Generally pestfree.

Myrtus communis
Myrtle

Myrtle loves a sunny place outdoors in summer.

The myrtle is one of those plants that have always attracted legends and stories. This evergreen from the Mediterranean regions, which in a pot or tub grows scarcely more than 1m (39in) tall, was once sacred to the Greek goddess Aphrodite and therefore a symbol of youth and beauty. Three hundred years ago the Greek and Roman custom of crowning a virgin bride with a wreath of myrtle was revived in parts of Europe, and since that time myrtle has been under cultivation. It is available in bush and elegant standard forms. The plant blooms in high summer with numerous small white blossoms and with good culture can live for many years. The small leaves smell spicy when bruised.

Family Myrtaceae, myrtle family.

Origin Mediterranean regions.

Location Bright to full sun and good air circulation. Myrtle loves to be outside in summer. Keep warm in summer, in winter if possible not more than 10°C (50°F).

Watering, feeding Use only softened water. In summer keep moist. In winter, when plants are less active, keep barely moist. *Avoid sogginess and dried-out root ball.* Feed weekly from early spring to late summer.

Further culture Mist often when indoors. Pot on young myrtles yearly, older ones as necessary in spring in good houseplant potting mixture. For generally compact plants, prune untidy or unwanted growth following flowering.

Propagating From non-woody end cuttings in spring or summer. Trim young plants for a bushy effect.

Pests, diseases Whitefly, scale.

Neoregelia
Neoregelia

Neoregelia carolinae *with red inner leaves.*

Neoregelias are chiefly found in the rain forests of eastern Brazil, where most of them grow as epiphytes. The rosette leaves form a large cup, in which the short-stemmed flowers 'nest', as in the nidularium (see page 174). These insignificant flowers do not last long. The most striking feature of the plant is the colour of the inner leaves, which often retain their brilliant coloration for months at a time. When they die, the mother plant dies too. Best known are *Neoregelia carolinae*, with red inner leaves and, in the variety 'Tricolor', creamy-white-striped outer leaves. *Neoregelia concentrica* has purple inner leaves.

Family Bromeliaceae, bromeliad family.

Origin Brazil.

Location Very bright, in winter also sunny. Warm all year round, in winter never below 18°C (64°F).

Watering, feeding Use only softened water and always pour it into the cup, keeping it full in summer, in winter barely full. Change the water occasionally to prevent it from stagnating. During the growing season add a weak solution of fertilizer to the water every 14 days.

Further culture Mist often or (a better alternative) provide for indirect humidity (see page 43).

Propagating From seed or from offsets, which should be detached and potted individually when of reasonable size. Plant in a good houseplant seeding medium with added polystyrene pieces.

Pests, diseases Dried-out leaf tips when air is too dry.

Nepenthes hybrids
Nepenthes hybrids — **Pitcher plant**

The pitcher plant is an ingenious insect trap.

The pitcher plant is the most striking of the insectivorous plants. The pitchers are not flowers but modified leaves and the most refined insect traps imaginable. Scent glands attract insects to the pitchers and smooth slippery surfaces help slide them into the liquid within, which contains the digestive enzyme pepsin. The insects drown and are subsequently digested. 'Lids' on the pitchers prevent rainwater from diluting the pepsin. The pure botanical species are available from specialist nurseries, the hybrids in garden centres. They are sold in hanging pots so that the dangling pitchers are set off to excellent effect.

Family Nepenthaceae, nepenthes family.

Origin Malayan archipelago, Sumatra, Borneo, Philippines, Australia, Madagascar.

Location Very bright but not sunny. Over 20°C (68°F) all year round. The plants need high humidity. The ideal situation is an enclosed flower window, terrarium or warm, humid greenhouse.

Watering, feeding Use only softened, room-temperature water. Keep potting medium slightly moist. In the growing season fertilize with a weak solution every three to four weeks.

Further culture Provide high humidity and mist the plants all over frequently. As necessary, pot on in spring in orchid potting medium. Use pots with good drainage or baskets. Take care that the roots are not injured when handling.

Propagating From cuttings, but very difficult for the non-professional.

Pests, diseases Devours all pests in the vicinity.

Professional tip Spray plants three or four times daily to combat dry air.

FOLIAGE PLANTS

Nidularium
Nidularium

The exotically contrasting foliage of the nidularium

Of the some 25 *Nidularium* species, all epiphytic inhabitants of Brazil, only a few are commercially available. *Nidularium fulgens* is very well known. As with the neoregelia (see page 173), the flowers of this cup bromeliad also nestle in the centre of the rosette of leaves; hence the name (from Latin, *nidus*=nest). It is easy to confuse the two genera, particularly as both develop their brilliant red inner leaves long before the flower. The neoregelia is particularly like *Nidularium innocentii*. *Nidularium billbergoides*, on the other hand, displays yellow inner leaves and inflorescence, which peeks up out of the nest to a height of as much as 20cm (8in). The leaves are green, glossy and may also be striped or spotted.

Family Bromeliaceae, bromeliad family.
Origin Brazil.
Location Bright all year round but not sunny; room temperature should never drop below 18°C (64°F). The plant loves high humidity.

Watering, feeding Use only softened, room-temperature water. Keep the cup filled all year round and never let dry out. In summer feed roots with a weak solution or treat leaves with a foliar feed.

Further culture Provide high humidity (see page 43). Every two years pot on in good houseplant potting mixture with added polystyrene pieces.

Propagating From seed or by offsets, which are separated when the plant is potted on if of reasonable size. Young plants usually bloom after two or three years.

Pests, diseases Dried-out leaf tips from dry air. Rot from cold, wet roots.

Professional tip In too dark a location the cream-white striped leaves of some species turn green.

Pachira macrocarpa (syn. Pachira aquatica)
Guiana chestnut, water chestnut

A very unusual plant and easy to grow

In its native habitat the Guiana chestnut becomes a small tree with a broad crown. The carmine-red flowers, up to 35cm (14in) in size, rise like a plume of egret's feathers over the leathery, palmate leaves. Unfortunately the flowers do not appear on the houseplant, but it is still a decorative little indoor tree, with a reputation for being undemanding and reliable. The water chestnut is a close relative of the baobab tree (*Adansonia digitata*) and of the Madagascan baobab (*Adansonia madagascariensis*) and like them has a trunk that stores water. Thus the former name for the species.

Family Bombacaceae, bombax family.
Origin Mexico to Costa Rica.
Location Sunny to semi-shady. Room temperature all year round, in winter also somewhat cooler, but not under 12°C (54°F). The plant loves high humidity.

Watering, feeding Keep slightly moist all year round. Fertilize with weak solution every week from early spring to late summer.

Further culture Provide for indirect humidity (see page 43), especially in winter. Pot on as necessary in spring in good houseplant potting mixture. Cut back plants that grow too large.

Propagating From seed or by top cuttings in a heated propagator at bed temperatures over 25°C (77°F).

Pests, diseases Sudden leaf drop from dry centrally heated air.

Pachypodium
Madagascar palm

The typical upright spiny stem of the Madagascar palm

In contrast to cacti and many other succulents, the Madagascar palm tolerates heated air and does not need cool overwintering. As a rule it grows better for novices who often forget watering than it does for very solicitous plant-lovers. The most likely species to be offered for sale is *Pachypodium lamerei*, with its broad, bright-green leaves. In its native habitat it will make a tree some 6 to 10m (20 to 33ft) high. Indoors after about ten years it may attain 1m (39in), and, in my experience, you may count on a very beautiful white-star blossom when it reaches 120cm (47in). (The Madagascar palm is not commonly grown in Australia and New Zealand.)
Family Apocynaceae, dogbane family.
Origin Madagascar.
Location Bright to full sun and warm all year round. In winter not below 18°C (64°F).

Tolerates warm, dry air.
Watering, feeding In summer always keep slightly moist, in winter keep almost dry. Plants enjoy a two- or three-month dry rest period. As soon as the first new leaves appear, start watering again. *Avoid sogginess.* From late spring to late summer feed every four weeks with cactus fertilizer.
Further culture Pot on as necessary with a good houseplant potting medium.
Pests, diseases Root rot and blackened leaves from cold, wet roots in winter. Total leaf drop from too much water or dryness. Dropping of lower leaves is normal for the species.
Warning Trunk and leaves of the Madagascar palm contain a highly poisonous milky juice. You can also receive injury from the thorns. Anyone with children or pets had better avoid this plant.

Pandanus
Screw pine

The screw pine needs lots of space.

Newly bought screw pines, usually juvenile plants of *Pandanus veitchii* or of *Pandanus sanderi*, have strap-like, cream- or white-striped leaves. In their native habitat, however, mature plants develop the species' typical, screw-thread leaves; bizarre prop roots emerge from the stem, become woody and anchor themselves in the ground; and the plant achieves a breathtaking breadth and height. When grown in pots indoors, plants will usually attain a height and spread of 1m (39in).
Family Pandanaceae, screw-pine family.
Origin Polynesia.
Location Very bright, also sunny. Shade from summer midday heat. Keep warm all year round, even in winter not below 18°C (64°F).
Watering, feeding During the summer growing-season always keep moist, in autumn and winter water sparingly. From early spring to late summer fertilize weekly.
Further culture Pot on young plants yearly, older ones as necessary in a good soil-based potting medium.
Propagating From rooted offsets about 20cm (8in) in length.
Pests, diseases Rare.
Professional tip Uneven whitening of the leaf surfaces is normal. You can receive injury from the spiny leaf edges so tie up the tuft of leaves when potting on.

The screw pine has a stately appearance and looks well when displayed alone on a pedestal.

FOLIAGE PLANTS

Pelargonium
Fragrant geranium, leaf geranium

The scent is released when the leaves are bruised.

These sisters of the ivy-leaved geranium have an exciting array of leaf patterns and scents. The leaf geraniums include wild species and hybrids of the bedding geraniums (*Pelargonium zonale* hybrids). The latter have more or less toothed leaves with white-red, white-green-red, very dark green or greenish-yellow markings. The simple, dainty flowers are white, yellow, red, white-red, white-pink or pink and appear in summer. They grow to various sizes, some remaining windowsill plants and others soon attaining tub size.

Scented geraniums
● *Pelargonium bland-fordianum* (almond scent)
● *Pelargonium × citrosum* (citrus scent)
● *Pelargonium crispum* (balm scent)
● *Pelargonium* 'Els' (strong flowery scent)
● *Pelargonium × fragrans* (citrus-pine scent)
● *Pelargonium gibbosum* (musky scent)
● *Pelargonium graveolens* (citrus scent)
● *Pelargonium odoratissimum* (lemon scent)
● *Pelargonium quercifolium* (camphor scent)
● *Pelargonium* 'Prince of Orange' (orange scent)
● *Pelargonium radens* (rose scent)
● *Pelargonium* 'Scarlet Pet' (orange scent)
● *Pelargonium tomentosum* (mint scent)

Leaf geraniums
'Masterpiece', 'Dolly Vardon', 'Madame Salleron', 'Bird Dancer', 'Freak of Nature'

Family Geraniaceae, geranium family.
Origin South Africa.

Location Full sun to bright, and airy. In summer also outdoors in a place protected from wind. Overwinter in bright, cool spot at 10 to 12°C (50 to 54°F).

Watering, feeding Water well in summer, in winter keep relatively dry. Fertilize weekly from early spring to late summer.

Further culture Tolerates dry air well. In spring or autumn cut back hard and pot on as necessary in good houseplant potting mixture.

Propagating Easy with top cuttings in spring or autumn.

Pests, diseases Aphids, whitefly, fungal and bacterial diseases.

Warning Anyone who gets headaches from powerful fragrances should not keep too many scented geraniums in a poorly ventilated room.

Pelargonium hybrid 'Prince of Orange'

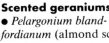 

Pelargonium Stellar hybrid 'Els'

Pelargonium hybrid 'Scarlet Pet'

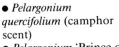 

Pelargonium gibbosum

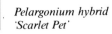

Peperomia

Peperomias *look good as a group of selected species.*

The small, herbaceous peperomias are favourite collector's plants. No wonder, with their multiplicity of pretty leaf structures and colours. More than a thousand species are said to exist. Characteristic of many of them are the thick stem and the fleshy upper side of the leaf, shaped like a water cushion. Peperomias grow upright, hang or creep. Many are epiphytes. The flower spikes that appear with some species are white. Well-known species and varieties include:

● *Peperomia argyreia*, with green-silvery-striped foliage on red stems, is propagated from leaves.
● *Peperomia arifolia* has oval, strongly pointed leaves, whose upper sides are glossy dark green.
● *Peperomia caperata* has puckered leaves; the variety 'Tricolor' has white-bordered foliage.
● *Peperomia clusiifolia* only shows its beauty when fully mature, when its fleshy leaves take on a strong red colour.
● *Peperomia fraseri* has fragrant leaves.
● *Peperomia griseoargentea* has silver-green leaves on red stems.
● *Peperomia incana* can be easily recognized by the grey tomentum that covers the fleshy leaves and is retained only in a bright location.
● *Peperomia magnoliaefolia* (desert privet) has fleshy leaves with pale green and cream variegation. 'Green Gold' is a popular variety.
● *Peperomia obtusifolia* is a very common species that can be found with green-and-white- or yellow-marbled leaves. Best-known varieties include: 'Jeli', 'Albo-marginata' and 'Minima' (dwarf form). They must be trimmed regularly to grow bushy.
● *Peperomia rotundifolia* has small round leaves, which develop from discs the size of the head of a knitting needle and sit on threadlike stems.
● *Peperomia scandens* bears heart-shaped leaves on long, creeping shoots and makes a very pretty hanging plant.

Family Piperaceae, pepper family.
Origin Tropical America.
Location Green-leaved species and varieties in bright location, in summer also semi-shady. Coloured-leaved plants very bright but not sunny. Warm all year round, but a little cooler in winter. Species with fleshy leaves tolerate dry centrally heated air, those with smooth leaves need higher humidity.
Watering, feeding Keep only slightly moist. *Avoid cold roots in winter.* Danger of rot. Feed every three weeks from mid spring to early autumn.
Further culture Provide for high humidity, especially for the smooth-leaved species from mid spring to early autumn. Mist often. In spring or summer pot on as necessary in good houseplant potting mixture. Carefully cut back plants that look bare in the spring.
Propagating From top and leaf cuttings.
Pests, diseases Leaf drop, leaf and stem rot from poor culture. Leaf eelworms.

Philodendron
Philodendron

For over a century philodendrons have enjoyed considerable popularity as plants for the conservatory and the home. There are approximately 275 recognized species, and both large- and small-leaved species are commercially available. All must have warm, moist conditions to thrive. Listed below are the best known for houseplant culture. The climbing species need a support.

● *Philodendron bipinnatifidum*, a spreading plant, with broadly oval, large leaves
● *Philodendron erubescens*, the red-leaf species; the best-known varieties are 'Red Wings', 'Green Emerald' and 'Burgundy'
● *Philodendron* 'Lynette' with atypical leathery, green leaves which are formed like a shuttlecock
● *Philodendron martianum*, one of the bushy, non-climbing species
● *Philodendron melanochrysum*, with black-green foliage
● *Philodendron scandens*, a climbing or trailing species with heart-shaped leaves
● *Philodendron selloum*, the trunk-forming species
● *Philodendron wendlandii*, the rosette-forming bird's nest philodendron

Left
On the wicker table is a magnificent specimen of Philodendron selloum *and beside it is* Philodendron erubescens *'Red Emerald'.*

Pilea, aluminium plant, artillery plant

The best-known variety: Pilea cadierei *'Minima'*

An indefatigable climber: Philodendron scandens

Family Araceae, arum family.
Origin Tropical South America.
Location Bright to semi-shady. Warm all year round, never under 18°C (64°F). Important: the soil temperature should never fall below the air temperature.
Watering, feeding Always keep slightly moist. Feed every 14 days from early spring to late summer.
Further culture Mist often, especially when new growth begins. Important: *do not use leaf polishes in sunny locations*.

Pot on young plants yearly, older ones as necessary, in good houseplant potting mixture.
Propagating From top or stem cuttings, by air layering or from seed.
Pests, diseases Scale, thrips if air too dry. Roots rot if kept wet and cold.
Warning Contains irritants to skin and mucous membranes.

Philodendron 'Lynette' has georgeous leaves.

These herbs are scarcely more than 20cm (8in) in height with attractive pointed or round-oval leaves, and are very closely related to the stinging nettle. They are especially good as ground cover for flower windows and for dish gardens. The important species and varieties are *Pilea cadierei* (the aluminium plant) with silver-green, slightly 'bumpy' leaf texture, *Pilea crassifolia* 'Moon Valley', with black-veined, crinkled leaves, and *Pilea spruceana*, with silver stripes on grey-green or bronze-green leaves. *Pilea nummulariifolia* is a pretty, small-leaved, hanging species. *Pilea microphylla* (syn. *Pilea muscosa*), known as the artillery plant, is rarely seen today. The name derives from the way in which pollen is expelled from the flower when it is touched.

Family Urticaceae, nettle family.
Origin Tropics.
Location Bright to semi-shady. Warm all year round. High humidity is desirable.
Watering, feeding Plants require more water when in active growth. From early spring to late summer feed weekly.
Further culture Provide for indirect humidity (see page 43). Pot on in spring as necessary and cut back. However, without artificial light in winter the plants soon lose their lower leaves and become unsightly. Provide for offspring by taking cuttings.
Propagating From top cuttings all year round. Pinch back young plants and keep bright and warm during winter.
Pests, diseases Spider mites from dry centrally heated air.

FOLIAGE PLANTS

Heimerliodendron brunonianum var.
Bird-catcher tree, para-para

Pisonia umbellifera 'Variegata'

The bird-catcher tree looks something like a coloured-leaved rubber plant, but it is related to the bougainvillea and the four-o'clock plant (*Mirabilis jalapa*). Of the 50 species, only *Heimerliodendron brunonianum var.* is cultivated as a houseplant. In its homeland it grows as a 6m (20ft) high tree or shrub with delicate, opposite leaves arranged almost in a whorl, up to 40cm (16in) wide. The variety commercially available is 'Variegata', which has green, white, and silver marbled foliage. In the home it grows to be about 1.2m (47in) high, provided you make sure that this South Seas beauty never has cold roots.

Family Nyctaginaceae, bougainvillea family.
Origin Australia, New Zealand, South Seas.
Location Very bright so that it does not lose its variegation, but no sun.

Warm air and soil temperature all year round, never under 18°C (64°F). The plant loves low-level heating or a heated underlay. The roots rot when cold.

Watering, feeding Always keep root ball moist. From early spring to late summer feed every 14 days.

Further culture Mist leaves often and wash occasionally so that they can 'breathe'. As necessary, pot on in spring in good houseplant potting mixture. Cut back branches that are too long to old wood.

Propagating From top or stem cuttings in heated propagator with bed temperature between 20 and 25°C (68 and 77°F).

Pests, diseases Scale and aphids from dry, heated air. Dry or soggy root ball can lead to brown leaf edges, yellowed leaves and leaf drop.

Plectranthus
Swedish begonia, Swedish ivy

Plectranthus coleoides 'Marginatus'

Since its introduction as a houseplant in the early nineteenth century *Plectranthus fruticosus* has been by far the most prominent representative of the genus. Our forebears successfully used the violet-flowered plant with the penetrating camphor odour to combat clothes moths. But today two other species have overtaken it in importance. They are, on the one hand, *Plectranthus oertendahlii*, with small, round, bright green, white-veined and red-margined leaves and, on the other, *Plectranthus coleoides* and its variety 'Marginatus', with white-bordered leaves. Both develop slightly trailing shoots and are lovely hanging plants or ground cover.

Family Labiatae, mint family.
Origin South Africa.
Location Bright to sunny and in a room with good air circulation. Can summer outside well. In winter keep no cooler than 15°C (59°F) but *Plectranthus fruticosus* will tolerate as low as 10°C (50°F).

Watering, feeding Keep moist. Water freely on hot summer days, in winter quite sparingly. From early spring to late summer feed every 14 days.

Further culture Potting on is not rewarding because older plants are often not particularly attractive.

Propagating In early spring or summer from top cuttings, which root easily. Pinch back often so that bushy plants will develop.

Pests, diseases Rare.

Pogonatherum paniceum (syn. *Saccharum paniceum*)
House bamboo

The house bamboo must be kept moist.

The house bamboo has the graceful elegance of evergreen culms in common with the bamboos and the subfamily of the sweet grasses. In fact, this plant, introduced as a houseplant around 1980, belongs with the grasses because it flowers each year, unlike the bamboos, which bloom very seldom. Its old name *Saccharum paniceum* points to close relationship with the sugar cane. The house bamboo has a bushy habit and forms thin, woody stalks, 15 to 60cm (6 to 23in) in length, with narrow leaves 7cm (3in) long.

Family Gramineae, grass family.

Origin South-east Asia.

Location Bright to full sun. Warm all year round, even in winter not under 15°C (59°F). Loves high humidity, but also tolerates dry air. May spend the summer outdoors in a semi-shady spot.

Watering, feeding Water well. *Never let the root ball dry out.* Dryness can be lethal. In summer can stand the pot in water. From early spring to late summer feed every two or three weeks.

Further culture Pot on as necessary in spring in good houseplant potting mixture.

Propagating By division or from root runners when potting on in spring.

Pests, diseases Rare.

Polyscias
Aralia

Polyscias balfouriana: *stately and slow growing*

The aralia's name indicates that it is a shade-loving plant (from Greek, *poly* =much, *scias* = shade). This preference is also indicated by the fernlike character of the leaves of many species. *Polyscias filicifolia*, *Polyscias guilfoylei* and *Polyscias paniculata* have pinnate or deeply incised foliage. To keep them successfully for any length of time, you need a warm, humid flower window. *Polyscias balfouriana* is more robust and therefore more widely available. It has round to kidney-shaped leaves with white margins, spots or veins.

Family Araliaceae, aralia family.

Origin Tropical Asia, Polynesia.

Location Bright to semi-shady. Never sunny. All year round at 20°C (68°F) and warmer; never under 18°C (64°F). The plant loves high humidity and grows best in tropical to sub-tropical areas.

Watering, feeding Keep slightly moist with softened, room-temperature water. *Avoid sogginess absolutely.* From early spring to late summer fertilize every two weeks.

Further culture Provide for indirect humidity (see page 43) and mist often. Pot on every two years in a slightly larger pot using good houseplant potting mixture.

Propagating From cuttings in a heated propagator. Difficult.

Pests, diseases Aphids, scale and spider mites from dry centrally heated air.

The aralia, especially the species *Polyscias fruticosa*, is wonderfully suited for training as an attractive indoor bonsai.

FOLIAGE PLANTS

Radermachera sinica
Emerald tree, Asian bell tree

The emerald tree hates cigarette smoke.

This exotic species is one of the more recent houseplants and has won a lot of admirers in a very short time; its genus name derives from the plant fancier Radermacher. With its doubly pinnate, glossy green leaves, it looks really very decorative. In its native habitat the plant grows as a small evergreen tree and blooms with large sulphur-yellow flower bells. In a roomy pot it will easily reach a height of 1.5m (59in). It will probably never set flowers under houseplant culture, but it is easy to care for as a foliage plant. There is only one thing it dislikes: cigarette smoke, to which it reacts by dropping its leaves. If you cannot find the plant under this name, it was formerly called *Stereospermum sinicum.*
Family Bignoniaceae, bignonia family.
Origin South-western China, Taiwan.

Location Bright and airy all year round. Keep warm in summer, in winter at 15°C (59°F).
Watering, feeding Keep only slightly moist. In winter water only enough to prevent the leaves from falling. From early spring to late summer feed every week.
Further culture Mist often. Pot on young plants every year, older ones as necessary in good houseplant potting mixture. There is still very little experience available to indicate whether it is suitable for water culture.
Propagating From seed or from cuttings.
Pests, diseases Aphids and scale as well as spider mites and thrips after overwintering too warm.
Professional tip Put the plant outside from early summer to early autumn in a sunny, wind-protected spot; it clearly does it good.

Rhoeo spathacea
Boat lily, Moses-in-the-basket

The white flowers develop in boat-like bracts.

Without flowers the *Rhoeo* might appear at first glance to be a dracaena or a bromeliad. But when the small flowers appear in early/mid summer, it is immediately clear that this is a strange, unique genus. For its inflorescences with delicate, white 'tongue flowers' are situated directly on the stem in pocket- or boat-shaped bracts deep down in the leaf axils. *Rhoeo spathacea* is the only species of the genus. The most widely available variety is 'Vittata', whose sword-shaped leaves, about 30cm (12in) long, have a green-and-white-striped upperside and glowing purplish-red undersides.
Family Commelinaceae, spiderwort family.
Origin Central America.
Location Bright but not sunny. Room temperature all year round, never below 18°C (64°F). The plant loves high humidity, especially during its growing season in summer.
Watering, feeding Only use softened, room-temperature water for watering. Always keep slightly moist in summer, drier in winter. Feed weekly from early spring to late summer.
Further culture Provide for indirect humidity (see page 43). Pot on as necessary in spring in good houseplant potting mixture.
Propagating From side shoots, top cuttings and seeds.
Pests, diseases Curling of leaves and brown leaf tips in air that is too dry. Crown rot from too much water, especially in winter.

Rhoicissus capensis
Cape grape, evergreen grape

The cape grape is a very vigorous vine.

The cape grape is a vigorous climber, for which you need a sturdy trellis. It develops heart-shaped, single, glossy green leaves up to 18cm (7in) wide, whose undersides are reddish and hairy. The soft, woody stems are hairy too. In Mediterranean regions you frequently see the plant used as a lush covering on balconies and pergolas. It tolerates cool temperatures as low as 5°C (40°F) and can be used for greenery in cool, frost-free conservatories.

Family Vitaceae, grape family.

Origin Cape Province, South Africa.

Location Bright to semi-shady, and airy. No sun. In summer not too warm, in winter best between 6 and 10°C (43 and 50°F). But room temperatures are certainly tolerated. The plant loves shady summer quarters.

Watering, feeding Keep reasonably moist, in winter water less. The cape grape has round tubers or storage organs, with which it can survive the dry spells in its native habitat. *Avoid sogginess because wet roots will kill it.* Feed every 14 days from late spring to late summer.

Further culture Remove dust from leaves often with careful washing. In spring pot on in larger containers in good houseplant potting mixture. Shoots can be cut back if overgrown.

Propagating From stem or top cuttings.

Pests, diseases Mildew and other fungal diseases from too much water. Spider mites.

Sansevieria trifasciata
Mother-in-law's tongue

Mother-in-law's tongue is almost indestructible.

This plant was already in cultivation in 1770 in Austria; today it still enjoys great popularity. Bowstring hemp is the name given to the genus on account of its hemplike fibres, from which West Africans traditionally made bowstrings. Of the 70 recognized species, *Sansevieria trifasciata* is the one most commonly cultivated as a houseplant. There are tall varieties with stiffly upright leaves almost 1 m (39in) long, like the yellow-margined 'Laurentii', and lower-growing rosette-like ones, such as the golden-yellow-striped 'Golden Hahnii' and the white-variegated 'Silver Hahnii'. All sansevierias have rhizomes, which become so tightly entwined with each other that eventually they burst their pots.

Family Liliaceae, lily family.

Origin Tropical West Africa.

Location Sunny to semi-shady. Room temperature all year round but can tolerate as low as 15°C (59°F).

Watering, feeding Water little. Always let the soil dry out. Only overwatering can kill the sansevieria. Tolerates hard water. Feed from early spring to late summer every two weeks with flower or cactus fertilizer.

Further culture Pot on when the roots/rhizomes break the container using a soil-based compost with the quantities of peat and loam reversed.

Propagating By removing mature side shoots and potting them individually. Or by leaf cuttings (but the bright yellow margin of a coloured-leaf parent is lost when using this method).

Pests, diseases Rare.

Professional tip It is not unusual for older plants to produce lime-green, fragrant flowers.

The mother of thousands is one of the prettiest hanging plants.

Saxifraga stolonifera
Mother of thousands, strawberry begonia, strawberry geranium

The threadlike runners, which can be up to 50cm (20in) long, have young plantlets (offsets) at the end. In summer panicles of tiny, white, star-shaped flowers appear.

Family Saxifragaceae, saxifrage family.

Origin China, Japan.

Location Bright to semi-shady, airy and cool; in winter frost-free, in mild regions with appropriate protection even winter-hardy. The coloured variety 'Tricolor' is suitable for indoor cultivation all year round and must be kept brighter and warmer (even in winter at least 15°C/ 59°F).

Watering, feeding Keep reasonably moist, in winter in a cool situation water less. From early spring to late summer fertilize weekly.

Further culture Pot on as necessary in summer in good houseplant potting mixture.

Propagating By offsets, which are often already rooted. Plant several of these young plants to a pot to produce lusher clumps.

Pests, diseases Aphids in too warm a location. Root rot from too much water.

Professional tip The runners of the mother of thousands can act as ground cover (for example, in a conservatory) as well as trailing attractively in a hanging container.

Saxifraga stolonifera means something like 'runner-growing stone-breaker'. In fact, the ability to create runners has made this little plant a popular hanging subject. Besides the pure species with roundish- to kidney-shaped hairy leaves (which are dark-green on the uppersides with grey-white veins and purplish on the undersides), 'Tricolor', a variety with green, white and pink leaves, is also commercially available.

Schefflera (syn. *Heptapleurum*)
Umbrella tree, parasol plant

Schefflera arboricola 'Capello' thrives on a moss pole.

The umbrella tree's exuberant growth indicates that it makes a shrub or tree in its natural habitat. Two species are commonly found as houseplants: *Schefflera actinophylla* and *Schefflera arboricola* (syn. *Heptapleurum arboricola*). The former's long-stemmed leaves, which look as though they were lacquered, can grow up to 30cm (12in) long. The latter's growth habit is daintier, its leaves are narrower and it is now also available in several variegated forms. The hand-like arrangement of the leaves is characteristic of both.

Family Araliaceae, aralia family.

Origin Taiwan, north-eastern Australia, New Guinea.

Location Bright to semi-shady. In summer airy; also possible to keep out of doors – temperatures of 10 to 18°C (50 to 64°F) in a place protected from sun and wind are ideal.

In winter, green species should be cool (12 to 16°C/54 to 61°F), variegated ones not under 18°C (64°F).

Watering, feeding Keep only slightly moist at all times, in a cool winter location water sparingly. From early spring to late summer feed every 14 days.

Further culture Mist often in a warm location. Pot on young plants yearly in good houseplant potting mixture, older ones only as necessary.

Propagating From seed at any time in warm conditions.

Pests, diseases Scale in too warm and dry a winter location. Leaf drop at temperatures under 12°C (54°F).

Warning Contains irritants to skin and mucous membranes.

Scirpus cernuus
Bulrush, sedge

A plant suitable for hanging baskets

The bulrush belongs to the sedge family and is an interesting plant to grow in a hanging container, where its pendulous foliage will be set off to best advantage. Moreover, grown as a hanging plant the tiny flowers formed on the tips of the narrow culms will also be seen to better effect. Smaller, wall-mounted containers are well suited to the compact growth habit of this plant. In its native habitat the 20cm- (8in-) long, rush-like culms are in full light and therefore grow more upright.

Family Cyperaceae, sedge family.
Origin Mediterranean, subtropics and tropics.
Location Bright to semi-shady, no sun. Room temperature all year round.
Watering, feeding Water well. *Never allow to dry out.* Like the umbrella sedge, the plants love standing in water. From early spring to late summer feed with a weak solution every two weeks.
Further culture In a heated living room provide indirect humidity (see page 43). Pot on as necessary using a well-drained potting mixture.
Propagating From seed or by division (when potting on in spring).
Pests, diseases Dry tips from too little humidity and soil too dry. Aphids. Caution: the bulrush finds many insecticides intolerable.
Professional tip Being lovers of moisture, these are fine plants for decorating the margins of a water feature. You could also grow bulrush in a pot with a face painted on it, so that the soft, green stems will resemble a head of hair.

Sedum
Stonecrop

Sedum morganianum *with its succulent leaves*

Of the some 600 succulent species, it is those from Mexico which have acquired most importance as houseplants. *Sedum morganianum* is an attractive hanging plant, whose 50cm (20in) or longer trailing stems are densely packed with grey-frosted, cylindrical leaves. Unfortunately, the little leaves drop easily at the slightest touch, as they do in all other species. One of the most exciting growth habits belongs to *Sedum rubrotinctum*, whose leaves turn red in sunlight. Very well known too is the winter-hardy *Sedum sieboldii*, which comes from Japan; its rounded blue-green leaves with a reddish border are not so dense as those of the first-named species. With the appropriate cool culture these plants become dormant in autumn and sprout anew in spring.

Family Crassulaceae, orpine family.
Origin Mexico; *Sedum sieboldii* from Japan.
Location Bright to full sun. Warm in summer, also in a protected spot outdoors. In winter cool (5 to 10°C/41 to 50°F). Warm room-temperatures will also be tolerated if need be in an extremely bright location, but this is not good for the plant in the long run. *Sedum sieboldii* should be cultivated as cool as possible.
Watering, feeding Water sparingly in summer, in winter only moisten the plants a little now and then. In summer give cactus fertilizer every four weeks. Too much fertilizer produces soft, less attractive growth.
Further culture Pot on in cactus soil as necessary.
Propagating From stem cuttings or single leaves. Allow cut surfaces to dry for a few days before planting.
Pests, diseases Rots in too damp places.

185

FOLIAGE PLANTS

Soleirolia soleirolii (syn. *Helxine soleirolii*)
Mind your own business, baby's tears, Irish moss

Mind your own business needs constant moisture.

From Corsica to Sardinia this small-leaved ground-cover plant is found in the cracks of walls, between paving stones and on rocks. Anyone who has a greenhouse knows how fast it can spread on the benches there, but mind your own business is a decorative plant for growing in pots and hanging baskets.
Family Urticaceae, nettle family.
Origin Mediterranean region.
Location Bright to semi-shady. Will accept room temperature in winter as well as cooler temperatures. The plants even tolerate cold down to the limits of frost.
Watering, feeding Keep reasonably moist, but in cool winter locations less water. *Do not allow plants to dry out*; they react to irregular watering with leaf spots and loss of leaves. Feed from early spring to late summer every four weeks.

Further culture Mist often. To retain freshness new plants should be propagated because older subjects deteriorate.
Propagating By division. Plant pieces in pots with good houseplant potting mixture. Or from cuttings, which root very easily. Always plant several in one pot.
Pests, diseases Rare.

Sparmannia africana
Wind flower, African hemp, indoor linden

With the increasing popularity of conservatories there is again a place indoors for decorative trees like the wind flower – a decidedly solitary plant. As they grow older they need a lot of space if they are to reveal their full beauty, and they also like a generous supply of light. The large velvety leaves of the tree-like shrub are linden-green, hairy on both sides and hang on long stems. In larger plants white umbels of flowers with yellow and red stamens develop from winter to spring. However, the flowering is very variable – some plants do not bloom at all.
Family Tiliaceae, linden family.
Origin South Africa.
Location Very bright, but not full sun, all year round. In a place with too little light, the plant develops unsightly long leaf stems. It prefers cool and airy conditions at all times.
Watering, feeding The large leaves indicate that the plant loses a lot of moisture through evaporation so keep the potting medium moist at all times, but *avoid sogginess.* In summer water more, in winter less, depending on temperature. From early spring to late summer fertilize weekly.
Further culture Pot on young plants yearly, older ones as necessary in good houseplant potting mixture. Bare stems on older plants can be cut back.
Propagating In spring or summer from firm cuttings placed in a heated propagator.

Pests, diseases Lack of leaves and leaf drop from deficiencies of light and nutrients and too warm a location. Spider mites and thrips from poor air circulation. Whitefly.
Professional tip The wind flower is likely to overbalance when grown in small pots. It is best to set the potted plant in a larger outer pot, filling the intervening space with moist peat. This will give the plant more support and in warmer areas will also provide increased humidity.

Small and delicate: the blooms of the wind flower

Opposite
The wind flower grows rapidly, and its large, velvety leaves lose a lot of water through evaporation.

FOLIAGE PLANTS

Syngonium
Goosefoot plant, arrowhead plant

Syngonium: *durable plants for poor light*

Green-white or green-silver variegated leaves are the distinguishing characteristic of the goosefoot plant, which can easily be confused with the philodendron (see page 178). As the mature plant produces its green arum flower with a spathe of glowing red, its leaves take on a purplish tinge. And they change in other ways too. Whereas juvenile plants generally have arrowhead-shaped, simple leaves, older specimens sometimes have compound or lobed ones. But in either case the goosefoot plant is an attractive, exotic climber, which thrives best on a trellis. The commonest variety by far is *Syngonium podophyllum* 'White Butterfly', of which coloured-leaved varieties are also available.
Family Araceae, arum family.
Origin Central America.
Location Coloured-leaved varieties bright; green-leaved species and varieties bright to semi-shady; no sun for either type. Warm all year round, even in winter not below 18°C (64°F). The plants need high humidity and warm soil.
Watering, feeding Keep slightly moist all year round with soft, room-temperature water. From early spring to late summer feed every 14 days.
Further culture Mist often and now and then dust leaves with a damp cloth. As necessary, pot on in good houseplant potting mixture.
Propagating From top or stem cuttings in heated propagator at soil temperature around 25°C (77°F).
Pests, diseases Scale from dry, heated air.
Warning Contains irritants to skin and mucous membranes.

Tetrastigma voinierianum
Chestnut vine, lizard plant

The chestnut vine is a very vigorous climber.

The chestnut vine is a climbing plant that grows in rampant spurts and can easily develop 5 to 6m (16 to 20ft) in a year so it needs a sturdy trellis. The plant develops naturally twining tendrils that enable it to climb any convenient support. It has three to five leaflets per serrated leaf – the uppersides are dark-green and the undersides have a brown tomentum – and the leaves are carried on sturdy stems. In pot culture it seldom flowers.
Family Vitaceae, grape family.
Origin Tonking, Vietnam.
Location Bright to shady. Room temperatures all year round, also cooler in winter, but never below 10°C (50°F). Tolerates dry, centrally heated air.
Watering, feeding Water freely in summer (especially during a growth spurt), in winter more sparingly, depending on temperature. Fertilize weekly during growth period.
Further culture Pot on every spring in good houseplant potting mixture; can be cut back as necessary at the same time.
Pests, diseases Rare.
Professional tip The young shoots are quite brittle so it is best to let them harden before tying them to a trellis. This is a truly rampant grower – you can almost see it grow.

Tolmiea menziesii
Piggyback plant

The piggyback plant likes airy, cool conditions.

The piggyback plant is a botanical curiosity: perfectly formed miniature plants develop at the base of the heart-shaped, hairy leaves, eventually growing into plants identical in appearance to the parent plant. Another of its popular names, youth-on-age, also reflects this curious development. The winter-hardy 25 to 30cm- (10 to 12in-) high plant is a splendid hanging specimen, and it is also ideal for ground cover.
Family Saxifragaceae, saxifrage family.
Origin Northern Pacific coast.
Location Bright to semi-shady and airy. In winter cool at 5 to 10°C (40 to 50°F). In summer outdoors in a shady spot.

Watering, feeding In summer water freely, in winter keep barely moist. From early spring to late summer feed every 14 days.
Further culture Young plants should be potted on as necessary. Mature plants can be maintained by regular feeding during spring and summer.
Propagating From plantlets (see photograph, below) which can be set in the soil with or without the mother leaf.
Pests, diseases Brown leaf margins from too warm a winter location.

A leaf with 'piggybacked' offsets

Tradescantia
Wandering Jew, spiderwort, tradescantia

Green-leaved Tradescantia fluminensis

This foliage plant can be recommended to anyone. It grows quickly, requires scarcely any care and is an especially fine hanging subject. Of the approximately 60 species, the following have shown themselves to be best for houseplant culture.
● *Tradescantia albiflora*, with tiny, pointed oval leaves, and its hybrid forms 'Rochford's Quicksilver' and 'Alba-vittata' with silver-striped leaves, 'Tricolor' with three-coloured leaves and 'Aureo-vittata' with yellowish leaves
● *Tradescantia blossfeldiana*, whose fleshy leaves have red undersides, and its variety 'Variegata', whose cream-green leaves are tinged with pink
● *Tradescantia fluminensis* 'Variegata', which looks very much like *Tradescantia albiflora*
Family Commelinaceae, spiderwort family.
Origin South America.

Location Coloured-leaved species and varieties bright, but not sunny; green ones bright but can tolerate semi-shade. Room temperatures all year round, also cooler in winter; will tolerate as low as 10°C (50°F) in a location that is not too damp.
Watering, feeding Always keep slightly moist. In a cool location in winter water less. From early spring to late summer feed every 14 days.
Further culture Mist often at room temperatures. Use a good-quality houseplant potting medium when potting on.
Propagating All year round from cuttings, which root easily in water or in seeding medium. Pinch back young plants and always put several in one pot.
Pests, diseases Aphids rarely.

Yucca

Yucca, Spanish bayonet

Long-standing favourites
as house- and tub plants
are *Yucca aloifolia*, with a
dense head of grey-green,
hard, sharp leaves, and
Yucca elephantipes, with a
tuberously thickened
stem at soil level and a
rather loose head of dark
green, sword-shaped
leaves, 50 to 100cm (20 to
39in) long.
Family Liliaceae, lily
family.
Origin Mexico, Central
and North America.
Location Very bright
and sunny. In summer
warm, preferably
outdoors on a sunny
terrace, in winter cool 5 to
10°C (40 to 50°F), but
room temperatures are
tolerated.
Watering, feeding In
summer out of doors,
water well, indoors
moderately; in winter less
depending on
temperature. Feed every
three weeks from early
spring to late summer.
Further culture Pot on
as necessary in good
houseplant potting
mixture.
Propagating From
stem pieces or side
shoots.
Pests, diseases Rare,
but very wet conditions
will cause leaf drop.
Professional tip In
spring you can shorten
yuccas that have grown
too tall by cutting them
back to the desired
height. Powder the cut
surfaces with charcoal.
Warning Watch out for
the leaf tips, particularly
of *Yucca aloifolia*; they
inflict nasty scratches.

Left
A Yucca aloifolia *with
a particularly luxuriant
leaf crown*

Xanthosoma lindenii
Indian kale, spoon flower

Zebrina
Zebrina

An unusual species, happiest in an enclosed window

The zebrina *also looks well in a hanging basket.*

Like its relative the alocasia (see page 143), the Indian kale is one of the most gorgeous foliage plants available. This tropical plant has wonderful, white-veined, arrowhead-shaped leaves (especially the variety 'Magnificum') and a tuber-like rhizome. Older plants develop the inflorescence common to the arum family with a white spathe. In temperate climates it thrives best in an enclosed plant window or warm, humid greenhouse.
Family Araceae, arum family.
Origin Colombia.
Location Semi-shady to shady all year round; humid and warm, over 20°C (68°F); in winter not below 18°C (64°F).
Watering, feeding Keep slightly moist from early spring to early autumn and feed every 14 days. In winter, during the rest period, water sparingly. Avoid sogginess.

Further culture Provide high (70%) humidity. Pot on every one or two years at the first signs of new growth, using a free-draining, peaty medium.
Propagating By division of the rhizome at potting on. Succeeds only at high soil temperatures.
Pests, diseases Spider mites when air is too dry. *Avoid cold, wet roots.* The rhizomes are very susceptible to rot and can be attacked by bacteria and fungus.
Warning *Xanthosoma lindenii* contains substances that can irritate skin and mucous membranes; but rare in cultivated plants.

The close relationship with tradescantia (see page 189) is obvious. All three recognized species also good for pot culture: *Zebrina pendula* is, as the botanical name indicates, an ideal hanging plant. But it is also very happy as ground cover in a roomy flower window or in a soil bed in a warm conservatory. The four-colour-striped 'Quadricolor' is the variety chiefly available. *Zebrina purpusii* is more vigorous in habit and has no stripes. Harder to find is the fluffy white hairy *Zebrina flocculosa*.
Family Commelinaceae, spiderwort family.
Origin Central America.
Location Bright, not sunny. In dark locations the beautiful colours pale. Room temperatures all year round, in winter not under 12°C (54°F). Tolerates dry air.

Watering, feeding Water moderately. From early spring to late summer feed every 14 days. Too much water and fertilizer have a bad effect on the leaf colours.
Further culture Pot on in spring in good houseplant potting mixture. But it is better to bring on new young plants every year.
Propagating From cuttings, which also root easily in water.
Pests, diseases Rare.

RARITIES

Foliage plants that are a little unusual: bizarre shapes with remarkable leaves, new arrivals from the Far East and old favourites rediscovered

Bambusa vulgaris 'Striata'
Common bamboo

Thick, yellow, green-striped culms, sawn-off and rooted, with lateral shoot or shoots bearing abundant foliage. The plant grows about 1m (39in) tall. Diameter of the culm 6 to 8cm (2 to 3in).
Family Gramineae, grasses.
Origin Tropics. **Location** In summer very bright and warm, from early summer onwards outdoors. Cooler in winter but not below 5°C (40°F). **Watering, feeding** Water well when warm, less at cool temperatures. Avoid sogginess. Feed every three weeks in summer. **Further culture** Pot on as necessary in good houseplant potting mixture. In too warm and dry a winter location, susceptible to spider mites.
Propagating Difficult. **Note** Also thrives in hydroculture.

Dionaea muscipula
Venus fly trap

Small, rosette-forming, insect-eating plants with leaves that snap shut when touched. The Venus fly trap is an interesting plant, but in the house it will thrive only in a cool, damp spot and even in winter it must have brightness.

Family Droseraceae, sundew family.
Origin South and North Carolina, USA. **Location** Bright, cool and airy. In summer out of doors, in winter at 5 to 10°C (40 to 50°F). **Watering, feeding** Stand the plant in a shallow dish of rainwater. **Further culture** Pot on as necessary, using a peaty compost. **Propagating** From leaf cuttings or division.

Dioscorea
Yam

These are climbing plants that grow from woody tubers that can be bumpy (*Testudinaria elephantipes*) or smooth (*Testudinaria sylvatica*). Leaves can be kidney- to heart-shaped and a fresh green in colour with interesting mottled variegation.

Bambusa vulgaris 'Striata': the variety name 'Striata' derives from the green-striped culm, which produces growth of varying lushness.

Family Dioscoreaceae, yam family.
Origin South Africa.
Location Bright to full sun, all year round not below 18°C (64°F).
Watering, feeding In summer the plant needs a rest period, during which it should be kept almost dry. In autumn/winter water moderately and feed with weak solution every four weeks. **Further culture** Pot on as necessary before new growth in late summer, using good-quality peaty compost. **Propagating** From seed or cuttings (difficult).

Senecio rowleyanus
String-of-beads

Creeping plant with thin, 1m (39in) long stems lined with pea-like, succulent leaves like beads. Blooms in spring with small cinnamon-scented flowers.
Family Compositae, composite family. **Origin** South-western Africa.
Location Full sun and warm, in winter also 10 to 12°C (50 to 54°F).
Watering, feeding Very little, in

winter keep almost dry; in summer feed once monthly. **Further culture** As necessary pot on in spring in a shallow pot, using cactus potting medium. **Propagating** Break off stems, dry for two days before planting in sandy seeding medium.
Note Similar in growth and appearance are *Senecio citriformis*, *Senecio herreanus* and *Senecio radicans*, all unusual hanging plants.

Nicodemia diversifolia
Indoor oak

Undemanding evergreen plant with oval, dark green leaves with indented margins and insignificant yellowish-green flowers, which seldom appear in houseplant culture.

Family Loganiaceae.
Origin Madagascar. **Location** Bright, semi-shady. The plant tolerates temperatures between 5 and 22°C (40 and 72°F). **Watering, feeding** Water well, in winter and in a cooler location somewhat less. From early spring to mid autumn fertilize weekly. **Further culture** Plants can be trimmed to shape as found necessary. Pot on, again as necessary, using good houseplant potting mixture. **Propagating** From half-woody cuttings.

Ophiopogon jaburan
Snakebeard, white lily-turf

Evergreen, grass-like plant with green or golden-yellow-striped leaves ('Variegatus') and white to violet flowers. Very robust.
Family Liliaceae, lily family.
Origin Japan. **Location** Bright. Plant tolerates temperatures between 12 and 18°C (54 and 64°F). Even cooler in winter. **Watering, feeding** Keep moist all year round, water less in winter in a cool location.

Mist in dry, heated air. From early spring to late summer feed every 14 days. **Further culture** Pot on as necessary in spring, using good houseplant potting mixture.
Propagating By division in spring.

Strobilanthe dyerianus
Persian shield

Herbaceous shrub with elliptical-lanceolate leaves. The dark green background of the uppersides glows with a metallic blue-silver-violet variegation and the undersides are red.
Family Acanthaceae, acanthus family. **Origin** Burma.
Location Bright to semi-shady all year round, humid and warm, in winter not below 16°C (61°F). Popular in tropical and sub-tropical frost-free

zones. The plants tolerate neither sunlight nor centrally heated air. **Watering, feeding** Keep moderately moist with soft water. In summer feed with a weak solution every 14 days. **Further culture/ Propagating** Since the Persian shield quickly becomes leggy and only the juvenile plants are beautifully coloured, take cuttings in spring; these root quickly in a heated propagator. Trim the young plants two or three times so they become bushy.

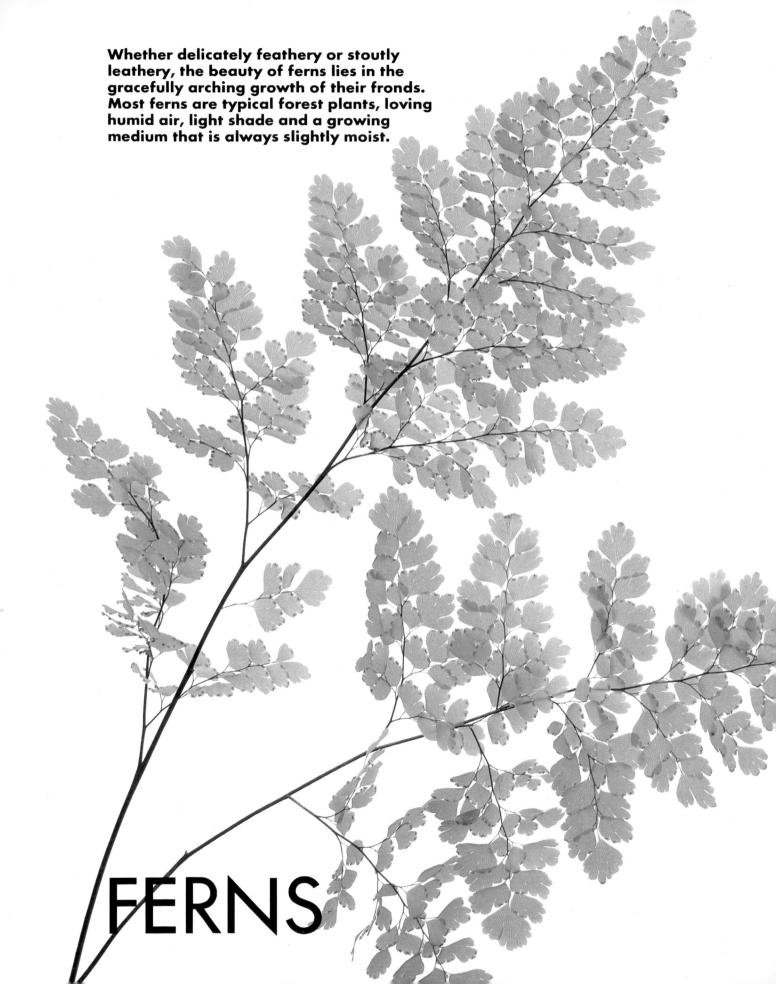

Whether delicately feathery or stoutly leathery, the beauty of ferns lies in the gracefully arching growth of their fronds. Most ferns are typical forest plants, loving humid air, light shade and a growing medium that is always slightly moist.

FERNS

'At once a dense parasol and a green tent roof, they spread their mighty fan of fronds and show the traveller who takes his midday rest beneath them the eternal blue of heaven through the most beautiful lace curtain that ever Nature wove or knitted.' Thus wrote a botanist about the ferns of the rain forest over a hundred years ago.

Exotic ferns were immensely appealing to our nineteenth-century forefathers, being far and away the first choice as plant ornaments for salons and hotel lobbies. The English of the Victorian era loved them so much that they artfully worked cast iron and glass to create 'ferneries', in which humidity and soil moistness were almost constant.

Ferns are still today, despite their limited lifespan, among the most popular of the foliage plants. They have been separated from the other 'green' plants in this book and given their own chapter for two reasons.
1. They do not, like the former two categories of houseplants, belong to the highly developed groups of plants which flower.
2. They can make a very individual contribution to home interiors but theirs is a more subtle appeal that needs careful handling.

The houseplant ferns introduced on the following pages all belong to the class of Filicopsida. Not included is the Japanese fern (*Cycas*), also called the sago palm, which belongs in another botanical category and is therefore found with the foliage plants (see page 157).

Primitive plant forms

The ferns on our windowsills date back to the time of the dinosaurs. They are among the oldest plants in existence and have undergone very few changes since they first appeared.

Today botanists number some 200 species and 9000 varieties in the division of fern plants (Pteridophyta), and it is a cosmopolitan group distributed all over the world. Ferns live on the ground in the light or deep shade of temperate-zone or tropical forests, perch high on the forked branches of primeval giant trees and colonize sunny cliffs or water surfaces. The floating fern (*Salvinia*) is just one extraordinary example. It clothes lakes in southern Africa so densely that it is possible to walk on the water and even shrubs can be supported by the 'raft' it creates.

Ferns do not flower. Unlike the highly developed flowering plants, ferns reproduce 'primitively', like fungi, through spores. These are situated on the undersides of mature leaves and, depending on the species, are arranged like tiny dots in loose little clumps or precise lines. Mature spore dust is powder-fine and can be distributed on the wind. On a warm, damp surface (earth, for example) this dust can develop a *prothallium* or small, flat, independent disc of tissue which bears both male and female reproductive organs. From the

This bird's nest fern is growing epiphytically in its natural tropical setting.

fusion of these organs young fern plants are created.

The dominant characteristic of most species is the more or less finely pinnate fronds. They can be light or dark green, striped with silver-grey or tinged with red, leathery and robust or extremely delicate. Also characteristic are the pretty curled 'snail' forms from which new fronds uncoil. In this way the fern protects its tender leaf tips – the most vulnerable part of the plant – from being eaten by animals.

Appropriate culture

Most of our house ferns are forest dwellers from warmer regions. This means that they do best in a loose, nutrient-rich, moisture-retaining potting medium, and that they tolerate neither blazing sunlight nor cold, especially cold roots. Through their lush and numerous fronds, ferns lose a great deal of water by evaporation so the medium should be kept moist at all times, using soft and room-temperature water.

Almost all species, but especially the tender-leaved ones, come from habitats where high humidity prevails: the main reason for the failure of houseplant ferns is heated, dry rooms. Unfortunately, many ferns do not like to be misted so that you must provide for indirect humidity (see page 43). However, there are a few species that tolerate drier air, such as the holly fern and other hard-leaved species, the staghorn fern, which protects its leaves from too much evaporation by a waxy coating, and the cliff brake, which as a xerophyte thrives in very dry locations.

Ideal sites for the indoor fern are the bathroom, a humid flower window or a greenhouse. Also suitable are terrariums and growing cabinets.

Epiphytic ferns grown as houseplants can be bound to a fibrous piece of bark to make them feel at home.

FERNS

Adiantum
Maidenhair fern

The delicate foliage is supported on wiry stems.

Most of the some 200 *Adiantum* species tolerate neither dry air nor draughts. There are only a few species commercially available. The best known are *Adiantum raddianum*, with its varieties 'Decorum', 'Fragrantissum' and 'Fritz Lüth', and *Adiantum tenerum*, the variety 'Scuteum Roseum' having red-tinged leaves. Characteristic for the maidenhair ferns are the thin, almost wiry, dark brown to black stems.
Family Polypodiaceae, polypody family.
Origin Tropics, especially the Americas.
Location Semi-shady. No sun. Air and bed temperatures above 20°C (68°F) all year. The plant needs high humidity and therefore lives longest in a terrarium, fernery or enclosed flower window.
Watering, feeding Keep root ball moist all year round with soft, room-temperature water. It must never dry out or withered leaves and fronds will result. From early spring to late summer feed every two weeks with weak solution.
Further culture Provide for indirect humidity (see page 43). Mist often, especially when using central heating. Pot on larger plants in spring as necessary, using good houseplant potting mixture.
Propagating By spores at bed temperatures between 24 and 26°C (75 and 79°F). Place a seed tray of damp peat under the fronds. Also by division.
Pests, diseases Hot, dry conditions will cause fronds to shrivel. Growth disturbances from cold roots and alkaline water.

Arachniodes
Arachniodes

Arachniodes aristata tolerates heated air.

This bushy fern has leathery leaves composed of two to three leaflets. The fronds can reach lengths of 70cm (27in). The plant grows epiphytically and in its native habitat forms great colonies where it settles on the trunks of tree ferns. The root stock is thick, creeping and densely covered with long, red-brown scales. *Arachniodes adiantiformis* and *Arachniodes aristata*, along with its variety 'Variegatum', are the best-known species of the genus. They manage very well with central heating because of their leathery leaves.
Family Polypodiaceae, polypody family.
Origin South Africa, Central and South America, Australia, Polynesia, New Zealand.
Location Bright to semi-shady, no sun. The plant loves high humidity. Room temperatures all year round possible, also somewhat cooler in winter; almost no growth below 12°C (54°F), however. Can take fresh air outdoors in summer.
Watering, feeding Keep moist with soft, room-temperature water. In winter in a cool location reduce water; water somewhat more in a warm location. From early spring to late summer feed weekly with a weak solution.
Further culture Mist often in warm winter quarters. Pot on as necessary in good houseplant potting mixture.
Propagating By division and by sowing of spores in a heated propagator at 22 to 24°C (72 to 75°F). Also by runners and rhizome division.
Pests, diseases Soft stems from light deficiency. Spider mites and scale from too warm, dry winter location with poor air circulation.
Note Sensitive to many insecticides.

Asplenium nidus
Bird's nest fern, nest fern

The bird's nest fern forms a rosette of greenery.

This tropical-forest fern, which in its natural habitat develops leaves almost 1m (39in) long, does best in a warm, humid environment, but it also manages astonishingly well with dry, centrally heated air, especially the variety *Asplenium nidus* 'Fimbriatur'. The plant lives on trees like a bromeliad, collecting humus and rainwater in its leaf-rosette 'nest'. Especially attractive are the dark central veins of the leaves. This fern is closely related to the wall rue (*Asplenium ruta-muraria*), a delicate fern that grows in the cracks of old walls.

Family Polypodiaceae, polypody family.

Origin Tropical Asia, Africa and Australia.

Location Semi-shady. All year round room temperatures of 20°C (68°F) and more; *never below 16°C (61°F).* A warm, humid location suits it best. Warm roots are important so place a heating mat underneath containers on cold windowsills.

Watering, feeding Water regularly with softened water. In spring and summer feed once weekly with a weak solution.

Further culture In heated areas mist often with soft water or provide for indirect humidity (see page 43). Pot on in summer every two years using good houseplant potting mixture.

Propagating By spores in a warm propagator.

Pests, diseases Scale. Brown leaf margins from too dry air or too low temperatures. Failure to grow because of cold roots. Bacterial leaf disease.

Professional tip Do not use leaf-polish sprays. The leaves can be cleaned with a damp sponge or cloth.

Blechnum
Blechnum

Blechnum gibbum *develops a 1m- (39in-) high trunk.*

These ferns from tropical and subtropical regions are very decorative with their sturdy rhizomes and feathery, dark green fronds, sometimes even with split leaflets. The best-known species, *Blechnum gibbum*, thrives satisfactorily either in rooms or in a conservatory. With increasing age, this fern develops a trunk 1m (39in) high, which frequently grows at an angle and thus looks very strange. *Blechnum brasiliense*, whose young fronds are brownish red, and *Blechnum moorei* need more warmth and humid air.

Family Polypodiaceae, polypody family.

Origin South America, New Caledonia.

Location Bright to semi-shady. In summer warm, *in winter never below 18°C (64°F).* Tolerates neither cold roots nor draughts.

Watering, feeding Use softened, room-temperature water. In summer keep moist, in winter water somewhat less. Never allow root ball to dry out. From mid spring to late summer feed every two weeks with weak solution.

Further culture *Do not mist* but provide for indirect humidity (see page 43). Pot on as necessary in spring in a good houseplant potting mixture.

Propagating From spores in heated propagator at bed temperatures between 20 and 25°C (68 and 77°F) or by division.

Pests, diseases Scale from poor air circulation, spider mites from dry air.

Professional tip In time these ferns develop into superb plants that are ideally suited for tub culture.

The potting medium for blechnum should be warm, airy and both water-permeable and water-retentive.

FERNS

Cyrtomium falcatum
Holly fern

The holly fern's leaves have a natural dark gloss.

The holly fern is a sturdy, undemanding fern for cool areas and conservatories that also thrives in quite shady locations indoors. Its finely serrated, leathery-hard leaves shine as if polished, and it can look particularly attractive when grouped with variegated-leaved plants. The most frequently cultivated variety is 'Rochfordianum', which has deeply incised, finely serrated leaflets. Rare, but especially unusual, is the *Cyrtomium caryotideum*, whose fronds look very like the fishtail palm (*Caryota mitis*) (see page 207).

Family Polypodiaceae, polypody family.
Origin Eastern Asia, India, South Africa.
Location Bright to shady, cool and airy. In winter if possible no warmer than 10 to 14°C (50 to 57°F). Can spend summer out of doors in a shady, airy place.

Watering, feeding Use softened, room-temperature water. From mid spring to late summer, depending on temperature, water moderately to freely (completely immersing the plant occasionally) and feed every four weeks. In winter at lower temperatures keep only slightly moist.
Further culture Mist often and pot on as necessary in spring in good houseplant potting mixture.
Propagating By division or from spores. Place a tray with damp peat under the fronds. Ripe spores will fall and germinate.
Pests, diseases Rare. In a location that is too warm and dry, scale.

Davallia
Rabbit's foot fern, hare's foot fern

Davallia mariesii, with hairy rhizomes

Of the some 40 *Davallia* species, those most often seen are *Davallia bullata*, *Davallia canariensis* and *Davallia mariesii*. All have bright green, finely pinnate fronds reminiscent of chervil and do not become very large. This epiphytic fern thrives best when it is bound to a trunk or a piece of bark and can enjoy the high humidity of a terrarium or an enclosed flower window. *Davallia canariensis* becomes a remarkable plant when grown in a hanging container made of terracotta because the rabbit's foot rhizomes can be seen growing over the edge of the pot. Each year new growth appears and the rhizomes can eventually completely encompass the container. Note: this fascinating development does not occur in a plastic pot.

Family Polypodiaceae, polypody family.
Origin Canary Islands, tropical Asia.
Location Bright, no sun. Warm all year, *never under 18°C (64°F)*. The plant needs high humidity.
Watering, feeding Keep moist with soft, room-temperature water. The rhizomes should not dry out. In summer feed with weak solution every two weeks.
Further culture Mist often. For culture in a shallow pot use coarse epiphyte potting mixture.
Propagating By sowing spores or from rhizome pieces which grow in a moist, peaty mixture in close, warm air.
Pests, diseases Scale in dry, centrally heated air.

Didymochlaena trunculata
Cloak fern

This fern is easy to grow but hates heated air.

Didymochlaena trunculata, which freely translated means 'shortened cloak', is found in all the tropical regions of the world and has a different name in every country. In its natural habitat it develops a 50cm (20in) high stem with a cluster of fronds a good 1m (39in) long. The leathery-seeming oval, doubly pinnate leaves are situated on brownish red stems. This ground-dwelling fern is relatively easy to cultivate but, like most ferns, it does not tolerate dry heated air.
Family Polypodiaceae, polypody family.
Origin Tropics.
Location Bright to semi-shady all year round. Keep warm from the beginning of new growth and over the summer, in winter keep cool 16 to 18°C (61 to 64°F). A north window is ideal.

Watering, feeding Use only softened, room-temperature water for watering and misting. Keep slightly moist the whole year round. With dryness of root ball and air, the fronds wither and the leaflets fall off. From early spring to late summer feed with weak solution every 14 days.
Further culture Mist often. Pot on in spring as necessary using a good houseplant potting mixture.
Propagating From spores or by division.
Pests, diseases Scale from too warm and dry a location.

Microlepia stringosa
Microlepia

In time, microlepia develops very long fronds.

Of the 45 known species that occur in tropical and subtropical regions, *Microlepia stringosa* has become the best-known houseplant. It has soft, light green, sparsely hairy fronds and, like *Davallia* (see page 198), creeping, hairy rhizomes. The fronds develop very lushly and so, of course, lose a lot of water through evaporation. This fern, which was first described a hundred years ago by the English botanist Thomas Moore, needs a lot of space to uncoil its 1m- (39in-) long fronds undisturbed.
Family Polypodiaceae, polypody family.
Origin Tropics and subtropics.
Location Very bright all year round, but *never sunny*. In spring and summer around 20°C (68°F), in autumn and winter not under 16°C (61°F). The plant loves high humidity.
Watering, feeding Use only soft, room-temperature water. Keep root ball quite moist, otherwise the fronds wilt. In winter in cooler temperatures water less. From late spring to late summer feed every four weeks with a weak solution.
Further culture Provide for indirect humidity (see page 43) and mist often. Divide each spring when growth is vigorous and pot on in good houseplant potting mixture.
Propagating By sowing of spores at bed temperature of 20°C (68°F). Or by division when potting on. Each portion of rhizome must show an active growing point from which the new fronds can develop.
Pests, diseases Troublefree if hot, dry conditions are avoided.

Nephrolepsis exaltata
Sword fern, fishbone fern

Pellaea
Cliff brake

Pellaeas are charming in hanging baskets or pots.

This sword fern cultivar has wavy, pinnate fronds.

The best known of the 30 species in this genus, countless large and dwarf cultivars with curly, wavy or multiple pinnate fronds are commercially available. Some form long runners that can be used for propagating.
Family Polypodiaceae, polypody family.
Origin Tropical regions worldwide.
Location Bright to semi-shady, warm and damp all year, in winter not under 18°C (64°F). In higher humidity even tolerates some sun.
Watering, feeding During the main growing season from early spring to late summer provide with plenty of room-temperature water and feed weekly with weak solution. From mid autumn water more sparingly but *avoid very dry conditions.*
Further culture Pot young plants as they become established, using a peaty potting medium. Older plants can usually be sustained by regular feeding while in active growth.
Propagating Mainly by runners (cut off in summer and plant), more rarely by spores.
Important: soil temperature must be over 20°C (68°F).
Pests, diseases Scale and mealy bugs.
Note The plant is sensitive to many insecticides.

One of the cliff brakes (*Pellaea rotundifolia*) has the appropriate common name 'button fern' because of its round leaves with a leathery sheen. In fact, the appearance of this *Pellaea* species is utterly untypical of ferns. It lacks the characteristic fern fronds and also lives differently from its forest relatives, being, in contrast to most ferns, not adapted to dampness but preferring to grow in relatively dry locations. There it forms trailing stems up to 20cm (8in) long, which look wonderful in a hanging basket. But there are also other species on the market that do not belie their fern origins: *Pelleae viridis* from South Africa and Madagascar with 50cm- (20in-) long green fronds, *Pellaea falcata* from southern Asia, Australia and New Zealand and *Pellaea atropurpurea* from North America, an almost winter-hardy rock fern with 25cm- (10in-) long red-brown fronds.
Family Polypodiaceae, polypody family.
Origin New Zealand, Australia, Norfolk Island, North America, Asia, Africa, Madagascar.
Location Bright but not full sun. Room temperature all year round. Keep *Pellaea rotundifolia* and *Pellaea atropurpurea* in winter around 15°C (59°F).
Watering, feeding Water only moderately all year round. *Avoid sogginess at all costs* because it kills the plant. From early spring to late summer feed every two weeks.
Further culture *Don't mist.* Pot on newly acquired or young plants every spring in shallow pots. Provide for good drainage.
Propagating From spores, which only appear on the undersides of leaves of older plants, and by division.
Pests, diseases Scale.

Cyclamen

Cyclamen persicum

Its delicate, shimmering flowers held elegantly above a mound of heart-shaped, patterned leaves, the cyclamen makes a pleasing display through the winter.

Secrets of Success

GENERAL CARE

This is a relatively easy plant to care for, but it does need careful watering and should be in a coolish position.

Potting: Repot in August after it has rested over the summer. Put it in a slightly larger pot and use fresh peat moss or a peat-based potting mixture.

WATERING

They enjoy high humidity. Mist and stand on a bed of pebbles. Water at the edge of the pot. Avoid wetting the tuber. You could also water by standing the pot in a saucer filled with tepid water for 20 minutes.

Feeding: Feed with diluted liquid plant fertilizer once a week during the growing period.

CONDITIONS

Light: Cyclamen need to be in a cool place with a little shade. Do not ever put them in fierce sunlight. Winter sunlight will not harm them.

Temperature: While flowering and growing keep it at a temperature between 10°–15°C (50°–60°F). While resting it will cope with normal summer temperatures out of doors.

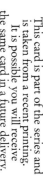

This card is part of the series and is taken from a recent printing. It is possible you will receive the same card in a future delivery.

Cyclamen leaves are very attractive. Keep them in good condition by cleaning them with a soft brush. Don't use proprietary brands of leaf cleaner or sprays on cyclamen leaves.

Above and right: *A white hybrid and a red variety with white edges. Some varieties have ruffled petal edges. Flower colours range from all the shades of red, through mixed colours to shiny white.*

Buying Tips

When to buy

Buy your plants from September to December so that you get the most from the long flowering period.

What to look for

Buy plants with fresh green, undamaged leaves. Check there are a lot of buds. Don't buy them if they are standing outside — they are often chilled.

Lifespan

You can save the tuber and grow it on from year to year although many people regard them as short-term gift plants.

Phlebodium aureum
Rabbit's foot fern, golden polypodium

In a bright location the fronds turn blue.

Two features distinguish this tropical fern: its very hairy rhizomatous parts, which look like rabbit's feet, and its bluish-green leaves with golden-yellow spore clusters on the undersides. The rabbit's foot fern, which can grow quite large, comes from a warm, humid region and with its tough leaves, which lose little water through evaporation, can handle dry centrally heated air astonishingly well. On the market are several varieties, including 'Areolatum' with broad wavy leaves, the most vigorously growing variety 'Mandaianum' with typical fern fronds, and the somewhat less vigorous 'Glaucum'.

Family Polypodiaceae, polypody family.
Origin South America.
Location For an intense blue colour, bright; semi-shade is also tolerated, but no blazing sun. Warm all year round, in winter cooler also but not under 12 to 16°C (54 to 61°F). Thrives best in warm, humid flower window.

Watering, feeding Keep root ball slightly moist at all times and feed every 14 days during the growing season with weak solution.

Further culture Mist often in heated room or provide for indirect humidity (see page 43). Pot on every spring in good houseplant potting mixture.

Propagating By spores or division of rhizomes.

Pests, diseases Occur very seldom.

Professional tip Be careful when potting on to leave the rhizomes sticking out of the soil, as they are a major feature of the plant.

Phyllitis scolopendrium
Hart's tongue fern

Phyllitis scolopendrium 'Crispum'

This winter-hardy fern, which is native to Europe, used to be a popular houseplant, and there were countless variations of it, especially in England. Today, when more and more people are installing unheated conservatories, the hart's tongue fern is coming into fashion again as an attractive foliage plant for cool, shady locations. But it thrives everywhere, with the exception of tropical heat and blazing sunshine. On the market are varieties with attractively long, wavy leaves like 'Cristata' or 'Crispum' or some with almost parsley-like leaves such as 'Ramosa Marginata' or 'Ramosa Cristata'.

Family Polypodiaceae, polypody family.
Origin Europe, Anatolia, North Africa, USA, Japan.
Location Semi-shady to shady all year round; a north window is ideal. In summer 15 to 18°C (59 to 64°F), in winter around 10°C (50°F). The plant loves an outdoor stay from late spring to early autumn.

Watering, feeding Keep moist but not wet. During the growing season from late spring to early autumn feed with weak solution every 14 days.

Further culture Needs high humidity. Mist all over often. Pot on in spring as necessary in good houseplant potting mixture.

Propagating The species by spores, the varieties by division or by rooting of stems with a little piece of rhizome.

Pests, diseases Scale and thrips in too warm and dry a location.

Professional tip You may not find the hart's tongue fern locally, but you can get the species and one or two varieties in any good plant nursery.

Platycerium
Staghorn fern

The leaves can grow over 1m (39in) long.

The staghorn fern is a remarkable looking plant that is clearly different from other ferns. Characteristic are the antler-like branching leaves, often 1m (39in) long, which develop brown-black, flat spore deposits on their undersides at particular points, according to the species. This epiphytic fern is also furnished with other, sterile leaves that serve to anchor it. These older, upright anchor leaves form a roughly cup-shaped receptacle for rainwater, but also for the falling leaves and rotting plant parts

A rarity: Platycerium angolense

from which the fern gains its nutrients. The ideal place for the staghorn fern indoors is an enclosed flower window, where it can be bound to a sturdy epiphyte support or placed in a lattice-work basket or a hanging pot. They are also excellent plants for attaching to sections of bark or timber which are used to decorate walls. Use a moisture-retaining material when affixing plant roots to chosen anchorage.

The genus *Platycerium* consists of some 17 species. Besides *Platycerium bifurcatum*, the best-known species and the easiest to look after, which was introduced to England in 1808, one encounters the much larger *Platycerium*

grande, which comes from the Philippine island of Luzon. Its sterile leaves are lighter green, slightly wavy and incised at the tips. The fertile leaves grow to be more than 1m (39in) long and when juvenile are tremendously hairy. Rarely seen in the market is the African species *Platycerium angolense* with simple fertile leaves.

Family Polypodiaceae, polypody family.
Origin Australia, Peru, Madagascar, New Guinea.
Location Bright to semi-shady, not sunny. Room temperatures all year, in winter even cooler (but never below 16°C (61°F).
Watering, feeding Water into the 'cup' using soft, room-temperature water or soak the fern once a week for 30 minutes. From mid spring to late summer add fertilizer to the water or use a plant-feed tablet pressed into the potting medium. However, make

sure you use a weak fertilizer.
Further culture Provide for high humidity. Do not use water to wipe the leaves or you will remove the pretty hairy covering. Potting on is not necessary for specimens on epiphyte supports. Potted plants should be placed in a peaty medium that is free draining.
Propagating From spores (difficult for the non-professional) or small plantlets that can be carefully removed and put into clay (not plastic) pots filled with a peaty mix.
Pests, diseases Scale on the undersides of fronds from dry, centrally heated air. Scratch off carefully or dot with spirit-soap solution (see recipe, page 52) and then wash off with lukewarm water.
Note *Platycerium* is sensitive to many insecticides.

Pteris
Brake, dish fern, table fern

Pteris ensiformis *'Evergemiensis' (left) and* Pteris cretica *'Albolineata'*

The genus *Pteris*, represented by about 280 species in the tropics and subtropics, offers a rich selection of coloured-leaved or green, small or vigorous species and varieties. Its genus name derives from the Greek word *pteron* = wing.

Characteristic of the brakes are the bush-like fronds, which arise from short, underground rhizomes. They grow upright at first and then bend, pointing their tips downwards. Some species have two kinds of fronds: short sterile ones and longer fertile ones, on which the spores are situated along the edges of the undersides of the leaves. Others have either fertile or sterile fronds. It is simple enough to distinguish between the two types of fronds. Fertile fronds curl the edges of their leaflets under to protect the spores so they appear to be smooth-margined. If you can see the leaf

serrations clearly, the frond is a sterile one.

The best-known brake or dish fern is the robust *Pteris cretica* and its green and variegated cultivars, such as 'Albo Lineata', the parsley-like 'Rowen' or 'Wimsettii'. *Pteris cretica* has either fertile or sterile fronds on 15cm-(6in-) long black stems. Needing more warmth is *Pteris ensiformis*, a charming small fern for the bottle garden, growing cabinet or fernery. This species has fertile and sterile fronds. Commercially available are varieties like the white-bordered 'Evergemensis', which was developed in Belgium in 1956, or 'Victoriae', which has been around since about 1890. Anyone with a climate-controlled flower window can also grow the especially beautiful *Pteris quadriaurita* as well as its cultivar 'Argyraea'. In roomy conservatories the brilliant green *Pteris*

tremula from New Zealand and Australia makes a very good show. It grows to be at least 1m (39in) tall.

All are terrestrial ferns and must be kept in pots and not bound to boards.

Family Polypodiaceae, polypody family.

Origin Tropical and subtropical regions.

Location Semi-shady to shady. Delicate species like *Pteris quadriaurita* and *Pteris ensiformis* all year round at 20°C (68°F); *Pteris cretica* can tolerate cooler winters – variegated cultivars at 16 to 18°C (61 to 64°F), green-leaved at 12°C (54°F). High humidity is important.

Watering, feeding Water only with softened, room-temperature water. In summer keep moderately moist, in winter at lower temperatures water somewhat less. From mid spring to late summer feed with weak solution every 14 days.

Further culture Mist now and then. In spring pot on as necessary in good houseplant potting mixture. *Pteris does not tolerate draughts.*

Propagating By division in spring when potting on or by spores, which form so abundantly that young plants often spring up in the pots of neighbouring pot plants. Prick out young plants into very small pots.

Pests, diseases Scale and aphids in too dry a location.

Professional tip Cut away the unsightly older fronds. The plant regenerates itself through the development of young fronds.

PALMS

All palms make a strong, graphic statement. Some grow to the ceiling, and over the years they can, like a beautiful piece of furniture or a painting, become the focus of an interior design.

Palms are the favourite plants of many interior decorators and are often used to soften the supercold glitter of modern entrance halls of glass and steel. With the exception of *Washingtonia*, the lady palm and palmetto, all the palms described in this section are species that should be kept warm indoors all year round.

Types of palms

More than 3000 species and over 200 genera belong to the palm family. Palms grow in shady tropical rain forests and in the intense light on mountain massifs 3000m (10,000ft) high. They are also to be found on savannahs, steppes, deserts and along seashores, and almost all are sensitive to frost. Palms are among the younger plants in the history of plant evolution. Proof of this comes from the fact that they are monoecious, that is they bear both male and female organs, and that they have long, parallel leaf veins.

Palms are divided into two distinct categories: the feather-leaved (plumose) palms and the fan-leaved (palmate) palms.
● Feather-leaved palms, like the parlour palm (see page 207), develop the conventional, branch-like palm frond.
● Fan-leaved palms, like the *Washingtonia* (see page 211), have fronds which are almost circular. However, a palm's true leaves sometimes do not appear until the plant reaches maturity. In almost all palms, feather leaves or fans are

The coconut, a giant seed, can float for thousands of miles before finally germinating on a new shore.

Only in a natural setting out of doors do palms' spadix-like inflorescences develop the vibrantly coloured fruits which contain seeds.

borne at the end of an unbranching trunk. With the exception of the parlour palm, they do not bloom indoors, for in the confined space of their pot they never progress beyond the juvenile stage.

The right culture

The best location for a palm is a very bright situation, but never a sunny one. Species with hard, tough foliage tolerate dry air better than those with soft, filigree-fine leaflets. Fan palms offer large surfaces for evaporation and must be provided with water more frequently than feather-leaved species. Dry, centrally heated air and a dry root ball are the chief causes of brown tips, frequent on palms.

When watering, the 'heart' of the palm must be avoided. This bulb-like thickened stem contains the vegetative cone from which the new leaves develop. When it rots, the palm is done for. Standing water or cold roots can be just as lethal.

In their homelands palms grow in inorganic soil – on sand, limestone, serpentine rock rich in magnesium and silicic acid – and in the tropical red soil type that is enriched with clay and iron. Inorganic fertilizers or horse-tail broth, which is rich in silicic acid (see recipe, page 52), does them good, in my experience. It is important when potting on not to use containers that are excessively large in relation to plant size and it is equally important to use a good-quality, properly prepared potting medium.

PALMS

Archontophoenix cunninghamiana
Piccabeen palm

This species dislikes centrally heated air.

This palm species, in which the feathery fronds broaden with increasing age, is frequently sold under its older genus names of *Seaforthia* or *Ptychosperma*. Moreover, its current name is easy to confuse with *Acanthophoenix*, a less well-known genus native to Mauritius. *Archontophoenix cunninghamiana* is native to Australia and there its trunk attains a height of 18 to 22m (59 to 72ft). If you see the mature plant in a botanical garden, you may be lucky enough to find it in bloom; from its lavender-blue flowers red berries later develop.

Family Palmae, palm family.
Origin Eastern Australia.
Location Bright but not sunny. Room temperatures all year round, in winter rather cooler (but not below 10°C/50°F). Tolerates dry, centrally heated air poorly; therefore better to place in a bright stairwell or conservatory at the beginning of autumn.

Watering, feeding Keep moist but avoid sogginess. From mid spring to late summer feed with weak solution.

Further culture Mist often, especially after heating is turned on. Pot on as necessary in good houseplant potting mixture.

Propagating By seed in a heated propagator, using a free-draining potting medium. This is a long, slow process so you need to be patient when waiting for germination.

Pests, diseases Spider mites and scale in a warm, dry location.

Professional tip As with the majority of palms, these are plants that are seen at their best when grown in decorative pots as individual specimens.

Areca catechu
Betel palm

High humidity and bed warmth are essential.

In its native habitat the betel palm grows to a height of 30m (98ft). It is frequently offered in trade as a relatively small seedling with 2 to 4 leaves, which at first looks like a fat 'V'. Only with greater age does the plant develop its characteristic pinnate leaves. Unfortunately, the life expectancy of this slender-stemmed palm is limited if you cannot offer it a warm, humid flower window or a roomy terrarium. The betel palm – famous for the betel nut chewed as a mild stimulant by millions of people between the tropics of Cancer and Capricorn – grows very slowly.

Family Palmae, palm family.
Origin Philippines, South-east Asia.
Location Bright but not sunny all year round and warm (over 20°C/68°F). The plant needs high humidity and warm roots.

Watering, feeding Keep moist. In a window give it an undersaucer constantly filled with water. From mid spring to late summer feed with weak solution every 14 days.

Further culture Provide for indirect humidity (see page 43) and mist often. Pot on seldom.

Propagating From seed, which germinates after two to three months at bed temperatures of 25°C (77°F), but the large seed with its outer husk is seldom available outside the trade.

Pests, diseases Growth disturbances in too cool a location with dry air.

Professional tip With a warming pad underneath, this plant will survive for a long time, even on the windowsill.

Caryota mitis
Burmese fishtail palm

Unmistakable leaves: like nibbled fishtails

Of the 27 species that belong to this genus, to date only *Caryota mitis* has been available as a houseplant. It has long been a prized houseguest in the United States and since 1850 in Europe. Its doubly pinnate leaves, looking like gnawed fishtails, are unmistakeable. It grows bushy relatively slowly and develops numerous suckers, which can be removed and used for propagating. In a warm, humid situation it can grow to a height of 1.5m (59in) and almost as wide. Its striking, deep green fruit clusters do not develop in pot culture.
Family Palmae, palm family.
Origin Burma, Java, Philippines.
Location Bright and warm all year round. No sun and never under 18°C (64°F). The plant needs high humidity. A climate-controlled flower window or growing cabinet is ideal.

Watering, feeding Keep root ball slightly damp at all times. *Avoid sogginess and dry root ball.* From spring to autumn fertilize weakly every week.
Further culture Provide for high humidity. Best to mist daily. Pot on as necessary, using good houseplant potting mixture.
Propagating From seed, which is generally difficult to obtain. Perhaps the best advice is to buy small plants and grow them on.
Pests, diseases Spider mites when air too dry; brown tips after dried root ball or sogginess.

Chamaedorea elegans (syn. *Neanthe bella*)
Parlour palm

The parlour palm blooms even as a young plant.

The attractive parlour palm, *Chamaedorea elegans*, has a stiff, closely ringed little trunk, which reaches 2m (78in) at the most, and fresh green, graceful foliage. It is at home in the impenetrable mountain forests of Mexico and Guatemala and adept at surviving in shade. Moreover, it is one of the few palms that bloom in their juvenile years. The parlour palm is possibly the best palm for growing in rooms offering limited space because of its neat appearance and because it never becomes invasive. In good culture the pale yellow flowers continue to appear regardless of the time of year. *Chamaedorea cataractum* from Mexico and Hawaii, with darker fronds, is a recent arrival in the marketplace.
Family Palmae, palm family.
Origin Mexico, Guatemala.

Location Bright to semi-shady. A north window is ideal. Keep at 20°C (68°F) in summer, cooler in winter.
Watering, feeding Keep root ball moist. From early spring to early autumn feed with weak solution every three weeks.
Further culture Mist often. Pot on as necessary in good houseplant potting mixture.
Propagating From seed.
Pests, diseases Attacks of spider mites in dry, centrally heated air; possibly root rot with too much dampness in too dark a location.
Professional tip If your parlour palm blooms very frequently and you do not want it to be unnecessarily weakened, cut the flowers off before they unfold.

Once the parlour palm has flowered, remove the blooms. Otherwise the plant will invest all its strength in the developing seeds.

PALMS

Chrysalidocarpus lutescens
(syn. *Areca lutescens*)
Yellow palm

A species which can grow 20cm (8in) a year

Under its old name of areca palm, this was once one of the most frequently propagated palm species. In fact, in elegance the yellow palm is quite the equal of the sentry palm (*Howea*, see page 209). It differs from the *Howea* in its lighter, green-yellow foliage and in its 'freckled' leaf shafts. In its native habitat it can reach heights of 10m (33ft). Indoors, with good culture, it will easily grow 20cm (8in) per year. The fronds are 1m (39in) long, comb-like, pinnate and very decorative. The palm is sold in all sizes and frequently as a clump of several young plants. The latter is the type of planting you should look for when purchasing.
Family Palmae, palm family.
Origin Madagascar.
Location Bright but not sunny, all year round very warm, never under 16°C (61°F).
Watering, feeding Keep slightly moist. At high temperatures will even tolerate standing in a saucer of water. From early spring to late summer feed weekly with weak solution.
Further culture *Avoid dry air* and provide for humidity at all costs. In winter mist daily. Every two to three years pot on in good houseplant potting mixture.
Propagating From seed but this is generally difficult to obtain. However, plants with lots of stems in the pot can be separated to make new plants at any time.
Pests, diseases When air is too dry, leaf drop, yellowed leaves or brown spots. Scale is also a common problem indoors in poor light. Spider mites.
Professional tip The yellow-stemmed palm is a superb subject for growing in a conservatory that offers good light and reasonable warmth.

Cocos nucifera
Coconut palm

Coconuts need light, humidity and warmth.

The coconut palm in its native habitat is seen as the quintessential exotic palm. The houseplants on offer from commercial growers are forced plants, tiny in comparison to the parent plant. They are often still attached to the large coconut seed, buried in the potting medium, and this adds to the attraction and interest of the plant. Located under the smooth outer skin of the seed is the buoyancy skin that enables it to float great distances before coming to rest on some seashore. This skin does not rot so quickly indoors as it does in its warm, humid native habitat, becoming instead dry and hard, and this can hinder the growth of a young plant. It is for this reason, and because the coconut palm lacks the light intensity and the damp warmth of its equatorial home, that most indoor specimens are short lived.

Family Palmae, palm family.
Origin Tropics.
Location As bright, warm and humid as possible. The plant tolerates full sun. In summer, shade at midday. In winter do not keep below 18°C (64°F).
Watering, feeding Keep root ball slightly moist at all times. From mid spring to early autumn fertilize every week with weak solution.
Further culture Provide for humidity. Mist often. Pot on as seldom as possible.
Propagating From seed (not as sold to eat but with outer husk intact).
Pests, diseases Rare. Wilting of the lower leaves is normal. Brown tips indicate dry air.
Professional tip In winter I place my coconut palm under a plant light and mist it daily with soft, warm water to prolong its life.

Howea
Sentry palm, kentia palm

Howea forsteriana *has a wide spread.*

On the market are two species: *Howea forsteriana* and *Howea belmoreana*. As young plants they are scarcely distinguishable from one another. Later you can tell them apart by their growth patterns: whereas *Howea forsteriana* grows faster and spreads wider, *Howea belmoreana* develops slowly and becomes stiffly upright. Both bear pinnate, dark green fronds, have a single trunk and are mostly offered in clumps of three.
Family Palmae, palm family.
Origin Lord Howe Island, Australia.
Location Bright to semi-shady. The plant tolerates no sun and can get by with little light, but it grows very little under such conditions. Room temperatures all year round, in daytime up to 25°C (77°F), cooler at night.
Watering, feeding Water well but always allow potting medium to dry out between waterings. *Absolutely avoid sogginess.* From early spring to early autumn feed weekly with weak solution.
Further culture The sentry palm tolerates dry, centrally heated air relatively well. Nevertheless in winter mist often. Pot on in good houseplant potting mixture only when plant is completely potbound.
Propagating From seed at bed temperatures between 25 and 30°C (77 and 86°F), but germination will be very slow and seed will be difficult to obtain.
Pests, diseases Spider mite and scale infestations in air that is too dry. The heart rots with constant sogginess.
Professional tip At least twice a year wash dusty fronds with lukewarm water so that it can 'breathe' better. Avoid the use of chemical cleaners.

Microcoelum weddelianum
(syn. *Cocos weddelianum*)
Weddel palm

The Weddel palm loves high humidity.

The weddel palm is one of the best-selling palms for the home, frequently even being offered as a 'beginner's palm'. However, this filigreed plant from the tropical rain forest is more realistically something for the advanced gardener who already has other exotics like orchids or bromeliads in a warm, humid flower window, growing cabinet or conservatory. For these are the conditions under which the weddel palm feels at home and where it can thrive for a long time, and even the oldest plants grow scarcely taller than 150cm (59in).
Family Palmae, palm family.
Origin Tropical Brazil.
Location Bright and warm, never under 20°C (68°F).
Watering, feeding Keep moist, in winter water somewhat less. In spring and summer feed once a month with weak solution.

Further culture Must be sprayed often and regularly in winter. Pot on as necessary in good houseplant potting mixture – as a rule every two to three years.
Propagating From seed at bed temperature of 30°C (86°F).
Pests, diseases Spider mites when air too dry. Brown tips with dried-out root ball and too little humidity; stunted growth with cold roots.
Professional tip Your weddel palm has a chance of longer life if you provide it with constant humidity. To do so, sink the plant in a larger pot filled with clay granules or peat (see drawing, page 43).

Phoenix
Date palm

Phoenix roebelenii *has natural elegance.*

Of the 13 recognized *Phoenix* species, there are three of any real interest to the houseplant enthusiast: the true date palm (*Phoenix dactylifera*, see photograph, page 64), the Canary Island date (*Phoenix canariensis*) and the miniature (dwarf) date palm (*Phoenix roebelenii*).

The first two are suitable for the home only as young plants. They quickly become large and are then wonderful tub plants for the warm, spacious conservatory. The miniature date palm, on the other hand, hardly grows taller than 1.5 to 2m (59 to 79in), even in age, and needs a great deal of warmth. In its juvenile form it produces slender fronds, which droop elegantly. They are covered with white fibres which make them look as though they were dusted with flour. Eventually the plant develops a handsome trunk with a bushy crown of fronds.

Family Palmae, palm family.

Origin Tropics.

Location Very bright but not full sun, warm all year round. In winter never below 15°C (59°F).

Watering, feeding Keep root ball slightly moist at all times but never wet. From mid spring to late summer feed with weak solution.

Further culture Mist often, daily in warm rooms with a dry atmosphere. Pot on as necessary in good houseplant potting mixture.

Propagating From seed in heated propagator, but seed is difficult to obtain and slow to germinate.

Pests, diseases Chlorosis when hard water is used. Spider mites when air too dry. Growth disturbances and brown fronds in a location where roots get cold, too much dampness in winter or hard water.

Rhapis
Lady palm

This is the only palm successfully used for bonsai.

Rhapis humilis, which grows only to 1m (39in), is suitable for an average-sized room; for the conservatory or as a tub plant, there is *Rhapis excelsa*, which in a large container can reach 2m (79in). Both have bamboo-like, slender trunks with brown fibres and were very popular as long ago as the turn of the century. Their fronds reach 15 to 30cm (6 to 12in) across. The individual leaflets in *Rhapis humilis* are narrower and more delicate and numerous than in *Rhapis excelsa*. *Rhapis* is the only palm genus that has been used successfully for bonsai. In the USA it is so popular that some nurseries deal exclusively in the lady palm.

Family Palmae, palm family.

Origin China, Japan.

Location Bright to semi-shady, no sun. In summer warm, in winter cool at 5 to 10°C (41 to 50°F). From late spring can be set outside in a semi-shady spot for the summer. Thrives well in stairwell, provided there are no draughts.

Watering, feeding Water freely in spring and summer. In winter water more sparingly. From late spring to late summer use weak solution.

Further culture Mist fronds occasionally. Pot on when the root ball begins to squeeze itself out of the pot, using a slightly heavier (loam-based) potting medium.

Propagating From seed or by shoots that are separated from the mother plant.

Pests, diseases Dried and brown fronds from too warm a location with dry air. Yellow leaves from spider mites.

Sabal
Palmetto

The palmetto loves a bright location.

Palmettos are striking primarily because of their deeply incised fans. There are stemless, bushy species and others with mighty trunks which taper steeply as they rise from ground level. In their habitat, the largest, with a trunk diameter of 1m (39in), reach a height of 25m (82ft). There are some 25 known species, distributed from Venezuela through Central America and Mexico up to the southern United States and the Antilles. In Cuba these stately palms command the landscape, and in Italy there were palmettos during the geological Miocene epoch.

Commercially available as a houseplant is *Sabal minor*, which grows to a height of barely 2m (79in), is rather bushy in habit and forms runner-like rhizomes. Its 1m- (39in-) long, deeply cut leaves sometimes appear bluish-frosted.

There is also *Sabal palmetto*, whose leaf-stalk scars create a beautiful trunk pattern. Both are splendid conservatory plants.

Family Palmae, palm family.

Origin Subtropical America.

Location Very bright all year round, especially in winter. Keep warm in summer, cooler (10 to 15°C/50 to 59°F) in winter. May be set outside in a warm, sunny place from late spring.

Watering, feeding Water abundantly in summer, in winter only enough to prevent the root ball from drying out. From late spring to late summer fertilize with weak solution every week.

Further culture Pot on as necessary in good houseplant potting mixture.

Propagating From seed, also may attempt with shoots of *Sabal minor*.

Pests, diseases Rare.

Washingtonia
Washington palm

This fast-growing palm needs a lot of space.

This splendid palm can be kept as a houseplant for only a limited time. Then it becomes too large and imposing and needs at least a conservatory. It grows very quickly and even in a tub can become over 2m (79in) wide and 3m (10ft) tall. Available are the Mexican species *Washingtonia robusta* (the thread palm) and the Californian *Washingtonia filifera* (the fan or petticoat palm). Both, because of the patterns left by base of their leaf-stalks, have particularly picturesque trunks. The leaves of *Washingtonia robusta* are glossy green, those of *Washingtonia filifera* grey-green.

Family Palmae, palm family.

Origin Arizona, California, Mexico.

Location Bright and airy, in summer warm, in winter cool at 10°C (50°F); in any event avoid high temperatures. Place outside from late spring.

Watering, feeding Water well in summer, more sparingly in winter. Feed with weak solution every 14 days from mid spring to late summer.

Further culture Pot on young plants yearly, older ones as necessary in a loam-based potting mixture.

Propagating From seed in heated propagator.

Pests, diseases Aphids and brown leaf tips in dry, stagnant air.

Warning Washington palms bear sharp thorns on the leaf stems that can cause injury. Position the plants in the conservatory or on the terrace where people will not brush against them when passing.

The petticoat of old leaves that wraps the trunk of *Washingtonia filifera* and earns it the name of the petticoat palm.

A growing-cabinet or a
climate-controlled flower
window are not
absolutely essential if
you want to grow
orchids. Many modern
cultivars will thrive and
bloom simply on a
windowsill.

ORCHIDS

The blooming of African violets or the kaffir lily is always a joyful occasion. But when the *Coelogyne* rains down its cascades of white flowers in early spring, when light-hungry cymbidiums are successfully brought into bloom or when the size of the lady's slipper orchids is increased year by year, there is truly a cause for celebration.

As a rule the modern hybrids are the easiest to cultivate. Produced from various species and genera, these beauties are selectively bred to be better adapted to indoor climatic and light conditions and usually bloom more profusely and more willingly than the wild forms. Anyone who chooses to buy them, rather than the wild forms, is also practising conservation by not encouraging the destruction of the species.

The orchids introduced in the following section are primarily hybrids that are easy to obtain and to grow.

Anyone who is interested in more demanding species will find some suggestions, with appropriate tips on culture, in the Rarities section (see pages 220–1).

Growth forms

In terms of evolutionary history orchids are the youngest flowering plants. They also represent the largest plant family, with some 750 genera, 10,000 to 30,000 species and more than 70,000 hybrids. With the exception of the ice-cold polar regions and the hot, dry desert regions they are represented all over the globe, but they settle primarily in tropical rain or mountain forests, in cool, damp, more northerly forests and on rocky or coastal wastelands near the sea. Most of them come from Asiatic regions, many from Central and South America, and mostly they live in trees, some on the ground, a few on rocks.

Orchids have two growth forms.
● Monopodial species, like the *Phalaenopsis*, form one main stem that grows vertically from the root and develops flowers at the side of the main axis.

● Sympodial species, like the *Cattleya*, grow on a horizontal axis, from which numerous shoots arise. The new growth emerges sideways from the base and in time overlaps the edge of the pot. Sympodial orchids have pseudobulbs. These storage organs for water and nutrients are evidence that in their natural habitat the plants have to survive periods of dryness.

The leaves of orchids are usually smooth-edged and supplied with parallel veins. Colour and texture signal the plant's natural location. Dark green leaves indicate a low light requirement, bright green normal and grey-green extremely high requirements. Orchids that tolerate cold or sun have quite hard leaves, whereas those of shade- and warmth-loving ones are rather soft. The orchid blossoms are extraordinarily beautiful and most are astonishingly long lasting.

Correct culture

Always ask when you are buying an orchid whether you are dealing with a species or hybrid for cool, temperate regions or for tropical or subtropical regions. It is important

Orchids living on or in trees derive their nutrients from the humus of decaying plant parts.

to know the climatic conditions from which the plant – in the case of hybrids, the dominant genes – come. Orchids from cool regions are

more difficult to keep in indoor conditions. The required humidity is achieved using electric humidifiers or by other measures (see page 43). Of course, all orchids thrive best in climate-controlled flower windows or growing cabinets.

The magic formula for successful blooming is: rest, cooler temperatures at night, a lot of light in autumn and the right humidity at all times. Orchids with tough leaves and thick bulbs need a dry resting period, those with soft, tender leaves must never get completely dry. The following is intended as a rough guide to the yearly cycle of a modern hybrid orchid, but there will naturally be many variations, depending on the species being grown.
● *Late winter/spring* The new growth begins. Watering is increased now.
● *Early summer/summer* Growth accelerates. Plants need fertilizer, water and warmth.
● *Late summer/autumn* The bulbs develop, the new growth matures and the formation of flowers is stimulated. Important: nightly temperature drop of about 4 to 6°C (7 to 11°F), full autumn light and less water.
● *Autumn/winter* The rest period occurs; this corresponds to the tropical dry season. Orchids need plenty of light and little water.

Unlike most houseplants, orchids will not grow in standard houseplant potting mixtures. They need a special medium which is loose, light and air permeable on the one hand, but on the other capable of storing nutrients and water.

The most bizarre flowers of all are probably found among the orchids. These of Encyclia cochleata *resemble insects.*

ORCHIDS

Cattleya
Cattleya

Cattleya bicolor *comes from Brazil.*

The free-flowering Cattleya bowringiana

Laeliocattleya *hybrid
'Creamton': more* Laelia
than Cattleya

Laeliocattleya *hybrid
'Culminari Recital':
particularly intense
colouring*

Laeliocattleya *hybrid
with yellow column*

In their natural habitat cattleyas usually grow epiphytically on branches or tree trunks. The buds develop from a sheath or spathe, and the flowers are large, magnificently coloured and have a conspicuous lip. The brown colour of the flower sheath is typical of the genus. So is the fibrous development around the bulb: it serves as a sunshade. On the market are *Cattleya* species, *Cattleya* hybrids and so-called multigeneric hybrids, for example,

Brassolaeliocattleya, *Epicattleya*, *Potinara* and *Sophrolaeliocattleya*. The flowers appear in white, yellow (in many shades), pink and various shades of red. Particularly good orchids for the home are crosses of *Cattleya* and *Laelia* (see page 216), called *Laeliocattleya* hybrids, for example 'Alma Wichmann' (spring bloomer), 'Max and Moritz' and 'Winter's

Tale' (winter bloomers). They are cultivated like cattleyas.

Flowering season Depending on species and variety, in spring, summer, autumn or winter.

Family Orchidaceae, orchid family.

Origin Central and tropical South America.

Location Very bright but not blazing sun. Ideal is an east or a west window. In summer and during growing season warm all day (to 25°C/77°F) and airy. The drop in temperature of several degrees at night is important. In winter temperatures of 18°C (64°F) in the daytime and 14°C (57°F) at night are acceptable.

Watering, feeding In summer water as needed or soak the plants; in winter water only enough to keep the roots and pseudobulbs from drying out. In summer add an orchid fertilizer to every third watering.

Further culture Mist leaves frequently from late spring to mid autumn. Every two to three years pot on in orchid potting medium. Spring and summer bloomers after flowering, autumn and winter bloomers in early/mid spring.

Propagating By separation of the pseudobulbs and potting individually when potting on.

Pests, diseases Scale from dry, centrally heated air. Watch out for ants, which are attracted by the sticky, sweet excretion from the spathe and bring aphids with them.

Professional tip To ensure that your *Cattleya* will bloom every year, put the plant in a cooler place as soon as the growth is mature and reduce the amount of water. In too warm a location the *Cattleya* will bolt and form only leaves.

Cymbidium
Cymbidium

Brown hybrids are especially sought after.

Cymbidium *hybrids offer a great range of colours.*

Of all the orchids, the cymbidiums provide the most cut flowers. From Thailand, mainly, thousands of panicles are dispatched to the flower markets of the world. Their popularity is not surprising. Cymbidium flowers last a particularly long time in a vase and offer a colour spectrum without equal. Cymbidiums are either terrestrial or epiphytic and have thick, fleshy roots and hard, long leaves, which usually grow out of oval pseudobulbs. The racemes of flowers appear at the bottom of the bulb.

Commercially available are the so-called standard type, *Cymbidium* hybrids that in a conservatory grow more than 1m (39in) tall, and the miniature indoor cymbidiums, which grow to a height of 80 to 100cm (31 to 39in). The latter have warmth-loving forebears, bloom from autumn, and tolerate heated rooms far better. The palette of flower colours ranges from cream-white through yellow, orange, pink, red, violet and brown to green. Well-known miniature cymbidiums, which bloom in winter/spring, are: 'Agnes Norton', 'Show-off', 'Dag Oleste', 'Excalibur', 'Mary Pinchess', 'Del Rey', 'Miniature Delight' (wonderful hanging plant), 'Minneken', 'Pink Tower' and 'Lemförde Surprise' (fragrant).

Flowering season
According to species and variety in spring, summer, autumn or winter.

Family Orchidaceae, orchid family.

Origin Tropical Asia, Australia.

Location All year round airy, very bright and sunny. Put standard types and older mini-cymbidiums out of doors from early summer to early autumn in a bright spot but not in full sun. Keep warm in summer but definitely cooler at night from late summer on.

Watering, feeding
Water well from early spring to early autumn and provide the plant with orchid fertilizer every four weeks. In late autumn and winter water less and do not feed.

Further culture Provide high humidity. Mist often. Every two years pot on after blooming in orchid potting medium.

Propagating By removing pseudobulbs and potting individually when potting on.

Pests, diseases Spider mites in dry air. Yellow spotted leaves and lighter leaves indicate a viral disease. Isolate plant so that it cannot infect others or destroy it. There are no remedies for viral disease.

Top left *Green hybrid with spotted lip*
Bottom left *'Silvia Müller Citronella'*
Top right *Cream-white hybrid with orange-red lip*
Bottom right *The well-known 'Starbright Capella'*

Professional tip The flowers that bloom from early spring to mid winter are set in late spring/early summer, those blooming from late winter to late spring are set in early autumn. During these periods the plants need much warmth in the daytime and plenty of fresh, cool air at night.

ORCHIDS

Laelia
Laelia

Laelia purpurata, *Brazil's national flower*

In their native habitat the some 50 species of *Laelia* mostly grow as epiphytes in tropical forests. But there are also some species that grow on rocks or on sandy ground, as for instance the stone laelias. Among them is the reddish-orange *Laelia cinnabarina*. This species is recommended for the beginner and, like the magnificent *Laelia purpurata*, blooms in spring. *Laelia crispa* blooms in summer. Laelias produce relatively few hybrids by crossing of the species, with the exception of the *Laeliocattleyas* (see *Cattleya*, page 214).

Flowering season According to species and variety in spring, summer, autumn or winter.

Family Orchidaceae, orchid family.

Origin Tropical America.

Location Bright to semi-shady, airy (but no draughts). In autumn full sun for *Laelia cinnabarina*. In spring and summer days 18 to 24°C (64 to 75°F); nights and in autumn/winter around 7°C (12°F) lower.

Watering, feeding In hot summer weather, water abundantly or soak. Water again only when the potting medium has dried out. In winter give only enough water to prevent the plants from wilting. At every third watering during the growing season add orchid fertilizer.

Further culture Provide for high humidity. Pot on every two to three years in fresh orchid potting medium. Epiphytic laelias can be bound to Portuguese bark supports or tree branches.

Propagating By removing the pseudobulbs and potting individually when potting on.

Pests, diseases Beware of stagnant air; it is not tolerated by laelias.

Miltonia, Miltoniopsis
Pansy orchid

The pansy flowers of Miltoniopsis

Miltonias have flat flowers with short stems which at first glance look like pansies. Today these epiphytic plants are roughly divided into two groups: *Miltonia* species, which are good for houseplant culture, and *Miltoniopsis* species, the so-called pansy miltonias, which come from cool, damp forest regions.

Both genera embrace 15 to 20 species. Most bear bright green flattened pseudobulbs with one or two small leaves. The flowers always arise from the base of the youngest pseudobulb and are multicoloured, often white with red or pink.

Species commonly available include the summer- or autumn-blooming *Miltonia clowesii*, *Miltonia flavescens* and *Miltonia spectabilis*, as well as various hybrids.

Flowering season Summer/autumn, some all year round.

Family Orchidaceae, orchid family.

Origin South America.

Location Bright all year round but not sunny. Also tolerates semi-shade. In summer not over 25°C (77°F), in winter around 20°C (68°F), at night 15 to 18°C (59 to 64°F).

Watering, feeding Keep slightly moist. In winter water sparingly. In spring and summer feed every three weeks with a weak solution.

Further culture Provide for high, indirect humidity (see page 43), but *do not spray the plants*. Pot on rarely and, when you do, use orchid potting medium for epiphytes in spring or autumn.

Propagating By removing the pseudobulbs and potting individually when potting on.

Pests, diseases Only with poor cultivation. If a slightly red tinge appears on the leaves, move to a brighter location.

Odontoglossum

Vuylstekeara cambria 'Plush' is a well-known variety.

Yellow-spotted hybrid

Most of the more than 100 species are cool mountain beauties, growing at heights of 1500 to 3000m (5000 to 9800ft). Some of them can even stand freezing temperatures for a brief time. From the unusual flowers, which sometimes have a tooth-like structure at the base, comes the botanical name (Greek/Latin: *odontos*=toothed; *glossa*=tongue). The pseudobulbs are smoothly oval, have one to three leaves at the tip and at the base develop racemose inflorescences, which as a rule point upward.

One of the least demanding species is *Odontoglossum grande* (tiger orchid), which today is classified in a special genus as *Rossioglossum*. The following hybrids and multiple-genera hybrids of *Odontoglossum* are of particular interest for houseplant fanciers:

● *Odontioda* (from *Odontoglossum × Cochlioda)*
● *Odontonia* (from *Odontoglossum × Miltonia*)
● *Ondontocidium* (from *Odontoglossum × Oncidium*)
● *Vuylstekeara* (from *Odontoglossum × Cochlioda × Miltoniopsis*)
● *Wilsonara* (from *Odontoglossum × Cochlioda × Oncidium*)

They are bred especially for windowsill requirements and outdo each other with luxuriant, frequently multi-coloured panicles of flowers, which come in yellow to brown (flecked or striped) and white with pink or red. Of the pure species, *Odontoglossum bictoniense*, *Odontoglossum pulchellum*, which has a lily-of-the-valley fragrance, and *Odontoglossum crispum* are good for culture as houseplants.

Flowering season Depending on species and variety, in spring, summer, autumn or winter.

Family Orchidaceae, orchid family.

Origin Central and South America.

Location Bright to semi-shady. East, west or north window; in winter south window. In summer 20 to 24°C (68 to 75°F), cooler at night. In winter 14 to 18°C (57 to 64°F).

Watering, feeding During the growing season keep moist. In winter water more sparingly. From early to late summer fertilize every 14 days through the leaves with a foliar feed.

Further culture Provide for high humidity with misting. Every two to three years pot on in fresh orchid potting medium after blooming.

Propagating By removing pseudobulbs and potting individually when potting on.

Pests, diseases Leaves grow wavy when humidity is too low.

Professional tip If you have a garden, hang your *Odontoglossum* in a tree with light leaf cover in early summer. It loves the fresh air, and particularly the summer warmth after a cool night, but do not forget to water in dry spells. On the other hand, it is best to bring the plant indoors during protracted rainy spells to keep the potting medium from going mouldy.

Give the plant full sun from early autumn on, letting it stock up on sunlight until mid autumn. This promotes the development of flowers and the maturing of the pseudobulbs. But be careful of night frosts. Then bring the plant indoors and place it in a bright, cool spot. Before long the new flower buds will appear.

The *Odontoglossum* is an important forebear of many orchid hybrids known under different names, such as the *Vuylstekeara*.

Oncidium
Dancing-lady orchid

Oncidiums – there are about 100 species – are at home in various temperature zones and are correspondingly various in form. The inflorescences bear delicate single flowers that are often banded or spotted. There are both hybrids and pure species on the market. When buying, always ask whether the oncidium you have chosen is at home in temperate or warm regions.

Flowering season Depending on species and variety, spring, summer, autumn or winter.

Family Orchidaceae, orchid family.

oncidiums 15°C (59°F), those requiring warmth around 20°C (68°F) and full sun.

Watering, feeding Keep plant slightly moist from early spring to mid autumn. From late autumn to early spring water only enough to keep the pseudobulbs and leaves from wilting. During the vegetative period give orchid fertilizer every three weeks.

Further culture Provide for high humidity but *mist carefully in winter and spring* because new growth rots easily. When the pseudobulbs swell out of the pot, pot on in orchid potting medium. The best time to do this is at the end of the rest period (early spring) when the roots and new shoots begin to grow.

Propagating By removing the pseudobulbs and potting individually when potting on.

Professional tip Do not cut off the flower stalks of

Oncidium hybrid with spotted flowers

Origin Subtropical and tropical Americas.
Location In summer bright to semi-shady, no direct sun and days warm, nights cool. In winter, temperate

Oncidium kramerianum and *Oncidium papilio* (*Psychopsis*) after they bloom. New buds develop on the same stem the following year.

Paphiopedilum (syn. Cypripedium)
Ladyslipper orchid

Paphiopedilum *hybrids are easy to look after.*

There are about 60 species of *Paphiopedilum*. Far larger, however, is the number of hybrids, to which plant fanciers should turn for reasons of conservation. These cultivars are much tougher than the botanical species and even thrive in heated areas. The ladyslipper has a special growth pattern: each leaf rosette produces only one flower shoot; subsequently new rosettes develop in the leaf axils, and these bloom the following year. The flowers are white, yellow, green, brown or purple, and often are striped, spotted or speckled.

Flowering season Depending on species and variety, spring, summer, autumn or winter.

Family Orchidaceae, orchid family.

Origin Tropical Asia.

Location In summer semi-shady, in winter bright but not sunny.

Room temperatures all year round, cooler at night. Exception: in early autumn, after growth stops, keep cool at night and sunny during the day for two to three weeks.

Watering, feeding Water only when the potting medium has dried out. In winter water more sparingly. From mid spring to early autumn feed every three weeks with a weak solution.

Further culture Provide for high humidity. Mist the leaves often. Pot on after blooming but only if the potting medium has 'clumped' or smells musty.

Propagating By separating the pseudobulbs and potting individually when potting on.

Pests, diseases Spider mites and scale. Bud, leaf and root rot from constant dampness.

Professional tip Ladyslippers thrive best when they grow in a clump so it is better not to divide.

Phalaenopsis
Moth orchid

The Phalaenopsis *has broad leaves.*

Phalaenopsis *hybrids flower almost all year round.*

Orchids that close at night do not develop pseudobulbs but roots that cling to whatever is offered them. The leaves are tongue-like and quite wide and the flowers show a range of forms, colours and markings, appearing in white, yellow, pink, red, violet, brown and green. Commercially available are *Phalaenopsis* species, hybrids (there is a large and beautifully coloured assortment – all ideal for beginners) and multigeneric hybrids like *Asconopsis*, *Doritaenopsis* and *Renanthopsis*. All require the same culture.

Flowering season Depending on species and variety, spring, summer, autumn or winter; hybrids bloom almost all year round.

Family Orchidaceae, orchid family.

Origin South-east Asia.

Location In summer semi-shade, in winter bright. *Never sunny under any circumstances.* Warm all year round. Days about 20 to 22°C (68 to 72°F) and even warmer in summer, nights not below 18°C (64°F). But in autumn keep plants around 16°C (61°F) for about four to six weeks. This stimulates the formation of flowers.

Watering, feeding Keep moderately moist all year round. The potting medium should never dry out completely but do not water while it is still damp. *Never water into the heart of the plant – danger of rot.* Feed with weak solution every 14 days in summer.

Further culture Mist the leaves often. Provide high humidity for *Phalaenopsis* species. The hybrids are better suited to dry air. Pot on the plants in late spring every two years, using coarse, airy orchid potting medium. Do not injure roots.

Propagating From the offsets that occasionally develop on the flower stems.

Pests, diseases Fungal infections from overwatering, scale in too dry a location and bud drop in too dark a position.

Professional tip The *Phalaenopsis* can bloom two to three times on the same stalk if you cut off the flower stalk above the third or fourth stem node before it has entirely finished blooming.

'Mambo' is the name of this green-gold hybrid.

The hybrid 'Cassandra' has a purple-red lip.

The hybrid 'Hokuspokus' has pink-spattered flowers.

219

From warm, humid tropical regions and damp, cool mountain forests, a selection of orchids with special requirements.

Coelogyne cristata

Coelogyne

For temperate areas. Epiphytic orchids with narrow, dark green leaves 15 to 30cm (6 to 12in) long, oval pseudobulbs and trailing white flowers with golden-yellow crests that appear in several clusters on stems up to 30cm (12in) long.

Flowering season Late autumn to early spring. **Family** Orchidaceae, orchids. **Origin** Himalayas, Nepal. **Location** Bright and airy all year round. No midday sun. Outdoors in summer. In winter 14°C (57°F) during day, 8°C (46°F) at night. **Watering, feeding** Water moderately from late spring to early autumn and feed with weak solution every two weeks. From mid autumn to mid spring keep almost dry. **Further culture** To prevent rotting, avoid misting new growth. Pot on as necessary after blooming in orchid potting medium. **Propagating** By separating the pseudobulbs. **Professional tip** The coelogyne blooms better when it has been outside in the full summer sun.

Brassia verrucosa

Brassia

For temperate areas. Orchid species with flat pseudobulbs, oblong,

leathery leaves and flowers that often have tail-like long petals and are situated on 50cm (20in) stems.

Flowering season Spring or summer, depending on species. **Family** Orchidaceae, orchids. **Origin** Tropical America. **Location** Very bright to semi-shady. In summer room temperature, dropping to 16 to 18°C (61 to 64°F) at night. In winter not over 18°C (64°F) in the daytime, 14°C (57°F) at night. **Watering, feeding** Water well with soft water from mid spring to early autumn and feed with weak solution every two weeks. From mid autumn to early spring water only enough to prevent bulbs from shrivelling. **Further culture** Mist regularly. Scale attacks when air is too dry. **Propagating** By separating the pseudobulbs.

Dendrobium densiflorum

Dendrobium, golden dendrobium

For temperate areas. Epiphytic species with bamboo-like pseudobulbs and golden-yellow cluster of flowers. **Flowering season** Early to late spring. **Family** Orchidaceae, orchids. **Origin** Himalayas, Burma, Indochina. **Location** Very bright but not sunny all year round. In spring/summer warm, from mid autumn 12 to 15°C (54 to 59°F). **Watering, feeding** In spring/summer water well and feed with weak solution every 14 days. From mid autumn water less, in winter water only enough to keep the bulbs from shrivelling. **Further culture** Mist often, especially in summer. **Propagating** By separating the pseudobulbs after blooming.

Zygopetalum
Zygopetalum

For temperate areas. Orchids with
thick roots, two or more narrow
lanceolate leaves, oval
pseudobulbs and strikingly
patterned and coloured
flowers. The
remarkable name
comes from the
Greek and alludes to
the thickened welt at
the base of the lip, which
holds the petals together like
a horse's yoke
(Greek: *zygo*=yoke,
petalon=petal). Both species
plants and hybrids are
available.
Flowering season Winter.
Family Orchidaceae, orchids.
Origin South America.
Location Bright to semi-shady and
airy. Room temperature all year
round. In winter 15 to 18°C (59 to
64°F). **Watering, feeding** Keep
moderately moist. From early spring
to early autumn feed with weak
solution every two weeks. **Further**

solution every two weeks. **Further
culture** Provide for indirect humidity
(see page 43), but do not mist or you
will have spotted leaves. Pot on yearly
after flowering. **Propagating** By
separating the pseudobulbs with
leaves.

Bulbophyllum

Masdevallia militaris
Masdevallia

For cool, damp areas (mountain
plants) so keep only in a cool
greenhouse. Orchids with fleshy root
stock and unusual flowers in which
the corolla has almost completely
disappeared and the calyx has
developed into a three-pointed
structure.
Flowering season Spring or
summer, depending on species.
Family Orchidaceae, orchids.
Origin Central and South America.
Location Bright to semi-shady. Airy,
moist coolness all year round.
Watering, feeding Keep orchid
slightly moist, no rest period. In
summer feed with weak solution every

three weeks. **Further culture** Pot on
in spring in orchid potting medium as
necessary. **Propagating** By division
of rhizomes; leave large clumps.

Bulbophyllum
(syn. *Cirrobopetelum*)
Bulbophyllum

For warm areas. This is a native of the
evergreen rain and monsoon forests of
the tropics. Epiphytic orchids with
elongated, creeping rhizomes and
slanted pseudobulbs, on which a
leathery leaf is situated (thus the
name, from Greek: *bolbos*=tuber,
phyllon=leaf). The bizarre flowers are
clustered, several in an umbel.
Flowering season Mid summer.
Family Orchidaceae, orchids.
Origin Tropics. **Location** Bright all
year round, 20°C (68°F) in the
daytime, never under 16°C (61°F) at
night. **Watering, feeding** Keep
moist, feed every 14 days with weak
solution during the growing season.
Further culture Provide for indirect
humidity (see page 43).
Propagating By separating the
pseudobulbs.

221

Cacti require little space and care, turn into brilliant flowering beauties overnight and excite a passion for collecting like no other plant group. Fall under their spell and you are a captive for life.

CACTI

Anyone who has a bright, sunny windowsill and cool, bright winter quarters can collect cacti. Even a tray offers space enough for a small collection. You may decide to begin with the easy-to-grow cacti (as shown on pages 224–5). Or perhaps you prefer the flowering succulents (see pages 226–7). Exclusively for the fancier with experience (and possibly also a growing cabinet) is the small selection of cacti described on pages 228–9. Plants with nearly identical culture requirements have been grouped together to give you a chance to assemble a small collection of different species. For cacti look best when displayed as a colourful group rather than individually.

The magic of the cactus lies in its contrariness. Defiant, even aggressive, are the impressions created by the flowerless 'thorn balls'. Yet when their flowers suddenly appear one after the other, shining like silk and exploding with joyful colour, they reveal an irresistible charm.

The first specimens are believed to have been introduced to Europe around 1500, when Christopher Columbus returned from his expedition to the New World. By about 1700 the melon, pillar, leaf and fig cactus were well known, but the passion for collecting cacti reached a peak in the first half of the nineteenth century. Today every country boasts its own specialist cactus society.

Structure of cacti

Cacti are American. They are found from Canada in the north to Patagonia in the south. Most of them inhabit prairies and blazing hot, desert-like, dry regions. Relatively few have colonized the warm, humid tropical areas, creeping under bushes or growing in the forks of forest trees. The cactus family, or *Cactaceae*, embraces some 200 genera and several thousand species. Like African violets and azaleas they are flowering plants, and yet they look completely different.

The characteristic cactus structure developed over millions of years through adaptation to a dry location. In order to keep the evaporation surface as small as possible and to protect themselves against sun and ultraviolet light, the cacti 'invented' the spherical and pillar forms, turned leaves into thorns and developed a thick skin furnished with a wax-like coating, corky deposits, dense thorns or a coating of silvery hairs. Some species have shallow, far-spreading roots that can make the most of even the briefest rain shower. Others grow thick, beet-like roots for water storage. All evolved succulence (from Latin: *succus* = juice), which means that their tissue has a capacity to store water.

A common growth form amongst young cacti is the sphere. But there are also species that form pillars or cushions. Mature specimens often appear as shrub, tree or candelabra shapes. Climbing cacti, like the queen-of-the-night, have long limbs and branch like bushes. The few epiphytes in the family, for example the Christmas and the Easter cactus, have leaf-like stems.

The flowers of cacti develop – depending on the species – either on 2- to 3-year-old specimens or only after they have reached a particular size. The flowering seasons for most species are spring and early summer. Every possible colour is available, with the exception of black and blue.

The right culture

Cacti are robust, to be sure, but they can easily be killed with kindness – if you give them too much water. In summer the plants can be watered quite liberally, but it is important to make sure there is no residual dampness around the roots and that they are watered again only when the potting medium has completely dried out. In autumn the amount of water is reduced, and in winter a cactus should have nothing at all to drink in a cool location under 10°C (50°F), and in a warmer spot only very, very little. Under no circumstances should growth be stimulated in the dark season.

The potting medium should have the character of desert sand, that is it should be inorganic, free-draining and well aerated. Work sand and lava granules into commercially prepared potting soil to improve its texture. But be careful when potting on: you could get hurt. Cacti are often equipped with extremely sharp thorns or spines and are best handled wearing gloves and wielding pieces of polystyrene (see drawing, page 41) or tongs.

Epiphytic cacti are cultivated entirely differently. They need a nourishing potting medium, more water and high humidity. And, in contrast to their desert brothers, they do not want sun.

Many cacti with a bushy growth habit grow only as pillars in a pot. Impressive candelabras like this occur solely in native locations.

*The giant barrel cactus (*Echinocactus ingens*) from Mexico can weigh as much as a ton in its native habitat and earned a gloomy reputation among the Aztecs as a sacrificial altar.*

Cacti for the beginner

All these little specimens bloom quite readily.

The cacti pictured on these two pages promise the beginner success at the first attempt and they can be made to bloom over and over again.

Family Cactaceae, cactus family.

Origin South-western USA, Central and S. America.

Location From spring to autumn very bright to sunny and warm. From mid autumn bright and cool (5 to 12°C/41 to 54°F). From late spring out-doors in a sunny place. But protect from rain.

Watering, feeding From late spring to early autumn water thoroughly, but always let potting medium dry first. From mid autumn keep dry. Do not water if overwintered in cool conditions, under 10°C (50°F); if warmer, water very little. In spring carefully resume watering. As soon as new growth shows, give cactus fertilizer every 14 days. Give a phosphorus-weighted fertilizer in the last watering before overwintering begins to promote flowering.

Further culture Pot on every two to three years in early summer in cactus soil with sand and lava granules added.

Propagating By seed in heated propagator at around 28°C (82°F); good seeding time at end of winter. When the seedlings become crowded, prick out.

Pests, diseases Mealy bug and root mealy bug.

Gymnocalycium

Large-flowered, very profusely blooming flattened-spherical to spherical cactus. Sprouts from the base and becomes some 15 to 20cm (6 to 8in) tall and 15cm (6in) thick. There are species with flat or projecting thorns. The flowers, up to 6cm (2in) in size, often appear on three-year-old plants.

Recommended species *G. andreae* (yellow), *G. baldianum* (red-violet), *G. bruchii* (pink), *G. denudatum* (cream-white).

Flowering season Spring to summer.

Notocactus

Spherical to short pillar cactus genus about 15 to 20cm (6 to 8in) in height and diameter. Usually sprouts only when older. The flowers appear near the crown and are about 8cm (3in) across.

Recommended species *N. apricus, N. concinnus, N. ottonis, N. submammulosus* (all yellow), *N. rutilans* (carmine pink), *N. uebelmannianus* (yellow-red and wine-red to violet-red)

Flowering season Spring to summer.

Mammillaria

The name in English, pincushion cactus, indicates that the mammillarias all have ribs studded with bumps that look like pinheads. Depending on the

Above
1 Gymnocalycium uruguayense
2 Notocactus concinnus
3 Mammillaria zeilmanniana
4 Rebutia ritteri
5 Rebutia minusculua
6 Echinofossulocactus
7 Lobivia vatteri

species, they may be flattened spheres, spherical, thin or thick pillars and have various kinds of thorns. They almost all sprout vigorously and form cushions. There are species that are 50cm (20in) in size and some only a few inches tall.

Recommended species All, including *M. bocasana* (cream), *M. zeilmanniana* (white)

Flowering season Spring.

Admirers find the thorn patterns just as attractive as the flowers.

Rebutia

At most 8cm (3in) thick and under 8cm (3in) tall, these cacti sprout very vigorously and soon develop small colonies. Fine spines cover the entire body. The cheerfully coloured flowers, 2 to 5cm (¾ to 2in) in size, are often so numerous that the entire cactus is covered.

Recommended species
All, but especially
R. marsoneri (yellow),
R. violaciflora (violet),
R. senilis (yellow, red)

Flowering season
Spring.

Echinofossulocactus

Characteristic of this spherical cactus genus are the deep, usually wavy, ribs from which it derives its common name, the brain cactus. The marginal thorns in each thorn cluster are light and thin, whereas the central ones are sturdy and often curved like hooks. The flowers, depending on the species, are whitish to blue-violet with dark central stripes or yellowish-white with darker stripes.

Recommended species
All types.

Flowering season
Early spring.

Lobivia

Spherical to short pillar and multi-ribbed genus. At most 30cm (12in) tall and rarely thicker than 10cm (4in) in diameter. The pattern of thorns varies from species to species. The flowers, up to 10cm (4in) across, appear at the side. Important: lobivias need a deep, wide container.

Recommended species
L. backebergiana (orange),
L. rebutioides and
L. famatimensis (yellow),
L. jajoiana (tomato red),
L. pentlandii (white, yellow, pink to violet),
L. wrightiana (pink)

Flowering season
Spring to summer.

Cleistocactus

Pillar cactus with dense, mostly needle-fine thorns. Blooms when reaches 30 to 80cm (12 to 31in) in height. The exceptions is *Cleistocactus wendlandiorum*, which can flower when it is only 15cm (6in) tall. The tubular flowers, up to 9cm (3½in) long, usually project pipelike at right angles to the cactus body and open only partially.

Recommended species
C. laniceps (red), *C. strausii* (wine red)

Flowering season
Spring to early summer.

Echinocactus grusonii

The barrel or golden-ball cactus grows to a height of 1.5m (59in) in its Mexican habitat. Its golden-yellow thorns are characteristic. The yellow flowers appear only in mature plants, at the earliest at a diameter of about 60cm (23in).

Flowering season
Summer.

Parodia

Small, relatively early-blooming cacti with flatly

Above
1 Cleistocactus straussii
2 Echinocereus pectinatus
3 Mammillaria bocasana
4 Echinocactus grusonii
5 Echinofossulocactus spec
6 Parodia mairanana
7 Mammillaria zeilmanniana

spherical to cylindrical bodies. Achieve maximum height of 20cm (8in) and thickness of 8cm (3in). Shape varies, depending on the species, but they sprout vigorously. The flowers appear on the crown.

Recommended species
P. chrysacanthion (yellow),
P. maassii (red),
P. mutabilis (yellow-orange)

Flowering season
Spring to summer.

Flowering succulents

Epiphyllum hybrids
Orchid cactus, pond-lily cactus

Leaf cacti bloom luxuriantly when they are able to spend the summer outside.

The name *Epiphyllum* means 'on the leaf' and indicates that here, against all the botanical rules, the flower appears to arise from the leaf. In reality, this leaf is a flattened stem, usually furnished with thorns, though insignificant ones. Epiphyllums live in their tropical habitats as trailing epiphytes, and they can therefore be

Red Epiphyllum *hybrid*

cultivated in hanging containers.

Of the many hybrids in existence, only a small number are ever commercially available. Depending on the species or variety, the flowers

Marniera chrysocardium
in bloom

measure from 5 to 35cm (2 to 14in) in diameter and are white, cream-coloured, yellow, orange, pink, red, purple or violet shades; many bicoloured forms are also available. Small varieties like 'Mimi' are especially in demand. Specialist nurseries have the largest selection.

Flowering season Late spring to mid summer.

Family Cactaceae, cactus family.

Yellow Epiphyllum *hybrid*

Origin Southern Mexico to tropical regions of South America. Only hybrid forms are available.

Location These are undemanding plants that can tolerate many locations, but they do best in semi-shade. Should spend the summer out of doors. From spring to autumn keep warm and humid, in winter around 10 to 15°C (50 to 59°F).

Watering, feeding Keep moderately moist all year round with soft, room-temperature water. Fertilize from early spring to late summer.

Further culture Mist now and again. As necessary pot on in bromeliad potting medium. Untidy growth should be trimmed to shape following flowering.

Propagating From cuttings. Let cut surfaces dry.

Pests, diseases Aphids (especially on buds), scale.

Note The pink-flowering *Nopalxochia phylanthoides*, known as 'Empress-of-Germany', which has

Above
1 *Red Epiphyllum* hybrid
2 *White Epiphyllum* hybrid
3 Nopalxochia phylanthoides

proved itself a useful hanging plant, is cultivated exactly the same way.

Professional tip A dormant period from late autumn to early spring in cooler temperatures is the recipe for successful flower development.

Rhipsalidopsis hybrids
Easter cactus

The Easter cactus is robust and eager to flower.

There are three kinds of Easter cactus.

● *Rhipsalidopsis gaertneri* with scarlet-red flowers 4 to 5cm (1½ to 2in) long

● *Rhipsalidopsis rosea* with five-sided, bristly stems and somewhat smaller, pink flowers.

● *Rhipsalidopsis × graeseri*, a cross of the two above, and obtainable with pink to violet flowers.

In spring all produce a profusion of brilliantly coloured flowers positioned at the ends of the leaf members. The Easter cactus grows as an epiphyte in its natural habitat.

Flowering season Early to late spring.

Family Cactaceae, cactus family.

Origin Brazil.

Location Bright to semi-shady and warm all year round. Keep at 10°C (50°F) for eight weeks from late autumn to mid winter. This promotes flower development.

Watering, feeding During the growing season (late winter to mid autumn) keep slightly moist with soft, room-temperature water; water sparingly for four weeks after blooming and during the rest period (late autumn to mid winter). In summer give cactus fertilizer now and then.

Further culture Mist often. Pot on only as necessary in bromeliad potting medium.

Propagating From leaf sections, best in late spring (but possible all year round). Allow cut surfaces to dry, and then cuttings root easily in moist potting medium.

Pests, diseases Not generally a problem. Root rot and leaf shrinkage from too much water; too little water can also cause leaf shrinkage. Falling buds from too cool a location or too much warmth with a deficienty of light at the same time.

Schlumbergera hybrids
Christmas cactus, crab cactus

The Christmas cactus loves humidity.

The Christmas cactus, as available today, is the result of a cross of the true Christmas cactus (*Zygocactus truncatus*) and *Schlumbergera russeliana*. Both species grow as epiphytes on trees in the Orgel Mountains near Rio de Janeiro in Brazil at heights of 900 to 1400m (3000 to 4600ft). There are enchanting hybrids on the market, with white, red, purple-red and violet flowers. With some luck you might acquire one of the newly hybridized yellow varieties like 'Gold Charm'.

Flowering season Early to mid winter (occasionally to early spring).

Family Cactaceae, cactus family.

Origin Brazil.

Location Bright to semi-shady, little sun. The plants love the fresh air outdoors in a semi-shady place through the summer (and until early autumn).

Watering, feeding Keep moderately moist in summer. Until mid summer feed every 14 days. From late summer water and feed less so that the leaves will mature.

Further culture Mist often. Bring the plants indoors again in early autumn and keep warm (18 to 22°C/64 to 72°F). The shorter periods of daylight will stimulate the development of flowers.

Propagating Accomplished easily by leaf cuttings, which should be dried before being planted in moist potting medium.

Pests, diseases Rarely a problem. Bud drop can result from altered light conditions following change of location.

Cacti for the enthusiast

The genera pictured here represent a small cross-section of cacti for the experienced admirer and have similarities in culture. A growing cabinet is recommended to cultivate most of them successfully. This guarantees the greatest possible amount of light and a controlled climate, both requirements for successful flowering. Some, like *Sulcorebutia* and *Mediolobivia*, actually come from mountain regions and are accustomed to intense ultraviolet light. (Due to import and quarantine restrictions, some of the cacti pictured may not be available in Australia and New Zealand.)

Opposite
1 Astrophytum
   capricorne *var.*
   niveum
2 Cephalocereus senilis
3 Thelocactus bicolor
4 Neoportaria villosa
5 Mammillaria nepina
6 Mammillaria laui
7 Thelocactus bueckii
8 Weingartia
   multispina
9 Astrophytum
   myriostigma
10 Astrophytum asterias
11 Mammillaria
   yaquensis
12 Mediolobivia
   schmiedcheniana
13 Sulcorebutia
   steinbachii

Flowering season
Spring and summer for most of the genera. *Thelocactus* blooms from spring to late summer.
Family Cactaceae, cactus family.
Origin Southern USA to South America.
Location From spring to autumn very bright to sunny and warm. From mid autumn bright and cool (5 to 12°C/41 to 54°F). From late spring the cacti can also be placed in a sunny warm situation outdoors. But protect from rain.
Watering, feeding As soon as they show new growth in spring, water regularly. But let potting medium dry out before each watering.
Further culture Mist now and again in summer and autumn. Pot on every two to three years, using a good-quality, free-draining cactus potting medium. When potting on, you should avoid the temptation to put plants into containers that are too large.
Propagating From seed at a bed temperature of about 28°C (82°F).
Pests, diseases Spider mites, mealy bugs, cactus rot from too much water, especially in winter.

Melocactus
Melon cactus

The crown or cephalum is the flowering area.

Tabernaemontanus, the German botanist, described this plant as a 'melon thistle' as early as 1588. Melon cacti differ from many other genera in the development of an accumulation of bristles, hairs and wool called the cephalium. Looking like a little crown, this is the flowering area of the *Melocactus*. It develops after seven years and signals the plant's maturity: from this time on, the cactus concentrates solely upon blooming. Melon cacti belong to the group of warmth-loving species and in winter prize a sunny place on the windowsill.
Flowering season Late spring to early autumn.
Family Cactaceae, cactus family.
Origin Central and South America.
Location All year round full sun, or at least very bright, and warm. In summer place outdoors in a warm, protected spot.

Watering, feeding
Water regularly in summer, reduce amount of water from mid autumn to early spring, but keep potting medium slightly moist at all times. In summer feed with cactus fertilizer every four weeks.
Further culture Mist frequently all year round. Pot on every two to three years in shallow container, using a very sandy potting medium. Do not injure the roots, especially of specimens that have a cephalium.
Propagating From seed in sandy soil at bed temperature of about 28°C (82°F).
Pests, diseases Cactus rot from too much water and cold temperatures.
Professional tip The old-man cactus (*Cephalocereus senilis*) is cultivated in exactly the same way; however, it may be kept cooler in winter, but not under 15°C (59°F).

INDEX

Page numbers in **bold type** refer to the main entry on the topic; those in *italic type* refer to illustrations. Entries in the Glossary are indicated by the letter G in front of the page number. Plants without common names, or commonly referred to by their genus names, are indexed under the genus name.

Indian azalea **127**, *127*
Indian banyan tree 165
Indian kale **191**, *191*
Indirect humidity 43
Indoor linden 26, *26–7*, **186**, *186, 187*
Indoor oak **193**, *193*
Indoor violet 28
Inflorescences 15, *15*, G74
Insect control
 Biotechnical 50, G69
 Chemical 51, G70
Insecticides **51**, 52, 68, 70, G74
 Natural 78
 Systemic 81
Insectivorous plants G74
Internodes G74
Ion exchanger *42*, G74
Iresine **170**, *170*
 I. herbstii 170, *170*
 I. lindenii 170
Iron-cross begonia 148, *148*
Iron deficiency 52
Iron sequestrin G74
Ivy 22, 25, 26, *27*, 55, *55*, 60, *60*, 141, **168**, *169*
 Aralia **163**, *163*
 Danish 28
 Devil's 26, *31*, 57, **162**, *162*
 English 163
 Grape 16, 25, 28, 141, **152**, *152*
 Spider **151**, *151*
 Swedish 28, **180**, *180*
 Tree 28, **163**, *163*
Ixora 15, 16, 26, **118**, *118*
 Hybrids 118, *118*
 I. coccinea **118**

Jaburan lily 28
Jacobinia **118**, *118*
 J. carnea 118, *118*
 J. pauciflora 118
Jade plant 25, **155**, *155*
Japanese fatsia 25, 163
Japanese fern 195
Japanese persimmon 63
Japanese sago palm **157**, *157*
Jasmine 25, 28, **119**, *119*
 Madagascar 28, **133**, *133*
Jasminum 25, 28, 31, **119**, *119*
 J. officinale 119
 J. polyanthum 19, 119, *119*
Jatropha *14*, 16, 28
 J. podagrica **119**, *119*
Jerusalem cherry 132, *132*
Jewelweed **117**, *117*
Joseph's coat 23, 25, 26, 57, 61, **153**, *153*

Kaffir lily 19, 58, 80, 89, **102**, *102*, 213
Kalanchoe 16, 24, 28, **120**, *120*
 K. blossfeldiana 120
 K. daigremontiana 58, 69, 120
 K. manginii 30, 120, *120*
 K. pinnata 58, 120
 K. tubiflora 120
Kale, Indian **191**, *191*
Kangaroo apple 132
Kangaroo-paw **137**, *137*
Kangaroo thorn *5*, 7
Kangaroo vine 48, 152
Keiki 58, G74
Kentia palm **209**, *209*
King's crown **118**, *118*
Kumquat *7*, **64**, *64*, 102

Labellum G74
Lady palm 25, 48, 205, **210**, *210*

Ladyslipper orchid 72, 213, **218**, *218*
Laelia 75, 214, **216**, *216*
 L. cinnabarina 216
 L. crispa 216
 L. harpophylla 216
 L. pumila 216
 L. purpurata 216, *216*
Laeliocattleya hybrids 214, *214*, 216
Lavender *4*, 7
Lavendula angustifolia *4*, 7
Layering 60, *60*, G74
 Air 61, *61*
Leaf begonia **148**, *148*
Leaf cactus 223
Leaf crowns 59
Leaf cuttings *58*, 59, *59*
Leaf eelworms 52, 55, *55*, G74
Leaf geranium **176**, *176*
Leaf loss G74
Leaf node *58*, 59, 75, 76
Leaf-polishing spray 51, 52
Leaf-section cuttings *58*, 59, *60*
Leaf succulents 81
Leaf vein G74
Leaves *14*, 15, 16, 20, 26, *26–7*, 45, *45*, 50, G68, 69, G76, G81, 82, 141
 Disease and pest signs **54–5**, *54–5*
 Healthy 54, *54*
 Seed *61*, 63, 71, 75, G79
Leea coccinea **171**, *171*
Legginess G75
Lemon 63, 83
Leopard lily *18*, *19*, 26, 68, **159**, *159*
Leptospermum 16
 L. scoparium **121**, *121*
Liana G75
Light 12, 13, 16, **20–1**, 26, 36, 45, *45*, 63, 73, G75, *77*
 see also Plant lights
Light germinators 60, G75
Light mark G75
Light spots 54, *54*
Lily
 African blood **113**, *113*
 Arum 19, 78, 81
 Barbados **114**, *114*
 Belladonna 19
 Blood 58, **113**, *113*
 Boat **182**, *182*
 Calla 28, *29*, 36, **135**, *135*
 Climbing **112**, *112*
 Glory 68, **112**, *112*
 Hidden 136
 Jaburan 28
 Kaffir 19, 58, 80, 89, **102**, *102*, 213
 Leopard *18*, *19*, 26, 68, **159**, *159*
Lime-hating plants 71, G75
Linden, Indoor 26, *26–7*, **186**, *186, 187*
Lipstick vine *15*, 16, **92**, *92*
Lisianthus resselianus 110
Lithophyte G75
Livingstone daisy *5*, 7, 81
Lizard plant **188**, *188*
Lobivia **225**
 L. backebergiana 225
 L. famatimensis 225
 L. jajoiana 225
 L. pentlandii 225
 L. rebutioides 225
 L. vatteri 224
 L. wrightiana 225
Lobster claws 135
Long-day plants G75

Lotus berthelotii *31*, **121**, *121*
Ludwig amaryllises 114
Luxmeter 21, 36, 45, *45*, G75
Lycaste skinneri 7
Lychee 63

Madagascan baobab 174
Madagascar jasmine 28, **133**, *133*
Madagascar palm **175**, *175*
Maidenhair fern 28, *33*, *35*, **196**, *196*
Magnesium 38, 70, G75, 76
Mammillaria **224**
 M. bocasana 225
 M. laui 228, 229
 M. napina 228, 229
 M. yaquensis 228, 229
 M. zeilmanniana **224**, *225*
Mango 63
Mangosteen 63
Manuka **121**, *121*
Maple
 Flowering *15*, 22, **138**, *138*
 Parlour **138**, *138*
Maranta 25, **171**, *171*
 M. erythroneura 171
 M. kerchoviana 171, *171*
Masdevallia militaris **221**, *221*
Mealy bug 52, 54, *54*
Mechanical control procedures 50
Medicinal aloe 144
Medinilla *15*, 16, 25
 M. magnifica 19, *122*, **123**
Mediolobivia 229
 M. schmiedcheniana 228, 229
Mediterranean plants 63
Melocactus 19, **229**, *229*
Melon cactus 223, **229**, *229*
Meristem tissue 56, 69
Metabolism G75
Metrosideros citrina 139
Microclimate G75
Microcoelum weddelianum **209**, *209*
Microlepia 28
 M. stringosa **199**, *199*
Micronutrients G75, 82
Mildew 50, 52, 55, *55*, G71, G75
Milky sap G75
Miltonia 43, **216**
 M. clowesii 216
 M. flavescens 216
 M. spoectabilis 216
Miltoniopsis **216**, *216*
Mimosa 28, 43, 79
Mind your own business 16, *18*, *19*, 22, 25, **186**, *186*
Ming arelia 48
Miniature plants 23, 25, G75, **102**, *102*, 105, *128*, 210, *210*, 215
Minimum-maximum thermometer G75
Mirabilis jalapa 180
Misting 31
Mites 52, 54, *54*, 55, *55*, G75, G80
Money plant 23, 48, *66–7*, **155**, *155*
Monocotyledonous plants G75, 79
Monoecious plants G75
Monopodial plants G75
Monopodial orchids 213
Monstera 25, 31, 44
 M. deliciosa **172**, *172*
Monterey cypress 22, 48, 141, **157**, *157*

Mosaic plant **166**, *166*
Mosaic virus 55, *55*
Moss, Sphagnum 71
Moss stake 44, *44*, G75
Mother-in-law plant **149**, *149*
Mother-in-law's tongue 25, 26, **183**, *183*
Mother plants 58, *58*, 60, G75
Mother of thousands 30, **184**, *184*
Moth orchid **219**, *219*
Mould 50, 52, 55, *55*, 73, G80
Multigeneric hybrids G75, 214, 217, 219
Mutation G75
Myrtle 22, 25, 26, *26*, 48, **172**, *172*
Myrtus 16, 22
 M. communis 48, **172**, *172*

Naegelia multiflora 137
Narrow-leaved bottle tree 48
Neantha bella **207**, *207*
Necrosis G76
Nematanthus 26
 N. glabra **116**, *116*
Neoporteria villosa 228, 229
Neoregelia 26, **173**, *173*, 174
 N. carolinae 173, *173*
 N. concentrica 173
Nepenthes 31
 Hybrids **173**, *173*
Nephrolepsis exaltata *33*, *34*, **200**, *200*
Nerium oleander *4–5*, 7
Nertera granadensis *33*, *35*, **123**, *123*
Nest fern **197**, *197*
New growth G76
New Zealand tea tree **121**, *121*
Nidularium 26, 173, **174**, *174*
 N. billbergoides 174
 N. fulgens 174
 N. innocentii 174
Nightshades **132**, *132*
Night-time temperature G76
Node G76
Nopalxochia phyllanthoides 226, *226*
Norfolk Island pine 12, 19, 22, 25, 75, 141, **145**, *145*
Notocactus **224**
 N. apricus 224
 N. cocinnus 224, *224*
 N. ottonis 224
 N. rutilans 224
 N. submammulosus 224
 N. uebelmannianus 224

Oak
 Indoor **193**, *193*
 Silky 22, 26, **166**, *166*
Odontioda 217
Odontocidium 217
Odontoglossum **217**, *217*
 Hybrids 52, *53*, 217
 O. bictoniense 217
 O. crispum 217
 O. grande 217
 O. pulchellum 217
 × *Cochlioda* 217
 × *Cochlioda* × *Miltoniopsis* 217
 × *Cochlioda* × *Oncidium* 217
 × *Miltonia* 217
 × *Oncidium* 217
Odontonia 217
Oedema 70
Offsets 58, *58*, 74, 75, G76
Oil-spot disease 55, *55*
Old-man cactus 229

Oleander *4–5*, 7, *66–7*
Oncidium **218**, *218*
 Hybrids 218, *218*
 O. kramerianum 218
 O. papilio 218
Ophiopogon jaburan 28, **193**, *193*
Opposite leaves G76
Orange 63
 Calamondin 102, *102*
 Dwarf 28, **102**, *102*
 Miniature 23, **102**, *102*
Orchid
 Dancing lady **218**, *218*
 Epiphytic *7*, 16, 22
 Ladyslipper 213, **218**, *218*
 Moth **219**, *219*
 Pansy **216**, *216*
 Poor man's **129**, *129*
 Tiger 217
Orchid cactus **226**, *226*
Orchids 12, 16, 22, 25, 38, 40, *41*, 42, 52, 55, *55*, 58, 71, 72, 74, 75, 76, 77, 78, 82, 212–21
Ornamental pepper **100**, *100*
Osiris plant 168
Ovary *15*, 72, *77*
Ovule 15
Oxalis **137**, *137*
Oxygen 73, G76, 78

Pachira 16, 28
 P. aquatica **174**, *174*
 P. macrocarpa **174**, *174*
Pachypodium **175**, *175*
 P. lamerei 175
Pachystachys 15
 P. lutea *21*, 25, 95
Pale leaves 54, *54*
Palm
 Areca 208
 Betel **206**, *206*
 Burmese fishtail **207**, *207*
 Canary Island date 210
 Coconut 205, **208**, *208*
 Date 64, *65*, **210**, *210*
 Fan *7*, 211
 Fishtail 198
 Japanese sago **157**, *157*
 Kentia **209**, *209*
 Lady 25, 48, 205, **210**, *210*
 Madagascar **175**, *175*
 Miniature date 210, *210*
 Parlour 205, **207**, *207*
 Petticoat 211
 Piccabeen **206**, *206*
 Sago 22, 141, **157**, *157*, 195
 Sentry 22, 28, 208, **209**, *209*
 Thread 211
 Washington **211**, *211*
 Weddel **209**, *209*
 Yellow **208**, *208*
Palm-Beach bells **120**, *120*
Palmetto 205, **211**, *211*
Palms 23, 25, 26, 48, 56, *62*, 63, 71, 75, 141, 204–11
Pandanus 22, 77, **175**, *175*
 P. sanderi 175
 P. veitchii 175
Panicle 15
Pansy miltonia 216
Pansy orchid **216**, *216*
Papaya 63, 64, *64*, 65
Paper flower **139**, *139*
Paphiopedilum **218**, *218*
 Hybrids 218, *218*
Papyrus plant 28, 158
Parasites 73
Parlour maple **138**, *138*
Parlour palm 205, **207**, *207*
Parodia **225**
 P. chrysacanthion 225

ACKNOWLEDGEMENTS

Photographs

Apel, page 107 right; BAMBOO/Descat: pages 213 right, 221 top; Becherer: pages 222, 224, 225, 226 top, bottom left and bottom centre, 228, 229; Becker: pages 62, 66-7; Benary: page 117 bottom (4); Bonsai-Centrum, Heidelberg: page 49 bottom; Busek: page 223 left; Eisenbeiss: pages 7, 53, 104 left, 136 top, 143 left, 144 right, 145 left, 150 left, 153 left, 154, 155, 156 right, 159 top left and top right, 163 right, 166 left, 168, 173 left, 175 left, 181 left, 182 left, 183 right, 184 right, 185 left, 189 top left and bottom, 191 right, 192 top, 196 left, 197, 198, 199, 202 top, 203, 212, 214 top right and bottom left, 216 right, 217, 218, 219 top left and top right, 220 top and right, 221 left and bottom, 227 right and back cover bottom right; Flora/Krampe/Gölling: pages 106 right, 201 left; GEO/George: page 13; Heitz: page 7 left; Lückel: page 220 bottom; mein schöner Garten/Krieg: page 201 right; mein schöner Garten/Stork: pages 12, 24, 216 left, 219 bottom right; Photoplant: pages 141 right, 195 top, 205 bottom; Pott: page 179 bottom; Rauh: page 223 right; Reuter: pages 214 top left, 215 left and top right; Riedmiller: pages 48 right, 150 right, 176 bottom (4), 206 left, 207 left, 208, 209, 210, 211; Sammer: pages 64 centre bottom, 65 bottom left; Sperling: page 132 left; Stork: pages 39, 48 left, centre top and centre bottom, 49 top, 51, 56, 57, 148, 158 left, 194, 214 bottom centre and bottom right, 215 centre top, centre bottom and right bottom, 219 bottom left and bottom centre; Wetterwald: pages 6, 80 right, 91 right, 92 right, 93, 95 left, 96 left, 101 top right and bottom, 103 left, 105 left, 106 left, 110, 111, 113 left, 118, 119 right, 122, 124 right, 126 top right, 128 left, 129 right, 132 right, 134 bottom, 136 right, 137 top left and bottom right, 142 right, 144 left, 145 right, 149 right, 152 right, 153 right, 157 left, 162 right, 163 top left and bottom, 165, 166 right, 167, 170 right, 171 right, 172, 173 right, 174, 175 right, 179 top left and top right, 180, 181 right, 182 right, 183 left, 184 left, 186 left, 188, 189 right, 190, 191 left, 192 bottom left and bottom right, 193, 196 right, 200 right, 202 bottom, 205 top, 206 right, 207 right, 227 left; Wothe: pages 89, 195 right, 213 left, 141 top; Strauss: all other pictures.

Illustrations

Marlene Gemke: page 59 top; György Jankovics: pages 14 left, 40 left, 42 left, 44 left, 50, 58 left, 60 left; Christel Langer: pages 16, 26, 36, 161, 165, 224, 225, 226, 229; Ushie Dorner: all other drawings.

The publishers and Fotograf Friedrich Strauss thank the following firms for their support: Gärtnerei Benedikt Wolf, Holzbrünnerstrasse 17, 80051 Haag a.d. Amper and Baumann Stoffe, Postfach 1107, 6057 Dietzenbach.

Warning

Some of the plants described in this book are poisonous. In the introduction to the plant portraits (see page 87) the plant families that are particularly poisonous are named and their effects listed. Furthermore, in the descriptions of individual genera and species (see pages 84-229) specific health hazards are pointed out under the heading 'Warning'. Lethal plants and those less poisonous ones that can upset specifically vulnerable adults or children are indicated with a skull and cross bones. Make absolutely sure that children and pets do not eat plants that carry the warning notice and skull and cross bones symbol. Some plants secrete substances which cause skin irritations, and these are also indicated under the 'Warning' heading. Anyone who suffers from contact allergies should always wear gloves when handling such plants.

United Kingdom

General houseplant suppliers

Allensmore Nurseries Ltd
Tram Inn
Allensmore
Hereford
Herefordshire
HR2 9AN
Tel: 098 121 221

Badger Hill Nurseries
Clophill Road
Maulden
Bedfordshire
MK45 2AD
Tel: 0525 61266

Barters Farm Nurseries Ltd
Chapmanslade
Westbury
Wiltshire
BA13 4AL
Tel: 0373 294/512

Blackwell Bros Ltd
Stephenson Road
Groundwell Farm Trading
   Estate
Swindon
Wiltshire
SN2 5BD
Tel: 0793 721063

Brentwood Moss Nurseries
New Moss Road
Cadishead
Irlam
Manchester
M30 5TJ
Tel: 061 777 9222

Brynawel Garden
   Centre Ltd
Sully Road
Penarth
South Glamorgan
CF6 2UB
Tel: 0222 702660

Buckels Nursery
Copplehouse Lane
Field Lane
Fazakerley
Liverpool
L10 0AG
Tel: 051 525 2712

Keith Butters Ltd
Fulnet Farm
Kellnett Gate
Spalding
Lincolnshire
PE12 6EH
Tel: 0775 768831

Bypass Nurseries
Capel St Mary
Ipswich
Suffolk
Tel: 0473 310604

Challis of York Ltd
Poppleton Nurseries
Poppleton
York
YO2 6NG
Tel: 0904 796161

Cuckoo Bridge Ltd
St Ives Road
Somersham
St Ives
Cambridgeshire
PE17 3ET
Tel: 0487 740255

Peter Eastwood Plants Ltd
Beardsfield Nursery
Common Lane
Ditchling
Hassocks
Sussex
BN6 8TN
Tel: 07918 5163

Elmbridge Gardens Ltd
Coniscliffe Road
Darlington
Co Durham
DL3 8DJ
Tel: 0325 462710

H Evans and Sons
   (Europa) Ltd
Ruxley Manor Nursery
Sidcup
Kent
DA14 5BQ
Tel: 081 302 7621

Ex-Cel Plants Ltd
397 Christchurch Road
West Parley
Wimborne
Dorset
Tel: 0202 593661

Findlay Clark Ltd
Boclair Road
Milgavie
Glasgow
G62 6EP
Tel: 0362 20721

Four Oaks Nurseries Ltd
Farm Lane
Lower Withington
Nr Macclesfield
Cheshire
SK11 9DU
Tel: 0477 71392

Gates Nursery
Hill House Hill
Liphook
Hants
GU30 7PX
Tel: 0428 725025

SW Green and Sons
Ringbeck
Ellerker
Brough
North Humberside
HU15 2DD

House of Zara Ltd
Bridge Farm
Hospital Bridge Farm
   Road
Whitton
Twickenham
Middlesex
TW2 6LH
Tel: 081 898 8100

Iver Flowerland Ltd
Norwood Lane
Iver
Bucks
SL0 0EW
Tel: 0753 655685

Linnell Plants Ltd
Hurst Lane
Egham
Surrey
TW20 8QJ
Tel: 0784 437677

Looe Garden Centre
St Martins
Looe
Cornwall
PL13 1PA
Tel: 05036 3866

Mantel (UK) Ltd
Barrow Farm
Halden Lane
Benenden
Kent
TN17 4BJ
Tel: 0580 241432

Frank P Matthews Ltd
Berrington Court
Tenbury Wells
Worcestershire
WR15 8TH
Tel: 0584 810214

Meldrum Nurseries
Silverwells
Montrose Road
Arbroath
Angus
DD11 5RA
Tel: 0241 72286

Munton and Fison plc
Cedars Factory
Stowmarket
Suffolk
IP14 2AG
Tel: 0449 612401

Northern Garden Supplies
Blyth Road
Oldcotes
Worksop
Nottinghamshire
S81 8JE
Tel: 0909 731024

Oakview Nurseries
Harwich Road
Ardleigh
Colchester
Essex
CO7 7LS
Tel: 0206 231134

Parkhill Nurseries
Parkhill
Dyce
Aberdeen
AB2 0AS
Tel: 0224 722167

School Lane Nurseries
School Lane
Torrington
North Devon
EX38 8AJ
Tel: 0805 26700

Smithills Garden Centre
Smithills Dean Road
Smithills
Bolton
Lancashire
BL1 7NX
Tel: 0704 45319

St Andrews Nurseries
Old North Road
Sawtry
Huntingdon
Cambridgeshire
PE17 5XN
Tel: 0487 830 482

St Dunstan's Nursery
Ham Street
Eltonsburgh
Glastonbury
Somerset
BA16 8AL
Tel: 0458 50037

Tamarisk Nurseries
Wing Road
Stewkley
Nr Leighton Buzzard
Bedfordshire
LU7 0JB
Tel: 0525 240747

Tickhill House Plants
Bawtry Road
Tickhill
Doncaster
South Yorkshire
DN11 9EX
Tel: 0302 742134

Trelawney Houseplants
Sladesbridge
Wadebridge
Cornwall
PL27 6JA
Tel: 0208 814204

P Van Zelst & Son Ltd
Barberry House Nurseries
Scriven
Knaresborough
North Yorkshire
HG5 9EL
Tel: 0423 863150

Withydale Nursery
Highleadon
Newent
Gloucestershire
GL18 1HG
Tel: 0452 79439

Woodlark Nurseries
Burhill Road
Hersham
Walton-on-Thames
Surrey
KT12 4JD
Tel: 0932 222746

Begonia suppliers

Gordon Smale (Dept GN)
2 St Bernard's Close
Buckfast
Devon
TQ11 0BA

Bonsai suppliers

Barthelemy & Co
262 Wimbourne Road
Wimbourne
Dorset
BH21 2DZ
Tel: 0202 874283

Bodiam Bonsai
Ewhurst Green
Robertsbridge
East Sussex
TN32 5RJ
Tel: 0580 830644

R Hore
The Bonsai Nursery
St Mawgan Village
Newquay
Cornwall
TR8 4ET
Tel: 0637 860116

The Bonsai Shop
Culver Garden Centre
Cattlegate Road
Crews Hill
Enfield
Middlesex
Tel: 081 367 3361

Bushukan Bonsai
Ricbra
Lower Road
Hockley
Essex
SS5 5NL
Tel: 0702 201029/524188

Cheshire Bonsai
'At Jardinerie'
Forest Road
Cotebrook
Tarporley
Cheshire
CW6 9EE
Tel: 0829 760725

Chobham Garden Centre
Bagshot Road
Chobham
Nr Woking
Surrey
Tel: 0276 856806

Fernwood Bonsai Trees
Fernwood
Onneley
Crewe
Cheshire
CW3 9QJ
Tel: 0782 750792

Glen Brook Bonsai
  Nursery
Tickenham
Clevedon
Avon
BS21 6SE
Tel: 0272 8585596

Harry and Christine
  Tomlinson
Greenwood Gardens
Ollerton Road
Arnold
Nottingham
NG5 8PR
Tel: 0602 205757

Dawn and Peter Chan
Herons Bonsai Ltd
Wiremill Lane
Newchapel
Nr Lingfield
Surrey
RH7 6HJ
Tel: 0342 832657

Hewett and Stewart
Arivgaig
Acharacle
Argyll
PH36 4LE

Kent Bonsai
Harwood
35 Chestfield Road
Chestfield
Kent
Tel: 0227 792962

Meads End Bonsai
Forewood Lane
Crowhurst
Battle
East Sussex
TN33 9AB
Tel: 0424 83388

Andrew Norfield Trees and
  Seeds
Lower Meend
St Briavels
Gloucestershire
GL15 6RW
Tel: 0594 530134

Ken and Ann Norman
Norman Miniatures
3 Westdean Drive
Brighton
Sussex
BN1 5HE
Tel: 0273 506476

Nursery of Miniatures
Honiton
Devon
EX14 8SX
Tel: 0404 42617

Pinewood Bonsai
8 Abbots Close
Formby
Liverpool
L37 6EY
Tel: 070 48 71315

Price and Adams
Cherry Trees
22 Burnt Hill Road
Wrecclesham
Farnham
Surrey
GU10 4RX
Tel: 0252 714266

Tokonoma Bonsai Nursery
14 London Road
Shenley
Radlett
Hertfordshire
WD7 9EN
Tel: 0923 857587/855670

Peter Trenear
2 Chantreland
Chequers Lane
Eversley Cross
Hampshire
RG27 0NX
Tel: 0734 732300

Cactus and succulant suppliers

DSP
6 Upton Grey Close
Harestock
Winchester
Hampshire
SO22 6NE

Greenacres Garden Centre
Nine Mile Ride
Wokingham
Berkshire
RG11 4NE
Tel: 0734 732544

Mayor Indoor Plants
W Mayor and Sons
Mayfield Nurseries
Southport Road
Ulnes Walton
Leyland
Lancashire
PR5 3LQ
Tel: 0772 600283

Carnivorous plant suppliers

Prop and Grow Ltd
Old Station Gardens
Ripon Road
Baldersby
Nr Thirsk
North Yorkshire
YO7 4PS
Tel: 076584 551

Conservatory plant suppliers

Advanced Biocentre Ltd
2 Brandon House
West Street
Somerton
Somerset
TA11 7PS
Tel: 0458 72295

P Bovill and Sons
Afton Park Farm
Freshwater
Isle of Wight
PO40 9TP
Tel: 0983 752980

Duncan and Davies
  (UK) Ltd
Highleigh Nurseries
Highleigh Road
Sidlesham
Chichester
West Sussex
PO20 7NR
Tel: 0243 56711

Fromefield Nursery
Church Lane
Awbridge
Nr Romsey
Hampshire
SO51 0HN
Tel: 0794 41123

Growforth Ltd
South Pargills
Clock Lunie Road
Hillend
Dunfirmline
Fife
KY11 5HS
Tel: 0383 415555

The Hawaiian Plant
  Co Ltd
The Nursery
Kimpton Bottom
Kimpton
Herts
SG4 8EU
Tel: 0438 832485

Heaves Nursery
Levels
Nr Kendall
Cumbria
Tel: 05395 61126

Charles Hill Nursery
Charles Hill
Tilford
Farnham
Surrey
GU10 2AT
Tel: 0252 703375

James McIntyre and Sons
Moyness Nurseries
Coupar Angus Road
Blairgowrie
Perthshire
PH10 6UT
Tel: 0250 3135

Pantiles Nurseries Ltd
Almners Road
Lyne
Chertsey
Surrey
KT16 0BJ
Tel: 0932 872195

Penheale Nurseries
Egloskerry
Launceston
Cornwall
PL15 8RX
Tel: 0566 85487

Alan Richmond
The Nurseries
Low Catton
Stamford Bridge
York
YO4 1EA
Tel: 0579 71149

Scarletts Quality Plants
Nayland Road
West Berhgolt
Colchester
Essex
CO6 3DH
Tel: 0206 240466

Seaforde Nursery
Seaforde
Co Downe
Northern Ireland
BT30 8PG
Tel: 039687 225

Webbs Nurseries
Wychbold
Droitwich
Worcestershire
WR9 0DG
Tel: 0527 861365

Fern Suppliers

Farplants Ltd
Toddington Lane
Littlehampton
West Sussex
BN17 7PP
Tel: 0903 722737

Hawksmill Nurseries
127 Hawkesmill Lane
Allesley
Coventry
West Midlands
CV5 9FP
Tel: 0203 402664

Highland Liliums
Kiltarlity
Beauly
Invernesshire
IV4 7JQ
Tel: 046 374 365

A Hill and Sons
Station Nurseries
Kirby Lane
Stokesley
Nr Middlesborough
Cleveland
TS9 7AB
Tel: 0642 711281

Kalm Oak Nursery
Hunters Chase
Ardleigh
Colchester
Essex
CO7 7LW
Tel: 0206 322877

JD Marston
Culag Ferns
Nafferton
East Yorkshire
YO25 0LD
Tel: 0377 44487

Mears Ashby Nurseries Ltd
Glebe House
Glebe Road
Mears Ashby
Northampton
NN6 0DL
Tel: 0604 811811

Stafford Lake Nursery
Stafford Lake
Knaphill
Woking
Surrey
GU21 2SJ
Tel: 04867 6367

Stone Cross Nurseries
Peelings and Saxon
  Nurseries
Hankham Road
Hankham
Pevensey
East Sussex
BN24 5AP
Tel: 0323 763355

Woodbridge Nurseries Ltd
Rectory Lane
Longworth
Oxon
OX13 5DZ
Tel: 0865 820300

Geranium and pelargonium suppliers

Beeches Nursery
Armroyd Lane
Elsecar
Barnsley
North Yorkshire
S74 7JB

Dermead Geranium
  Nurseries (GN)
Dermead
Waterlooville
Hampshire
PO7 6PS
Tel: 0705 240081

Hollycare Plants Ltd
Toddington Lane
Littlehampton
West Sussex
BN17 7PP
Tel: 0903 724541

M and J Lacey
7 Stour Valley Close
Upstreet
Canterbury
Kent
CT3 4DB

Milllbern Geraniums
Pye Court
Willoughby
Rugby
Warwickshire
CV23 8BZ

Redvale Nurseries
St Tudy
Bodmin
Cornwall
PL30 3PX
Tel: 0208 850378

Seddington Nurseries
A1
Beeston
Sandy
Bedfordshire
Tel: 0767 691758

Thorpe's Nurseries
257 Finchampstead Road
Wokingham
Berks
RG11 3JT
Tel: 0734 781181

Ivy Suppliers

Whitehouse Ivies
Tolleshunt Knights
Maldon
CM9 8EZ
Tel: 0621 815782

Orchid suppliers

Ken Evans Orchids
48 Thundersley Park Road
Benfleet
Essex
Tel: 0268 751619

Northern Orchid
  Enterprises
66 James Street
Helensburgh
G84 9LF
Tel: 0436 76952

Palm suppliers

The Palm Centre
22 Guildford Road
London
SW8 2BX
Tel: 071 720 8635

The Palm Centre
563 Upper Richmond Road
  West
London
SW14 7ED
Tel: 081 876 3223

Palm Farm (Dept GA)
Thornton Hall Gardens
Ulceby
South Humberside
DN39 6XF
Tel: 0469 31232

Poinsettia suppliers

Bradbrook and Hannah
Ravensworth Nurseries
Ravensworth
Richmond
North Yorkshire
DL11 7HA
Tel: 0325 718370

Briarlee Nurseries
49 Chapel Lane
Banks
Southport
Merseyside
PR9 8EY
Tel: 0704 26568

PJ Fillery
Ferndale Nurseries
273 Glazebrook Lane
Warrington
Cheshire
WA3 5AU
Tel: 061 775 2977

Roundstone Nurseries
Roundstone Lane
Angmering
West Sussex
BN16 4AF
Tel: 0903 776349

John Train and Sons
Benston
Station Road
Tarbolton
Ayrshire
KA5 5NT
Tel: 0292 541336

Water Gardening

Ampthill Aquatics Ltd
Abridge Road
Theydon Bois
Essex
CM16 7NR
Tel: 037 881 4545

Blagdon Water Garden
  Products Ltd
Units 6 & 7
Warlow Industrial Estate
Highbridge
Somerset
TA9 4AG
Tel: 0278 781556

Edge Aquatics Ltd
156 High Street
The Strand
Bromsgrove
Worcestershire
B61 8AR
Tel: 0527 33272/70677

Hawthorne Garden
  Supplies
Machine Farm
Bishampton
Pershore
Worcestershire
WR10 2NE
Tel: 0386 861026

Heatherwood Nurseries
Merley Park Road
Ashington
Wimborne
Dorset
BH21 3DD
Tel: 0202 883597

Honeysome Aquatics
  Nursery (Dept 5)
The Row
Sutton
Nr Ely
Cambridgeshire
CB6 2PF
Tel: 0353 778889

JMC Aquatics Ltd
59 Stubley Lane
Dronfield
Sheffield
S18 6PG
Tel: 0246 415275

Meare Close Nurseries Ltd
Tadworth Street
Tadworth
Surrey
KT20 5RQ
Tel: 0737 812449

Prestopets Ltd
Weald Bridge Nursery
Kents Lane
North Weald
Essex
CM16 6AX
Tel: 037 882 2421

Stapely Water Gardens
  (Dept GN1)
Stapely
Nantwich
Cheshire
CW5 7LH
Tel: 0270 628111

Trident Water Garden
  Products Ltd
Stoke Place Farm
Stoke Road
Stoke Poges
Slough
Bucks
SL2 4NL
Tel: 0753 692595

Australia

The Conservatory
62 Unley Road
Unley
SA 5061
Tel: (08) 272 9657

The Greenery
107 Porters Street
Templestowe
VIC 3106
Tel: (03) 846 2255

Hawkins Nursery Garden
  Centre
632 Albany Creek
QLD 4035
Tel: (07) 265 1022

Sunshine Nursery
Channel Highway
Kingston
TAS 7050
Tel: (002) 29 5755

Swanes Nursery
490 Galston Road
Dural
NSW 2158
Tel: (02) 651 1322

Waldecks Garden Centre
173 Wanneroo Road
Kingsley
WA 6026
Tel: (09) 409 9521

New Zealand

Botannix Garden Centres
  Ltd
Head Office
1 Forest Hill Road
Takapuna
Auckland

Palmers Garden Centres
Head Office
Great North Road
Glen Eden
Auckland